Three and A Half Powers

The New Balance in Asia

Three and
A Half Powers

*The New Balance
in Asia*

HAROLD C. HINTON

INDIANA UNIVERSITY PRESS
Bloomington & London

Published in Canada by Fitzhenry & Whiteside Limited, Don Mills,
Ontario

Manufactured in the United States of America

Library of Congress Cataloging in Publication Data

Hinton, Harold C.
    Three and a half powers.

    Bibliography
    Includes index.
        1. Asia—Politics.   2. Asia—Foreign relations—
United States.   3. United States—Foreign relations—
Asia.   I. Title.
DS35.H56   1975   320.9′5′042   74-17565
ISBN 0-253-36013-7 cl.
        0-253-20184-5 pa.

Contents

XVI. Conclusion: A Multipolar Balance?   273

      Suggestions for Further Reading   297

      INDEX   301

Preface

Asia is a word with many meanings and associations, a huge region whose importance and interest no one would deny. This book concentrates on the international politics of that part of Asia east of the Persian Gulf (excluding the Middle East, in other words), and on the interaction of the major powers—the United States, the Soviet Union, the People's Republic of China, and to a lesser extent Japan—in particular. My aim has been to write a book that would say something significant and interesting about Asia to the general reader, the student (whether in connection with a formal academic program or not), and if possible even the specialist in some aspect of contemporary Asian affairs.

Some people may wonder why, in view of Asia's proverbial complexity, a single person should have ventured to deal with its international politics as a whole in a single volume. To this there are several answers. One is that to the best of my knowledge there is no satisfactory overall treatment of this important subject in any language, whether by an individual or by a team, and a need therefore obviously exists. Secondly, it is a subject that I have been studying and teaching from various points of view—mainly that of a China specialist—since 1950. In the process I have accumulated substantial, although not necessarily unique, files that have proved indispensable in the writing of this book. To a large extent the files consist of newspaper clippings, and it is my firm belief that if used with care and if drawn from the best sources—my favorites are easily *The New York Times, The Washington Post,* and *The Christian Science Monitor*—these are enormously valuable although not sufficient by themselves. Some of the other published sources that I have found helpful are listed at the end of the book. In addition to these; I have learned a great deal over the years from academic colleagues and American officials—with whom contact is made a little, although not dramatically, easier by having a base in Washington—and from fairly extensive travel in Asia, especially in recent years. I have unfortunately not yet visited South Asia or the mainland of China; in the latter case, my request for a visa in 1973 was refused, on the ground that all facilities for tourists were already booked. But much of value can be learned about such areas without actually visiting them. I have nevertheless learned a great deal from visiting most of the other countries of the Far East and Southeast Asia and talking with local officials, journalists, students, scholars, and political figures, as well as foreign (including American) diplomats.

My approach to the subject has been to try to present it in its own terms, from the perspective of political history and political analysis rather than from that of one of the newer theories cum-methodologies currently fashionable in political science and the study of international relations. An approach that is not quantitative can still make statements that are significant and reasonably precise and have a high probability of being correct. Since the subject is one that arouses my intellectual interest but not to any great extent my political emotions, I believe I have managed to keep the latter out of the book to a reasonable degree. As for the area where this question naturally arises, that of American policy toward Asia, I am selectively critical rather than totally hostile or uncritically laudatory; above all, I have tried to understand and convey the reasons for American decisions and behavior. I have introduced some material on the domestic politics of the countries involved, including the United States, but always with the larger aim of analyzing international politics in mind.

Part I consists of relatively short chapters covering from the Second World War down to approximately 1969 and therefore dealing with an era in which the American role and American influence were the outstanding single feature of Asian international politics. Part II contains generally longer chapters treating in greater detail the period since about 1969; of the various important trends or situations that began at that time, the most significant seems to me to be strategic parity between the United States and the Soviet Union, a state of affairs that has profoundly influenced the whole of international politics. The others are the Sino-Soviet military confrontation, the American military disengagement from Asia, and the Sino-American détente.

I should like to express my appreciation to the Joint Committee on Contemporary China of the American Council of Learned Societies and the Social Science Research Council for a grant that made possible a trip to the Far East and Southeast Asia that was of great value in the preparation of this book in May-July 1973, and to Nancy Hallsted for typing the manuscript. The Joint Committee is of course not responsible for any of the opinions or conclusions expressed.

WASHINGTON, D.C.   HAROLD C. HINTON
SEPTEMBER 1974

Glossary of Acronyms

ABM	Antiballistic missile
AFPFL	Anti-Fascist People's Freedom League
ASEAN	Association of Southeast Asian Nations
ASPAC	Asian and Pacific Council
BCP	Burma Communist Party
CIA	Central Intelligence Agency
CPC	Communist Party of China
CPI (M)	Communist Party of India (Marxist)
CPI (M–L)	Communist Party of India (Marxist–Leninist)
CSCE	Conference on Security and Cooperation in Europe
DMZ	Demilitarized Zone
DRV	Democratic Republic of Vietnam (North Vietnam)
FUNK	Cambodian National United Front
GRUNK	Cambodian Royal Government of National Union
ICBM	Intercontinental ballistic missile
ICCS	International Commission for Control and Supervision
IRBM	Intermediate range ballistic missile
KMT	Kuomintang
MBFR	Mutual and Balanced Force Reduction
MCA	Malayan Chinese Association
MIRV	Multiple independently targetable re-entry vehicle
MRBM	Medium range ballistic missile
NATO	North Atlantic Treaty Organization
NLF	National Liberation Front
PAP	People's Action Party
PKI	Indonesian Communist Party
PRC	People's Republic of China
PRG	Provisional Revolutionary Government (of South Vietnam)
SALT	Strategic arms limitation talks
SEATO	Southeast Asia Treaty Organization
SLBM	Submarine-launched ballistic missile
UMNO	United Malay National Organization
WASAG	Washington Special Action Group

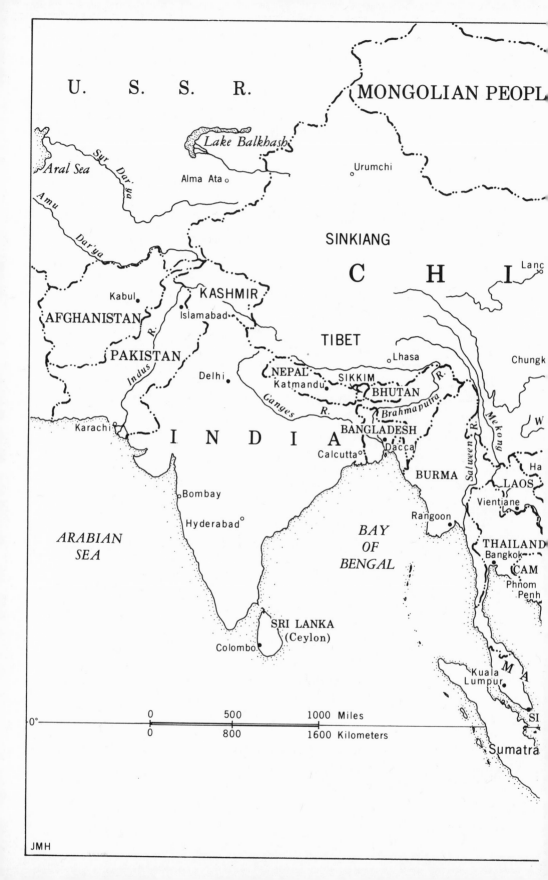

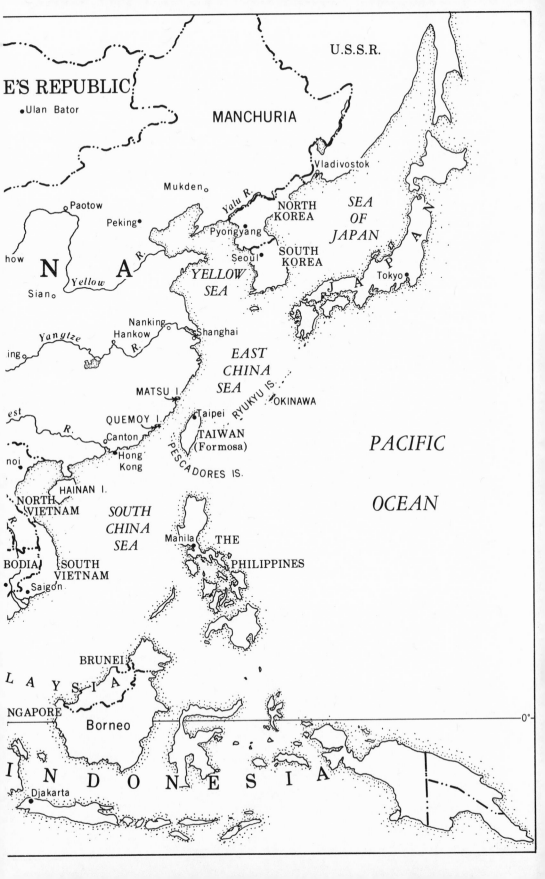

Three and A Half Powers

The New Balance in Asia

PART ONE

Asia in the Era of American Ascendancy

CHAPTER I

Japan's Defeat and Re-emergence

BY STARTING the Pacific War and then conquering its vast empire, Japan ensured the eventual elimination of Western domination from Asia and its replacement by independent nations. But Japan also earned the hatred of many Asians and, lacking adequate defensive capabilities and the means of deterring the United States by the threat of a direct attack, it found its sea communications with its empire virtually cut off and its home islands subjected to rapidly escalating American bombing by early 1945.

The Collapse of the Japanese Empire

From this untenable situation there was only one way out; after the arguments of the peace party in Tokyo had been strengthened by the two atomic bombs and the Soviet attack on Manchuria, the Emperor announced his country's surrender on August 15.

Japan's situation could hardly have been less promising. The home islands were devastated and demoralized and faced the prospect of six million more mouths to feed as millions of personnel and civilians were repatriated from the fallen empire.

In various other parts of Asia, the Japanese military attempted, through their behavior at the time of the surrender, to complicate the problems of whoever might replace them. Broadly speaking, this

meant the United States as the major power in the northwestern
Pacific, the Soviet Union in Manchuria, and the Chinese (Nationalists and Communists) south of the Great Wall; the situation in
Southeast Asia was more complex as the returning representatives
of the prewar colonial powers confronted emergent nationalist
movements.

Even though Japan was defeated, Asia has never been the same
since its defeat. By building an anti-Soviet "military-industrial complex" in Manchuria without actually attacking the Soviet Union,
Japan had inevitably involved Moscow in the affairs of postwar
Asia. By trying unsuccessfully to reduce the Chinese Nationalist
government of Chiang Kai-shek to satellite status, the Imperial
Japanese Army had so weakened it that the Chinese Communists,
for whom Japanese military and other conservatives had always felt
a strong ideological antipathy, were able to challenge and then overthrow it. By using the Western colonial empires in Southeast Asia
and encouraging anti-Western nationalism among the former subject peoples, Japan had helped to release a force that from then on
would almost inevitably resist domination by any alien power, beginning with Japan itself. Through the defeat brought on by its
own aggressiveness, Japan had been eliminated not only as a great
power but as a potential force—one whose potential had never
been realized—for international stability in an Asia badly in need
of such an influence.

The Occupation: The Punitive Phase

For practical purposes, the "Allied" occupation of Japan was an
American show. There were no occupation zones as there were in
Germany; Stalin's demand for such a zone in Hokkaido, the northern island, was flatly rejected by President Truman in 1945. If it
had not been, Japan might be divided today into a Communist
"North Japan" and a non-Communist "South Japan," with uncertain but obviously important consequences. Behind the merest semblance of "Allied" control, occupation policy was set jointly by the
United States government and by General MacArthur (the Su-
preme Commander for the Allied Powers) in Tokyo.

Confused by and ashamed of their defeat, and accustomed to
obeying their leaders, the Japanese people were in a cooperative
mood. The same was true of the Japanese government. It was pos-

sible, therefore, for the United States to avoid setting up a full-fledged military government and establish instead a "civil affairs" situation in which occupation policies were transmitted to and implemented by the Japanese government, suitably purged and "democratized."

This spirit of cooperation was all the more remarkable because the initial purpose of the occupation was strongly punitive. Japan was to be made to stew in its own juice as a reward for having started, and lost, the Pacific War. The Japanese armed forces were demobilized and their equipment destroyed. Thousands of people were purged, or debarred from public life, for having supposedly instigated or supported the waging of aggressive war. Some who were regarded as war criminals were executed or imprisoned. In theory, Japan was to pay reparations to the countries it had occupied, but because of the battered state of the Japanese economy almost none were actually paid in the lifetime of the occupation.

Reform and "democratization" of the Japanese political system, with the aim of immunizing it against the temptation to resort to aggression again, got under way at the beginning of 1946, when the Emperor announced that, contrary to previous official theory, he was in no way divine. MacArthur believed that all major reforms should be introduced within the first year, while the favorable atmosphere lasted; the pace accordingly was rapid, probably too rapid. Under strong American prodding, the Japanese government reluctantly adopted a new constitution from which the numerous authoritarian features of the old one (the Meiji Constitution of 1889) were missing and which instituted a full-fledged parliamentary system based on universal suffrage. Perhaps the most striking feature was Article 9, which owed its inspiration directly to General MacArthur; Japan renounced war and the maintenance of armed forces. In addition, the huge prewar industrial holding companies (the Zaibatsu) were deconcentrated somewhat, although not broken up entirely; a rather thoroughgoing land reform was instituted; the educational system was reformed along American lines; and a considerable degree of local autonomy was substituted for the previous overcentralized arrangement under which the Home Ministry (now abolished) in Tokyo controlled the political life of the prefectures and localities.

Under this new regime, Japanese political life promptly reasserted the prewar tendency toward conservative political dominance. Except for a brief interval of Socialist rule in 1947–48, the leading right-wing party (known since 1955 as the Liberal Democratic Party) has been in power since the first postwar general election of April 1946. It has stood essentially for stability, not necessarily reaction, in domestic affairs, and for a close relationship with the United States as the cornerstone of its foreign policy.

The Occupation: The Recuperative Phase

In 1948–49 a sharp change occurred in the spirit and purpose of American occupation policy. The cost of letting Japan stew in its own juice had been high and there was a strong desire in Washington to "get Japan off the American taxpayer's back" by actively promoting economic recovery (still without a military resurgence) rather than continuing to preach perpetual austerity alleviated by American relief aid. American experts began to advise the Japanese government on how to improve the economy's performance. A still greater stimulus to recovery was the beginning, in 1950, of massive "offshore procurement" of supplies from Japanese firms by the United States government in connection with the American military effort in the Korean War.

Another important phenomenon was the intensification of the Cold War in Europe after early 1947, and especially after the Communist coup in Czechoslovakia in February 1948, as well as the Communist takeover in China in 1949. In this difficult international environment the United States government promptly came to desire Japan as a stable friend, although not an active military ally, rather than as a defeated and repressed enemy.

After 1949, accordingly, the occupation authorities began to tolerate the natural tendency of the Japanese government to embark on a "reverse course" that undid some of the occupation's innovations while leaving their essence intact. There was some "depurging" of purged individuals and some recentralization at the expense of local autonomy. A "police reserve" was created in 1950 mainly to cope with possible Communist violence, some of which actually occurred in the spring of 1950 in connection with the impending Korean War and led MacArthur to purge the leadership of the Japan Communist Party without actually being able to catch it.

The Peace Settlement

One of the most important manifestations of the new American policy toward Japan was an intensification of efforts dating from about 1947 to negotiate a peace teaty. The moving spirit in this difficult diplomatic process was John Foster Dulles, later to become Secretary of State. The essence of the American proposal was to leave the status quo in Japan undisturbed, apart from the termination of the occupation, to deprive Japan formally of all territory outside the home islands, and to avoid further controversy on this point by refraining from specifying in the treaty the new ownership of the territories that Japan had lost. The main reason for this evasiveness was the dispute between the Chinese Communists and the Chinese Nationalists over Taiwan, which had been a Japanese colony for half a century before 1945 but had become the Nationalists' main base since their defeat on the mainland. For similar reasons neither of the contending Chinese parties was invited to the conference that met at San Francisco in September 1951 to consider the American proposal for a peace treaty. The Western and pro-Western governments that participated in the conference signed the treaty, which went into effect in 1952. The Soviet and Indian governments withheld their approval and expressed strong, but opposing, objections to the American-sponsored treaty, the Russians asserting in effect that it was too easy on Japan and the Indians that it was too hard.

The United States government regarded the peace treaty as part of a package deal the whole of which the Japanese government would have to accept, and the American view necessarily prevailed. Another part was a separate bilateral treaty between Japan and Nationalist China (or Taiwan), which was accordingly negotiated along lines very similar to the San Francisco treaty; a corollary was that Tokyo, partly willingly, and partly at American insistence, maintained diplomatic relations with the Chinese Nationalists rather than the Communists. The third part was a mutual security agreement (in effect a treaty of alliance) between the United States and Japan; this pledged the United States to defend Japan against external attack, a reasonable idea inasmuch as Japan lacked the power to defend itself, but it embodied some other provisions not necessarily acceptable to Japanese national pride; it gave the

United States the right to maintain bases and forces in Japan (including Okinawa) for the security not only of Japan but of the Far East as a whole and to intervene in Japan itself (with the consent of the Japanese government) if civil order were seriously threatened by a Communist rising.

The fact that a peace treaty was negotiated for Japan as early as 1952 stands in strong contrast to the case of Germany, for which no peace treaty has been concluded even today. The main reason for this difference is the fact that the occupation of Japan was essentially an American affair, whereas the occupation of Germany was shared by the Soviet Union as well as the Western Allies. But just as Stalin successfully opposed a peace treaty for a united Germany on terms that the Western powers would accept, so he opposed, although unsuccessfully, the idea of a Japanese peace treaty without his own participation, and, therefore, on terms unacceptable to him. As early as 1948, George Kennan, then the State Department's chief policy planner, saw that American insistence on reviving Japan and negotiating a peace treaty with it would probably produce serious complications with the Soviet Union. This prediction was borne out even before the San Francisco Conference.

Independent Japan

The termination of the "Allied" occupation of Japan in the spring of 1952 left Japan formally and fully independent, and led to some further movement along the "reverse course," notably further "depurging."

Given the immense dynamism and practical competence of the Japanese people, the legacy of the remarkable period of development down to 1945, a favorable international environment, and some further factors already mentioned, the Japanese economy moved rapidly ahead in the late 1950s. Its problems soon became those of a mature developed economy—inflation and pollution in particular—aggravated by occasional adverse payments balances with the outside world and the necessity to import nearly all industrial raw material.

The associated processes of a limited "reverse course" in domestic politics, rapid economic growth, and continued close association with the United States produced some dramatic results during the premiership of Nobusuke Kishi (1957–60). He aroused the violent opposition of the Japanese left, including many students, by his "high posture," which took such forms as a bill increasing the powers of the police and pushing through the signature of a revised mutual security agreement with the United States (which in reality eliminated the American right to intervention in Japan and was more favorable to Japanese interests in other ways as well). His pro-American stand antagonized Peking, which, in 1958, launched a program of intense although largely ineffective economic pressures against his government and the Japanese business community.

These difficulties led to Kishi's resignation in 1960 and his replacement by Hayato Ikeda, who consciously adopted a "low posture" de-emphasizing political initiatives and stressing economic growth, a program that could hardly fail since the economy was already growing at an extremely rapid rate.

Premier Eisaku Sato (1964–72) reverted in part to Kishi's pro-American "high posture," but he took care to cultivate popularity by declaring himself in 1965 in favor of the reversion of Okinawa to Japanese civil jurisdiction in the near future. Another important, although considerably less popular, step was the "normalization" of relations (i. e., the establishment of normal diplomatic and commercial relations) with South Korea, also in 1965. In the same year a seriously divisive issue arose in the form of the escalation of the war in Vietnam. The Sato government stuck loyally by its political and security commitments to the United States, which made considerable, although declining, use of Okinawa as a base in connection with operations in Vietnam, and the business community profited enormously from another round of offshore procurement. The left (the Communists, the Socialists, and the intellectual and academic activists), on the other hand, objected strenuously to American policy toward Vietnam, partly because one of its effects was to strengthen the Japanese Establishment, and increased its opposition to the Sato government, the Liberal Democratic Party, and the American connection.

By the late 1960s, Japan was a significantly different country from the Japan of a decade or more earlier. Its economic performance was astonishing, although subject to the strains of maturity. Its political system, while parliamentary and essentially democratic, was dependably dominated by a conservative leadership with the result, however, of a growing frustration and proneness to illegal tactics on the part of the left. Japanese foreign policy was growing somewhat more assertive, although within the framework of the American alliance, and the memory of 1945 continued to inhibit rearmament at anything above the level of a modest defensive capability.

CHAPTER II

De-colonization
and Nation-Building
in Southern Asia

IN 1940 Nazi Germany, convinced that the British Empire was finished, tried unsuccessfully to interest its then Soviet partner in taking over the eastern half of the sick man's estate while the Germans seized the western half. The analysis was rather too dramatic and certainly premature. But by the end of the war Britain was exhausted and unable to hang on to more than a few of its holdings "east of Suez" in the face of rising Asian nationalism. The Labor government elected in 1945, as well as the public opinion that had brought it into existence, was anticolonial in any case. The United States had been committed since 1933 to independence for the Philippines in 1946. The French and Dutch, on the other hand, were not similarly pledged to free their colonial empires in Southeast Asia.

Partition and Independence in South Asia

Since the 1920s British rule in India had been under active political pressure from the Congress, a nationalist movement that purported to be secular but in fact was dominated by Hindus and above all by the saintly Mohandas K. Gandhi and the brilliant,

secular-minded Jawaharlal Nehru. One reason for Hindu dominance of the Congress was the relative backwardness of the important Moslem minority in the subcontinent. Its Establishment,
consisting to a large extent of princes and landowners, wanted to
prevent the Congress, and especially the socialist Nehru, from
organizing the Moslem masses and eliminating the privileges of
the Moslem elite. Accordingly, during the late 1930s the latter
appealed to the Moslem masses by insisting, more loudly than the
facts warranted, that the Congress was threatening Islam in India.
The result was the rapid growth of the Moslem League, previously
little more than an elitist club, to the level of a mass party representing the Moslem community almost to the extent that the
Congress, in fact if not in theory, represented the Hindu community. In 1940 the League went on record as demanding that the
British give separate and equal status to the Moslem community
under the label of Pakistan, when and if they granted India its
independence.

When peacetime political activity resumed in 1945, the League
began to press its demand by adopting Gandhi's technique of
"nonviolent noncooperation," or passive resistance. This approach,
which was directed against the Congress as much as against the
British, tended to escalate all too readily to violence, and under
the circumstances violence carried the seeds of religious warfare.
Under this threat the British and the Congress agreed reluctantly
by 1947 that India must not only be given its independence but
must be partitioned into two separate states in the process. The
Congress leadership consoled itself with the hopeful thought that
a state founded on religion could not survive and would be reab-
sorbed sooner or later into India, without war. This scenario
appeared all the more plausible because the areas that opted to
join Pakistan rather than India were split geographically into two
wings separated by nearly a thousand miles of Indian territory.

Whatever its prospects, Pakistan emerged into independence
at the same time as the Republic of India, in August 1947, amid
an appalling upsurge of Hindu-Moslem violence in the two provinces that had voted to split themselves into Indian and Pakistani
portions, Punjab and Bengal. Gandhi was assassinated by a Hindu
fanatic in January 1948, as he tried vainly to calm the violence.
His death left Nehru the unchallenged leader of the Congress and
of India. The vast majority of the 562 princely states, now deprived

of British protection and strongly advised to join either India or Pakistan, did exactly that with a minimum of controversy. The outstanding exception was Kashmir, whose Hindu ruler tried to join India in defiance of the fact that a large majority of his subjects were Moslem but then saw the western and northern parts of his territory invaded by regular and irregular Pakistani forces. The result was a local war between India and Pakistan that was terminated by United Nations intervention and followed by an informal partition of the state into Indian-held and Pakistani-held areas.

Nehru's India

The most remarkable thing about Nehru's India was that it did not succumb to its problems: overpopulation, poverty, underdevelopment, and social disunity (linguistic regionalism, caste barriers, etc.). But there were major positive achievements as well; India preserved and adopted the parliamentary system inherited from the British, strengthened its claim to the title of the world's most populous democracy, and launched a massive and reasonably successful program of economic development.

This impressive record can be credited plausibly to three factors. One was the size and competence of the elite in all major fields of activity (political, business, scientific, etc.) that had emerged within the Hindu community during the period of British rule. Another was the unifying influence of the Congress, which dominated political life—although by a gradually decreasing margin—sufficiently to be effective and yet operated in a reasonably democratic manner as compared with most such "umbrella" parties. The third was the personality and leadership of Nehru, who provided a focus of loyalty for the population and an intelligent and dynamic, although, of course, fallible, source of decision making.

Nehru was very worried over the backward and centrifugal pull of traditional influences in India, which have fairly free play within India's complex federal constitution. He therefore opposed, unsuccessfully, the creation of "linguistic states" (i. e., states whose boundaries had been redrawn so as to correspond approximately with those of India's major languages) in the mid-1950's. He was also worried about a possible growth of Communist influence in some of the non-Hindi-speaking states, Hindi being India's official language and the one often associated by non-Hindi speakers with the Congress leadership, as a result of local Communists exploiting local issues effectively against the Congress. In this way the Communists did in fact come to power in Kerala, in southwestern India, after the general election of 1957. In 1959, Nehru felt safe in overthrowing the Communist government in Kerala, which had gotten into serious difficulties, under his emergency powers. Moscow, which in effect valued him more highly than it did the Indian Communists, did not protest.

Nehru's reaction was to improve his already rather close relations with the Soviet Union, to insure against the possibility of Moscow inciting the Communists in Kerala or other Indian states to revolt against him. He had always admired what he thought to be the Soviet Union's approach to its domestic problems, including the ethnic and cultural minorities, and he appreciated the economic development aid and the diplomatic support on Kashmir that had been forthcoming from Moscow since Khrushchev's rise to effective leadership in 1954. He also tended to sympathize with the Soviet Union as against the United States in the Cold War, although he kept India formally "nonaligned" (uncommitted, neutral) and deplored the existence of military "blocs" (alliances) anywhere, and although he accepted American economic aid. The rather close relationship with the Soviet Union under Nehru has survived, in spite of some strains, down to the present.

Nehru also had strong, friendly feelings for the People's Republic of China. He considered that independent India and the "new" (i. e., Communist) China together could lead Asia gently and constructively along the path to national development and freedom from Western influence. The Chinese, who like the Soviets appreciated the value of Nehru's diplomatic support during the Korean War, seemed to reciprocate his friendship for a time (approximately from 1954 to 1957). Even then, however, there were strains. There were fairly serious disagreements over the location of the Sino-Indian border. Most Indians sympathized with the Tibetans, who were being harshly treated by the Chinese, and Peking resented that sympathy. A little later, as the Sino-Soviet dispute developed after the mid-1950s. Peking resented Nehru's continuing closeness to Moscow. From these differences arose some clashes on the Sino-Indian border in 1959, Nehru's rejection in the spring of 1960 of a Chinese compromise offer on the border dispute, an intensive but unsuccessful effort to solve it through further negotiations (1960–61), and an Indian decision to occupy the strategic and disputed Aksai Chin area, adjacent to northeastern Kashmir, across which the Chinese had built an important military road linking western Sinkiang with western Tibet. This decision, which began to be implemented in the spring of 1962, when the Chinese leadership was in a militant mood on account of domestic difficulties and crises elsewhere (in the Taiwan Strait, in Indochina, and along the Sino-Soviet border in Central Asia), produced protests and warnings from Peking as Indian troops moved toward the Chinese road and then, in October-November, 1962, a brief border war, in which the Indian Army was badly defeated in fighting that occurred entirely on disputed territory (so that Peking could claim not to have invaded India). The border dispute remains unsettled, but the Indian Army, although now much stronger, seems to have given up any idea of occupying the whole of Aksai Chin in the near future.

The virtual collapse of his relationship with Peking and the defeat in the border war greatly shocked Nehru and contributed to a rapid decline of his health and vigor. Another disturbing problem was an erosion of the Congress's effectiveness and popular appeal, as a result of which six cabinet members resigned in 1963 in order to devote themselves to strengthening the Congress. One of them, Lal Bahadur Shastri, was soon brought back as Acting Deputy Prime Minister and therefore presumably as heir apparent to Nehru, who died in May 1964.

The Failure of Parliamentary Government in Pakistan

Apart from poverty and (at least in East Pakistan) overpopulation, the situation in Pakistan after 1947 differed unfavorably from the one in India. Leadership talent was much scarcer and tended to devote itself primarily to maintaining its control over the masses and opposing India on every conceivable issue. The Moslem League lacked the maturity and roots among the people that the Congress had developed under Gandhi and Nehru. Mohammed Ali Jinnah, the League's senior figure, was much more autocratic than Nehru; he insisted on assuming the ceremonial title of Governor General (appointed by the British Crown, as in Canada and other members of the Commonwealth), and yet also on dominating the work of the government in a way incompatible with the parliamentary system. A later Governor General, Ghulam Moham-med, behaved in a similar way, also with serious damage to the parliamentary system in Pakistan. Politics were dominated by an alliance of army officers, bureaucrats, and to a lesser extent land-lords, against which party politicians butted their heads without much effect except to bring about the adoption of a constitution in 1956 (India's was adopted in 1950) followed by two years of unstable party politics. The elite and people of East Pakistan (con-sisting of East Bengal) felt oppressed by the West, which domi-nated politics and the army and siphoned off much of the foreign exchange earned by the East's exports. As a result, the Moslem League lost an election in 1954 in East Bengal to the (local) Awami League and declined rapidly thereafter in the country as a whole.

At first Pakistan was as nonaligned in its foreign policy as India, but it began to incline toward the United States in the early 1950s in the hope of increasing the flow of American aid. Soon afterward the Eisenhower administration decided to seek an alli-ance with Pakistan as a means of getting bases from which to moni-tor Soviet missile tests in Central Asia and of helping to block a largely mythical Soviet drive to get control of Middle Eastern oil. Pakistan reciprocated mainly in the hope of getting support against India, which the United States had no real interest in providing; the military aid agreement concluded in 1954 specified that the arms provided by the United States could be used only against pos-sible Communist aggression. Always in the vain hope of support against India, Pakistan joined the Southeast Asia Treaty Orga-nization, of which the United States was the founding member, and the United States-sponsored Central Treaty Organization in 1954. One of the main effects of these actions by Pakistan was to arouse great excitement in its two unfriendly neighbors, India and Afghanistan, drive them closer to the Soviet Union, and worsen their relations with the United States.

By 1958, Pakistan's domestic problems, including the ineffec-tiveness of its parliamentary system, the tension between East and West, and the stagnant state of the economy, were reaching the proportions of a crisis. The army, with the support of the bureauc-racy, accordingly seized power from the politicians in October 1958 and proclaimed martial law. The senior figure of the military leadership, Mohammed Ayub Khan, emerged as President, and for a time provided reasonably effective leadership. The overall performance of the economy was improved, but at the cost of corruption and inequalities of wealth favoring a few dozen business families that were to cause trouble later. Ayub inaugurated a substitute for the parliamentary system, which he regarded as too sophisticated for Pakistan, that he called Basic Democracy, under which a system of local indirect elections was balanced by firm presidential rule. Ayub's popularity declined, and in a presidential election held in 1965 the opposing candidate, Miss Fatima Jinnah, a sister of the late Mohammed Ali Jinnah, made a surprisingly strong showing against him. A sense that he was slipping then began to tempt Ayub into adventurous behavior that was to contribute to his downfall.

De-colonization and Independence in Southeast Asia

De-colonization in Southeast Asia was inevitable, for reasons already suggested, but it was not inevitably peaceful. France and the Netherlands, which had been occupied by the Germans during the Second World War, had a subconscious need to compensate themselves by holding on to as much of their colonial empires as possible. The result was colonial wars in Indochina and Indonesia, the former of which in view of its importance is treated separately in another Chapter (VII). The United States and Britain, on the other hand, felt no similar urge to hold on where it would have been difficult or unpleasant to do so.

The United States had already promised independence to the Philippines for July 4, 1946, and delivered precisely on schedule, partly for genuinely idealistic reasons and partly to begin the process of getting the islands outside the American tariff barrier so that duties could be charged on Philippine exports to the United States. Another indication that the American attitude was far from disinterested was the fact that the United States insisted that, in return for independence and decreasing partial exemption of Philippine goods from American duties, American citizens be allowed equal investment rights in the Philippines with Philippine citizens. Existing American military base rights, as well as an American obligation to defend the islands, were confirmed in a mutual security agreement. The Philippines' American alignment was rounded out with membership in SEATO. Unfortunately, the islands' American-style presidential constitution and formally democratic elections masked a political system dominated by powerful families and bossism and riddled with corruption.

The Attlee government toyed briefly with the idea of trying to restore colonialism in Burma but changed its mind in 1947, mainly because the strong unpopularity of prewar British rule persisted. The Burmese nationalist leadership, organized in the Anti-Fascist People's Freedom League (AFPFL), opted for independence outside the Commonwealth, which was granted at the beginning of 1948. The AFPFL had been seriously weakened by the assassination of its leader, Aung San, in July 1947. The leadership as a whole was not only nationalist but Marxist in outlook. U Nu, the first prime minister of independent Burma, followed a foreign policy of nonalignment, partly because of Nehru's influence and partly because of fear of China. Almost from the beginning, independent Burma was plagued by revolts on the part of Communist groups and various ethnic minorities who resented the domination of the state by the Burmans (the majority ethnic group). Another problem was the so-called KMT (Kuomintang) Irregulars, former Chinese Nationalist soldiers who had settled in northern Burma (as well as some other parts of Southeast Asia) and who by their occasional raids into China created a risk of retaliatory Chinese Communist incursions into Burma; in 1953 the Burmese government repudiated American economic aid because it suspected the United States of collusion with the Chinese Nationalists on Taiwan to direct and supply the KMT Irregulars.

The British did not grant independence promptly to Malaysia (including Singapore), because there was less active demand for it than in Burma, because it was of great economic importance to the United Kingdom (Malaya was and is a major rubber and tin producer), and because the antagonism between the economically prosperous and numerous Malayan Chinese (about 40 percent of the total population) and the comparatively backward Malay majority complicated the problem of moving toward independence. Nevertheless, Malaya was given internal self-government in 1955 and complete independence, supported by British security guarantees, in 1957. Its politics were overwhelmingly dominated by the Alliance, composed of the leading Malay party (the United Malay National Organization) and the main Chinese party (the Malayan Chinese Association). By Asian standards the Malayan economy, founded on rubber and tin, was extremely prosperous. Singapore, overwhelmingly Chinese in population, was kept separate from Malaya so as not to tip the ethnic balance there against the Malays, but it was granted increasing degrees of self-government. In 1959 a sweeping electoral victory on the part of the leftist People's Action Party (PAP) alarmed the British and the Malays with the spectre of "another Cuba" in Singapore. But the PAP and its able and energetic leader Lee Kuan Yew soon shed its Communist elements, partly because the island is heavily dependent on foreign trade and investment and could not afford to frighten them away. When the Communist ex-allies of the PAP, organized in the Barisan Sosialis Party, scored some electoral gains in 1961, the PAP, the British, and the Malay government decided to cope with the problem of possible further gains for the Singaporean extreme left by federating the island together with Malaya and the British territories in North Borneo in a new state to be called Malaysia, which was inaugurated in 1963 over strong protests from China and Indonesia.

The Dutch returned to Indonesia in the last months of 1945 to find that a republic under the presidency of the prominent nationalist leader Sukarno had been proclaimed on August 17, with the consent of the Japanese occupation authorities. There ensued four complicated years of fighting (in particular two Dutch "police actions" in 1947 and 1948) alternating with negotiations, the latter sometimes taking place under American auspices. During this period the Republic, based largely on Java, grew stronger, while the ability and will of the Dutch to suppress it weakened. At last, in late 1949, an agreement was reached that created a federal Indonesian state formally under the Dutch Crown, with the Republic as its major component but with the others still under considerable Dutch influence. West Irian (Dutch New Guinea) was retained by the Dutch and became a major issue between Indonesia and the Netherlands. The central internal relationship of the new state was the one between nominally Moslem, but actually more nearly Hindu, Java and the predominantly Moslem but partly Christian Outer Islands (nearly all the others beside Java); the problem is intensified by the fact that Java is densely populated and needs extensive financial support, which it likes to get from the foreign exchange earned by the exports of the Outer Islands (petroleum, rubber, tin, etc.). The relationship was settled predominantly in

Java's favor in 1950, when the Republic established direct control over the other components; the formal union with the Dutch Crown was broken off in 1954. After the inconclusive general election of 1955, Sukarno began to favor the replacement of parliamentary democracy by what he called Guided Democracy, which in effect was a left-wing presidential dictatorship based to some extent on the Chinese and Soviet models, and with a minimal role for the political parties. This move exacerbated the tensions with the Outer Islands, in which revolts led by both military and civilian Moslems erupted in 1958. Their fairly prompt suppression enhanced the power of the largely Java-based central Establishment but also opened the way to increased tensions within it, mainly between the rapidly growing Communist Party (PKI) and the essentially anti-Communist army. The PKI successfully sought the support of Sukarno for the sake of protection, and of Peking in exchange for support in connection with the Sino-Soviet dispute. A clash between this leftist coalition and the army was postponed first by a politico-military conflict with the Dutch over West Irian, which the Dutch agreed to give up in 1962, and a "Confrontation" with the British and Malaysia in Kalimantan (Borneo) after 1963, but it could not be postponed indefinitely.

Communist Risings in Southeast Asia

Armed Communist-led guerrilla movements emerged to one degree or another during the Second World War in the Philippines, Burma, Malaya, and Indonesia, in addition, of course, to Vietnam. They were naturally opposed to a restoration of colonial rule and tended, like their Soviet and Chinese colleagues, to regard the independent governments that emerged from the process of decolonization as not really independent at all and therefore as suitable targets of what Communists called "armed struggle" (i.e., revolutionary warfare).

As the Cold War escalated in 1947 with the announcement of the Truman Doctrine and the Marshall Plan, Stalin apparently decided that the United States was in effect asserting a claim to hegemony over the western half of the vast British Empire-cum-sphere-of-influence of the south of Europe, and that it would be appropriate for him to do something similar to the eastern half before the United States could establish a presence there as well.

This would mean of course working through local Communist Parties. The general rationale for this offensive was proclaimed in more indirect language, by Stalin's heir apparent Zhdanov, at the time of the founding of the Communist Information Bureau (Cominform), an organization of nine European Communist Parties including the Soviet, in 1947. It appears that at the Communist-dominated Calcutta Youth Conference (February 1948), and through other channels at the same time, unpublished directives to revolt were passed from Stalin to at least some of the Southeast Asian Communist Parties, and that these were supplemented by more generalized encouragement from the Chinese, Vietnamese, and Yugoslav parties.

The first revolt was that of the Stalinist wing of the Burma Communist Party, often known as the White Flags, under Than Tun. He refused to be appeased by a program of leftist legislation pushed through by U Nu (nationalization of land and of foreign enterprises, etc.) and launched a guerrilla war against the newly independent government simultaneously with the outbreak of other revolts mounted by various left-wing groups and ethnic minorities. These insurgents could perhaps have overthrown the government if they had cooperated effectively with one another and if they had received significant support from the Chinese Communists. Since neither of these things materialized, the Burma Army under General Ne Win was able by about 1950 to reduce the insurgencies to fairly minor proportions, although it was unable to stamp any of them out.

The Malayan Communist Party, which had grown into a formidable guerrilla movement by fighting the Japanese with British support, was composed largely of overseas Chinese and was responsive to guidance from the Chinese Communists as well as from Moscow. After a series of disputes with the British authorities, it went into revolt against them in 1948. Because of the importance of Malayan exports to the economy of the United Kingdom, the British mounted a huge politico-military operation against what they called the Communist terrorists and soon confined them to the jungle. The British used air transport to establish and maintain jungle forts from which combat patrols could find and fight the Communist guerrilla units, and the latter were progressively isolated from their major source of supplies and recruits, the Chinese squatter population settled near the edges of the jungle, by reconcentrating the latter in new communities where their movements could be controlled and they could be protected from Communist pressures. In these ways the Communists were soon reduced to a minor nuisance, and, after unsuccessfully seeking in 1955 to gain a legal role in Malayan political life, they were forced to transfer their base to the remote jungle area astride the Malay-Thai border, where they remain to this day.

Stalin admired Sukarno's Republic of Indonesia for fighting the Dutch, and it is not clear what attitude he wanted the PKI to adopt toward it. A prominent PKI leader who returned from the Soviet Union in 1948, Musso, apparently thought that Stalin wanted him to take over the Republic by largely political action, as the Communists in Czechoslovakia had recently done. Some of his colleagues, on the other hand, precipitated an armed revolt against the Republic at Madiun, in eastern Java, which was promptly suppressed by the Republic. It took about five years for the PKI, now under the leadership of the young and able D. N. Aidit, to begin to recover from this disaster by repudiating violence, expanding its membership through various forms of political action, and seeking Sukarno's favor. Partly because of the refreshing contrast it appeared to present with most of the other parties, which were tarnished by corruption and office holding, the PKI grew so rapidly that by the early 1960s it was the largest nonruling Communist Party in the world.

The Communist-led Hukbalahap (Huks) in the Philippines capitalized effectively on the corruption and ineffectiveness of the newly independent government. By 1948 they were in revolt, although not necessarily on account of a directive received from Moscow, China, or any other external source. The revolt grew rapidly until the direction of the counterinsurgency operations was assumed in 1949 by a new Secretary of Defense, the honest and energetic Ramon Magsaysay, who leaned heavily on the advice of his chief of staff, General Jesus Vargas, and his American adviser, Colonel Edward Lansdale. They intensified the efforts of the Philippine Army against the Huks, as well as improving its behavior toward the civilian population, and offered surrendered Huks not found guilty of individual crimes an amnesty and a homestead in the sparsely populated southern islands. In this way the Huk menace was rapidly reduced, and Magsaysay was elected to the presidency in 1953. He attempted to break the power of the

Establishment and institute needed social reforms (notably land reform) but was unable to accomplish much before his death in an airplane crash in 1957.

With the perennial exception of Vietnam, then, Communist "armed struggle" did not prosper in Asia. Just as this fact was beginning to become evident, the Chinese Communists came to power full of the belief that their revolutionary experience, which can be described as highly politicized guerrilla warfare exploiting hatred of real or alleged "imperialist" influence in the country concerned, was uniquely valid in Southern Asia. As part of a complex process of bargaining with Mao, Stalin admitted the relevance of the Chinese revolutionary model. When Mao was in Moscow at the beginning of 1950, Stalin appears to have conceded the Chinese a supervisory role with respect to revolutionary movements in Southern Asia in exchange for Chinese recognition of Soviet pre-eminence in Northeast Asia (Korea and Japan). Recognizing the poor progress of the insurgencies in Southeast Asia (again except for Vietnam), Peking advised a more political and less military strategy and after 1952 began, as did Moscow, to de-emphasize "armed struggle" altogether in its advice to the Southeast Asian Communist Parties. This shift reflected Chinese and Soviet appreciation not only of the generally unpromising status of "armed struggle" but of the need to conciliate rather than antagonize the newly independent governments of Asia as a source of possible political and diplomatic support against the United States. One of the high points in this process of conciliation, at least where China was concerned, was the Asian-African Conference at Bandung, Java, in April 1955.

The Bandung Conference

Since few African countries had attained independence by 1955, most of the participating countries were Asian. The Soviet Union was not invited, on the ground that it was not truly an Asian country, but China was. The main moving spirit was Nehru, who fancied himself the leading statesman of the Third World. He was correspondingly annoyed when the star of the conference turned out to be the Chinese Premier and Foreign Minister, Chou En-lai.

Chou realized as soon as he reached Bandung that Peking was

widely disliked, especially by the Western-aligned governments of Asia but also to a considerable extent by the neutrals, for its recent incitement of "armed struggle," its pressures on Buddhism and Islam within its borders, and its boundary disputes with its neighbors. Above all, Chou was concerned to combat the effort of the United States to forge an anti-Chinese alliance in the form of SEATO; he was particularly conciliatory to the delegates from Thailand and the Philippines, the two Southeast Asian members of SEATO. At the end of the conference, Chou impressed the delegates favorably by offering to negotiate the issue of Taiwan, which had been under American protection since 1950, with the United States.

While at the conference, Chou negotiated a treaty with the Indonesian government, dealing with the status of persons of Chinese descent living in Indonesia who were considered to have dual citizenship (Indonesian and Chinese). As with the Chinese communities in the other Southeast Asia countries, many of them were economically prosperous, and they were disliked for that and other reasons in Indonesia more than in any other country of the region. Peking, having largely given up the idea of manipulating overseas Chinese for its own purposes because of their vulnerability to local retaliation, wanted as many as possible of the dual citizens to become Indonesian citizens exclusively so as to minimize future disputes; Indonesia preferred to deny Indonesian citizenship to most Chinese so as to be better able to discriminate against them as noncitizens. The treaty adopted a compromise formula, but the Indonesian government for various reasons refused to ratify it until 1960, by which time Sukarno had decided to seek a partnership with Peking for the main purpose of expelling Western influence from Southeast Asia.

Although Chou En-lai's performance was the most interesting, and probably the most important, aspect of the Bandung Conference, it was not the only aspect. The conference enabled the leaders of the countries represented to know each other better and enhanced their sense of solidarity as against the West. The conference adopted a ringing declaration against colonialism.

Another conference of the same kind, but called an Afro-Asian Conference, was scheduled at Algiers for June 1965. It failed to convene, however, nominally on account of a coup in Algeria at that time, but actually because the Chinese and Indonesians intended to use the conference as a major propaganda forum against the United States, the Soviet Union, India, and Malaysia, to the point where some of the other countries preferred not to see the conference held. With the collapse of the Algiers Conference, the Asian-African (or Afro-Asian) movement also collapsed, although a parallel series of conferences of nonaligned nations continued to be held. The lesson in all this seems to be that the Third World countries do indeed have important common interests, notably some genuine and some imaginary grievances against the West, but that common action on the basis of those interests is difficult to achieve.

CHAPTER III

The Soviet-American Cold War

IT WOULD be hard to deny that the most important single phenomenon in international politics since the Second World War has been the relationship, essentially an adversary one, between the United States and the Soviet Union, which is often known as the Cold War. Its ending has been hailed by American optimists and Soviet propagandists, but these reports of its death have always turned out to be greatly exaggerated. Every responsible leader on both sides has recognized the suicidal risks of a direct confrontation and has so far successfully avoided one, with a partial exception for the Cuban missile crisis. But if the Soviet-American crises that have occurred from time to time have never escalated to the level of war, neither have the periodic swings toward détente yet produced a condition of true harmony. In Trotsky's famous phrase, the relationship has been one of neither war nor peace. An objective analysis must assign more than half, although not all, the responsibility for this unhappy situation to the Soviet Union.

Planning for the Postwar Period

During the last years of the Second World War, there were two main schools of thought among American leaders about the postwar period; both recognized the crucial importance of the Soviet

Union's wartime role and its postwar relations with the United States. The first school, led by President Roosevelt himself, was the idealistic or universalist school in the tradition of Woodrow Wilson. By prolonging the spirit of the wartime alliance somehow into the postwar period, and by bringing both the United States and the Soviet Union into the United Nations Organization as Wilson had tried unsuccessfully to bring the United States into the League of Nations, this school hoped to blur the edges of the Soviet Union's Marxist-Leninist ideology and its tendency to regard the Western democracies as its adversaries. Regional spheres of influence for any major power were rejected in principle by this school as relics of the bad old power politics of an earlier era. The other school, which can be labeled the realistic, accepted the inevitability if not the desirability of power politics and spheres of influence and generally took a less optimistic view of the possibilities for postwar cooperation with the Soviet Union. The most articulate exponent of this view was George F. Kennan, a Foreign Service Officer stationed in Moscow at the end of the war, whose penetrating despatches did a great deal to awaken official Washington from its tendency toward euphoria about Soviet intentions and to a more accurate perception of the problem. As a result of interaction with the American realists, and still more with foreign realists such as Churchill and Stalin himself, the universalists modified their position reluctantly to the extent that they conceded to the Soviet Union, as the strongest power on the European continent, a sphere of influence in Eastern Europe, which Soviet arms were in the process of liberating from the Germans. But Roosevelt naively insisted on seeking and accepting Stalin's assurance that the countries in the Soviet sphere would be allowed to have democratic governments, for the first time in their history (except in the case of Czechoslovakia).

To Stalin, this would have meant no sphere of influence at all. Since about the time of the decisive victory of his armies over the Germans at Stalingrad early in 1943, he had been planning on the assumption, a virtual certainty, that the Soviet Union would not only defeat Germany but would be in a position to dominate a considerable area in Eurasia outside its current borders, especially in Eastern Europe. As he once indicated at a Kremlin banquet, he expected another war with Germany, and perhaps with other enemies as well, in fifteen or twenty years. Against that contin-

gency he wanted a buffer zone wider and more securely defended
than the mere eastern half of Eastern Europe, which he had acquired as his sphere through his famous pact of 1939 with Hitler,
but which had been overrun two years later by the Germans on
their way to attack the Soviet Union. To Stalin, a true buffer zone
consisted of satellite states run by local Communist Parties controlled from Moscow. But he was prepared to move fairly cau-
tiously toward this goal, for two main reasons. He did not want to
disrupt the wartime alliance too soon or too violently, if only because one of his allies, the United States, had the atomic bomb
(after 1945) whereas he did not (until 1949). Secondly, he did not
want to endanger the promising political future of the vigorous
French and Italian Communist Parties by embarrassing them in
the eyes of their countrymen through obviously heavy-handed behavior in Eastern Europe or elsewhere.

By late 1943 Stalin felt confident enough of the basic strength
of his position to begin negotiating face to face with Roosevelt
and Churchill on wartime strategy and postwar arrangements and
to promise something that he regarded as being in the Soviet interest and that the Americans also wanted for their own reasons,
namely that he would enter the war against Japan shortly after the
defeat of Germany. It was mainly at his conferences at Yalta
(February 1945, with Roosevelt and Churchill) and Potsdam (July
1945, with Truman and Attlee) that the initial shape of the postwar arrangements was worked out, generally to the Soviet Union's
advantage.

It was agreed that the Soviet Union should annex some islands
(mainly the Kuriles) from Japan, East Prussia from Germany, and
the eastern part of Poland (so that the Soviet Union now bordered
for the first time on Czechoslovakia and Hungary). Poland was to
be compensated with German territory, an arrangement calculated
to help insure Polish dependence on Soviet support in the face of
probable German irredentism. Eastern Europe, apart from Greece,
was to be in effect a Soviet sphere of influence; Stalin promised to
allow free elections and democratic governments in these countries, but it was soon to become clear that there was no effective
way to compel him to fulfill this commitment. Stalin also received
Western recognition of the Mongolian People's Republic (Outer
Mongolia), which had been a Soviet satellite for twenty years, as
his sphere of influence, and of his freedom to press Chiang Kai-

shek's government for the right to use the main railways and ports of Manchuria. He was to be awarded reparations from the Axis powers, principally Germany and Japan. Germany, and possibly Japan, were to be divided into occupation zones, including one for the Soviet Union; the boundary of the Soviet zone in East Germany was drawn considerably to the west of the farthest point reached by the Soviet armies at the time of V-E Day, so that Berlin (which was divided into four occupation sectors) found itself well within the Soviet zone. Roosevelt conceded Stalin's demand for a veto (for the other permanent members as well as the Soviet Union) in the United Nations Security Council and for three seats in the United Nations for the Soviet Union (one each for the Russian, Ukrainian, and White Russian Republics, all of which were completely controlled from Moscow). In exchange for all of this, as well as valuable wartime support and the possibility of postwar credits, Stalin conceded that Western Europe was outside his sphere and in effect could be an American sphere to the extent that the United States had the ability and desire to make it so, although he probably expected the United States to retreat into postwar isolationism after a time.

Breakdown of the Wartime Alliance

The uneasy wartime partnership between the Soviet Union and its Western allies began to collapse in favor of the Cold War as Soviet armies moved westward on non-Soviet territory, against crumbling German resistance, in 1944. Poland was the first country whose fate became a major issue between Stalin and his Western partners, both because its geography made it the first (apart from Romania) to be occupied by the Soviets and because of its political importance to the West: Britain had gone to war with Germany in 1939 on account of the German attack on Poland, and Roosevelt could hardly forget in an election year that the United States contained several million voters of Polish extraction. Ignoring these sensitivities, Stalin promptly showed his ruthless determination to crush all non-Communist leadership in Poland and bring it rapidly under the control of Soviet-dominated Polish Communists. A similar objective was implemented, with some variations, in the other Soviet-occupied countries as well: East Germany, Hungary, Romania, and Bulgaria. Yugoslavia and Albania escaped full-fledged Soviet military occupation but were taken over by their local Communist Parties after an anti-German guerrilla war; Czechoslovakia was occupied only briefly by Soviet forces but came under the control of its own Communist Party, the only strong one in prewar Eastern Europe, in 1948, without a civil war.

The Soviet victory brought difficulties to other countries as well. There was a flourishing Communist insurgency in Greece for a few years after 1944, although it was supported mainly from Yugoslavia and Bulgaria and Stalin regarded it as expendable, since he conceded that Greece was in the Western sphere. Soviet forces remained in occupation of northern Iran after the end of the war and tried to set up a local Communist regime but withdrew in the spring of 1946 under the pressure of an international crisis in which the United States supported the Iranian government. The Soviet Union tried unsuccessfully to pressure Turkey into ceding some territory.

It was reasonably clear that this behavior was part of an overall design whose main theme was hostility to the West, even though Stalin never gave any sign of an actual intention to invade Western Europe. He told his own people as early as February 1946 that they would have to continue sacrificing under stern discipline in view of the tense international situation. The Soviet Union's armed forces were demobilized after the war only to a limited extent, whereas those of the United States were reduced drastically, so that there was no effective American military restraint on Soviet behavior apart from the atomic bomb. The latter, as well as the Soviet Union's state of exhaustion after the defeat of Germany, was probably what prevented Stalin from behaving in an even more expansionist manner in the early postwar period than he did in fact.

It soon became obvious in Washington that more than nuclear deterrence was required to cope with the problem presented by Stalin and to alleviate the conditions around the Soviet periphery that seemingly tempted him to expand. The answer was the concept of containment, defined by its intellectual father George Kennan as "the adroit and vigilant application of counter-force at a series of constantly shifting geographical and political points, corresponding to the shifts and manoeuvres of Soviet policy." The first official expression of this concept was the Truman Doctrine, announced in the spring of 1947, which promised economic and military aid to Greece and Turkey and to other countries that might be threatened by Soviet pressures in the future.

The Cold War passed from an undeclared to what amounted to a declared state over the central problem of Europe. Stalin not only refused an American invitation in 1947 to participate in the Marshall Plan for European economic recovery but vetoed the desire of the Polish and Czechoslovakian governments, Communist-dominated though they already largely were, to take part. He tried unsuccessfully to sabotage the operation of the Marshall Plan in Western Europe through a campaign of political violence on the part of the French and Italian Communist Parties, outraged by their expulsion from coalition governments in their respective countries in the spring of 1947. Stalin's failure in Western Europe was symbolized by the defeat of the Italian Communists by the Christian Democrats in a hard-fought election in April 1948. Meanwhile, in the summer of 1947, he had established the Communist Information Bureau (Cominform), an organization representing the Soviet and the major European Communist Parties including the French and Italian, as an aid to carrying on the political and propaganda aspects of the Cold War. The Cominform's potential for international credibility and influence was badly shaken in the spring of 1948 by a crisis arising from Tito's open and successful resistance to Stalin's efforts to reduce Yugoslavia to the status of a satellite.

This great internal crisis was paralleled, in Stalin's eyes, by an external one. By mid-1948 the American, British, and French governments, exasperated by the negative and obstructive character of Stalin's German policy, were beginning to move toward the creation of a non-Communist German state through the merger of the three Western occupation zones. Stalin tried to stop this trend, which was highly objectionable to him, by blockading the land routes to West Berlin (i. e., the three sectors of Berlin occupied by the Western powers) in July 1948. But West Berlin managed to survive through the following winter on the strength of the toughness of its people and the famous American airlift, with which the Soviet Union chose not to interfere. Stalin quietly lifted the blockade in the spring of 1949. Later that year the Western occupation zones were formally merged in the Federal Republic of Germany

(West Germany), and the Soviet zone was proclaimed the German Democratic Republic (East Germany) while still under Moscow's military occupation and political control.

The Berlin Blockade and the seemingly final breakdown of any hope for a common policy on Germany for the Soviet Union and the West produced an atmosphere of crisis in Western Europe, even though there was no evidence of an impending Soviet attack. In order to create instead an atmosphere of security and confidence that would promote West European economic recovery and political cooperation, the United States took the lead in forming the North Atlantic Treaty Organization (NATO) in April 1949. It included all the West European countries except Spain, Switzerland, and West Germany (which was admitted in 1955), as well as the United States, Canada, Greece, and Turkey (the two latter countries joined in 1950). For some years at least, NATO's existence did promote the goals for which it was established, even though there was probably no strictly military necessity for it in view of the possession by the United States of a nuclear deterrent.

Soviet-American Interaction in the Postwar Far East

The United States had two primary objectives in the Far East in 1945: to ensure that Japan would never again threaten the peace of the region, and to prevent a renewal of civil war between the Nationalists and the Communists in China. Stalin's objectives were at the same time more flexible and more self-interested. George Kennan, the best authority on this subject then and now, described Stalin's policy at the time as "a fluid resilient policy directed at the achievement of maximum power with minimum responsibility on portions of the Asiatic continent lying beyond the Soviet border." This meant, in the Far East as in Europe, annexations and the creation of a buffer zone-cum-sphere of influence to the extent consistent with the overriding aim of avoiding a war with the United States. Stalin was considerably helped toward the fulfillment of his objectives by the eagerness of the United States that he should enter the war against Japan and save American lives by knocking out the supposedly powerful, but actually rather weak, Japanese forces in Manchuria. Stalin was determined to enter the war in any case and was delighted at the willingness of his naive

American allies to reward him for what turned out to be a relatively easy military operation. He entered the war on August 8, 1945, so as to be sure that Japan would not collapse under the impact of American atomic bombs before he could stake a claim to be one of the victors.

Since Stalin had no presence in and little leverage on Japan, where he was refused an occupation zone by President Truman, there was no significant Soviet-American interaction over the major defeated Asian power. It was another story in Korea, which was within reach of the Soviet armies. Probably with the idea of giving Japan a buffer against the Soviet sphere of influence on the Northeast Asian continent, American planners and negotiators persuaded their Soviet counterparts, at and after the Potsdam Conference, to agree to American occupation of the peninsula south of the 38th parallel, for the purpose of disarming and evacuating Japanese military personnel, the remainder to be occupied by Soviet forces, supposedly for the same purpose. American military government authorities in the South wrestled after V-J Day, valiantly but rather clumsily, to operate an occupation regime and at the same time to foster a democratic Korean political system, something for which there was no basis whatever in Korean tradition. The result was the Republic of Korea (South Korea), which was inaugurated in 1948 under the nominal auspices of the United Nations, under the actual rule of the dictatorially inclined President Syngman Rhee, and with limited economic and military aid from the United States. In the North, the Soviet occupation forces set up a full-fledged satellite regime under the even more dictatorially inclined Korean Communist Kim Il Song and then withdrew in 1948, at which time the Democratic People's Republic of Korea (North Korea) was proclaimed. Soviet-American negotiations in 1946–47 aimed at unifying the country foundered on Soviet insistence that only Communist and pro-Communist Korean parties could even be consulted on the formation of a provisional democratic government for the entire country, a demand that was completely unacceptable to the United States.

Soviet and American interests in China were somewhat closer to being parallel. Neither wanted to be drawn into a war with the other over that vast and unmanageable country (or over anything else), and this meant that each was bound to try to restrain the known warlike impulses of its respective Chinese client, the Nationalists in the case of the United States and the Communists in the case of the Soviet Union.

Since Moscow had not played a very obvious role in China for nearly twenty years, and since the Communists were essentially operating a revolutionary movement rather than a government, the interaction between them was relatively inconspicuous. It is known, however, that Stalin privately advised the Chinese Communists to enter a genuine political and military coalition with the Nationalists under Chiang Kai-shek's leadership at least for the time being, a demand that the Communists rejected in essence while complying outwardly. There is reason to believe that Stalin wanted the Communists to confine their activities and influence to North China and Manchuria, where they were relatively strong but where he could also exert comparatively direct influence on them, and that the idea of their controlling the whole of China struck him as neither very probable nor very welcome. Soviet forces occupied Manchuria in August 1945, by agreement with the United States, and remained there for about six months. While in occupation they tilted the local power balance in favor of the Communists by admitting their troops, turning over captured Japanese weapons to them, and making entry difficult for Nationalist forces. The Soviet military authorities also removed about one billion dollars' worth of Japanese industrial equipment, in order to ensure at the minimum that the region, regardless of who came to control it, could not again become a strategic base aimed at the Soviet Far East for a long time.

On the other side, the United States, which had played a very active diplomatic and military role in China since Pearl Harbor in support of the Nationalist government, undertook a difficult and in retrospect hopeless effort to mediate between the Nationalists and Communists and bring about a coalition government representing both of them as well as certain minor parties. This effort, which was conducted under the prestigious auspices of General George C. Marshall, was of course a failure. Each side was determined to crush the other and confident of its ultimate ability to do so. Each therefore put forward conditions it knew the other would not accept and waited only until the United States and the Soviet Union withdrew their military presences from China in the spring of 1946 to launch a full-scale civil war.

For a variety of political and military reasons of which limitations on American aid and support were one, but not a decisive one, the Nationalists then acquired the dubious honor of being the first Asian client of the United States to fall victim to a Communist insurgency.

Dulles versus Khrushchev

An important change in the personalities and atmosphere associated with the Cold War occurred in early 1953. Stalin died and after more than a year of struggle among his heirs was succeeded by the more flexible and less bloody-minded Nikita S. Khrushchev. In the United States, there was a transition from the Truman to the Eisenhower administration, whose foreign policy was designed and executed to a considerable extent by the formidable John Foster Dulles as Secretary of State. Dulles was keenly aware of the trouble that his predecessor Dean Acheson had suffered from the conservative Republicans in Congress and was determined not to have the same problem. This consideration, even more than his own inclinations, imposed on him a rigid and indeed militant stance with respect to the Cold War, among other things. Where Acheson had preached and practiced containment, Dulles spoke—sometimes but not always as a bluff—of liberation (of Eastern Europe), brinkmanship (the art of getting the adversary to back down by going to the brink of war without actually going over), and Massive Retaliation. The latter concept, or slogan, was understandably misinterpreted by many people to indicate a willingness to launch a nuclear war in retaliation for virtually any military move by the Communist powers. What Dulles actually had in mind was a far more flexible strategy based on the fact that in 1954 both hydrogen bombs and tactical (battlefield) nuclear weapons entered the American military inventory alongside other types of nuclear and conventional weapons. The nervousness that Dulles's threatening aura and brinkmanship inspired in his adversaries, as well as in nearly everyone else, helped considerably to extract relatively favorable settlements of the Korean (see Chapter IV) and Indochinese (see Chapter VII) conflicts.

Khrushchev emerged as the temporarily unchallenged head of the Soviet leadership in early 1955 after a series of successful power struggles against police chief Lavrenti Beria, who advocated

concessions to the West on Germany and whose fall was precipitated by popular risings in East Germany on June 17, 1953;
Premier Georgi Malenkov, who had advocated an only slightly
less passive policy toward the West based on an acceptance of an
inferior Soviet nuclear posture that would however, it was hoped,
amount to a minimum deterrent; and Foreign Minister Vyacheslav
Molotov, who advocated a cautious and "Stalinist" line in foreign
policy without conciliation of the West. Khrushchev's own policy,
at least initially, was one of outward militancy toward the West
short of serious provocation, combined with an active cultivation
of major Third World neutrals designed to undermine Western
influence in that region. In 1954–55, accordingly, he initiated
major programs of military aid to Egypt and economic aid to
India.

Khrushchev's tough line on Europe contributed to the admission of West Germany to NATO, in the spring of 1955, something
that was most unwelcome in Moscow since it seemed to increase
the likelihood of American (and therefore Soviet) involvement in
a military confrontation between East and West Germany if one
should occur. The Soviet response was a round of conciliatory
diplomacy: a new (but still essentially propagandistic) disarmament proposal; agreement on a state treaty (in effect, a peace
treaty) for Austria; and a summit conference with his American,
British, and French counterparts at Geneva. Khrushchev exploited
the enhanced nervousness of his East European allies about West
Germany, which has been one of the main sources of Soviet influence over them, by forming the Warsaw Pact (the Communist
counterpart to NATO) in the spring of 1955.

At his party's Twentieth Congress in February 1956, Khrushchev made clear his determination to avoid a thermonuclear war
with the United States. To counter the impression of weakness
that this line tended to convey in some quarters, especially Peking,
he initiated a tactic of "rocket rattling" a few months later; in
other words, he began to make carefully timed and essentially
meaningless nuclear threats against various Western powers (not
including the United States, until 1958). The classic example
occurred at the time of the Suez crisis of November 1956, when
Britain and France joined Israel in military operations against
Egypt. Once he had seen the United States oppose the Anglo-
French action in the United Nations, Khrushchev "rattled

rockets" with a sense of impunity at Britain and France, which had already made it clear that they were terminating their military operations.

The Suez crisis also gave Khrushchev an opportunity to distract international attention to some extent from a major crisis in Eastern Europe growing out of his emotional (although secret) attack on Stalin at the Twentieth Congress. An upheaval in Poland in October was resolved by political means to Khrushchev's satisfaction, but a similar affair in Hungary rapidly turned into an armed popular rising against pro-Soviet elements and gave rise to an independent Communist regime that promised to introduce a multiparty system into Hungary and to withdraw from the Warsaw Pact. This situation, which was intolerable to Moscow if only because it might have encouraged similar trends in other countries, was resolved when Soviet troops drowned it in blood in early November. The Hungarian freedom fighters, as they are known to their sympathizers, had hoped for some sort of American military support even though the United States had not actually incited the rising, but there was none. "Liberation" was shown to be nothing but a slogan.

In 1957–58 Khrushchev came under powerful political pressure from the Chinese to take a tougher line toward the West, especially on the Taiwan issue. He made some gestures in this direction but was unwilling to go farther on Taiwan than verbal militancy, which he displayed when Peking whipped up a politico-military crisis in the Taiwan Strait in August-October 1958. Instead of pressing the United States in that direction, Khrushchev issued a seemingly stern demand in November 1958 for drastic changes in the status of West Berlin.

As this demand was still pending in the spring of 1959, Dulles died. No later American statesman has been willing to use threats as an instrument of diplomacy to the same extent or would have been credible if he had tried to do so. His passing marks a more important watershed in the history of the Cold War and in international politics than is generally realized.

Peaceful Competition and "Harebrained Scheming"

Instead of applying increased pressure on Eisenhower now that he had lost Dulles, Khrushchev launched into a phase of détente diplomacy stressing peaceful (largely economic) competition between the two systems. The high point of this phase, which began with a dropping of the demand regarding West Berlin, was Khrushchev's visit to the United States in the summer of 1959, at the conclusion of which he hailed Eisenhower as a "man of peace." But Khrushchev's personal impulsiveness, as well as political pressures from some of his colleagues, rendered his détente diplomacy highly unstable. In May 1960 he canceled a scheduled summit conference at Paris, from which he expected little in any case and which was objectionable to the Chinese, when an American U-2 reconnaissance aircraft crashed on Soviet territory and President Eisenhower assumed personal responsibility for such flights.

At first Khrushchev saw little reason either to like or to respect President Kennedy. He was enraged by American support for the disastrous effort by Cuban exiles to overthrow the pro-Soviet regime of Fidel Castro at the Bay of Pigs in the spring of 1961. During and after a conference with Kennedy at Vienna the following June, Khrushchev apparently formed the impression that Kennedy was very unsure of himself and would raise no serious objection if the East Germans were to put up a barrier to isolate East Berlin from West Berlin, into which refugees from East Germany were then streaming at an enormous rate. He was right; the raising of the Berlin Wall in August, in violation of the 1945 agreements, was not met with any effective counteraction from the Western side.

The granting of independence to the Congo by Belgium in 1960 was followed by a period of chaos during which Khrushchev tried in various ways to give support to left-wing elements. He failed and order began to be restored, largely because of effective action by the United Nations under the leadership of Secretary General Dag Hammarskjöld. In a rage, Khrushchev demanded that the post of Secretary General be made into a troika (a three-horse Russian carriage), in other words a collectivity in which the top post should be held by a neutral (in the Cold War) and the two deputies be picked one each from the Communist and Western countries, each with a veto. The proposal, which if adopted would have seriously impaired the working of the United Nations, was blocked by Western opposition. On the other hand, the next Secretary General, the Burmese U Thant, took much greater care than his predecessor not to antagonize the Soviet Union.

By the summer of 1962, after several years of wrangling, the
United States and the Soviet Union had come close to an agreement on banning nuclear testing. Moscow suddenly backed away,
under Chinese pressure it was later learned.* Khrushchev, then
in one of his erratic swings, was temporarily in a mood to conciliate
Peking, and for this purpose he needed strategic leverage with
which he might compel the United States to abandon its protection
of Taiwan. He also wanted leverage with which to extract a settlement of Berlin and Germany more satisfactory than the essentially
stopgap measure of the Wall. He was vastly inferior to the United
States in intercontinental ballistic missiles (ICBMs) but had relatively large numbers of medium range ballistic missiles (MRBMs)
and intermediate range ballistic missiles (IRBMs) as well as a
potential forward launching platform in the shape of Cuba. It
was mainly for these reasons that in September 1962 he began,
secretly and in great haste in the hope of avoiding premature dis-
covery, to install in Cuba what was apparently intended to be a
total of 64 offensive missiles. He believed that once operational
these missiles could be used to pressure Kennedy into making
concessions along the lines already indicated. But to his enormous
surprise and discomfiture, a combination of firm and judicious
American counterpressures, which appeared to create some risk
of general war, forced him to agree in late October to withdraw
his missiles, which he did soon afterward.

Both sides were sufficiently nervous over their apparent trip
to the brink over Cuba so that the latter was followed, as soon as
Khrushchev had coped with some domestic opposition and
strengthened his hand by taking the lead in a new round of
polemics against the Chinese, by an important move toward
détente. After suspending the jamming of the Voice of America,
he reached at last an agreement on a nuclear test ban in late July.
The difficult problem of verification through inspection, on which
the Soviet leadership was very sensitive for security reasons, was
bypassed by banning only tests in the atmosphere and under water,
which could be verified without on-the-spot inspection.

Having contributed in this way to a considerable improvement
of Soviet-American relations, Khrushchev was abruptly ousted

* Cf. Helmut Sonnenfeldt, "The Chinese Factor in Soviet Disarmament
Policy," *The China Quarterly*, no. 26 (April–June 1966), pp. 129-130.

from power in October 1964 by a coalition of his colleagues, who objected to what they called his "harebrained scheming" in domestic and foreign policy. Among the counts against him were undoubtedly his adventurism in sending missiles to Cuba, and probably also his heavy-handed policy toward the Chinese, to whom he may have been contemplating applying military pressure by the time of his fall.

After Khrushchev

Khrushchev's successors, who were (and are) led by party First (now General) Secretary Leonid Brezhnev and by Premier Alexei Kosygin, were determined to avoid his swings between the extremes of demonstrative friendliness and dangerous provocation in dealing with the United States. Their attitude was to be hostile, but their behavior was not to be bellicose, at least for the time being.

The dramatic escalation of American military involvement in Vietnam in 1965 (see Chapter VII), although not entirely unexpected in Moscow, came as a considerable shock to the new Soviet leadership. North Vietnam, a Communist state and a member of the "socialist camp," was being heavily bombed by the American "imperialists" and was therefore presumably entitled to expect effective Soviet support. If it were not forthcoming, the effects on Soviet influence not only in North Vietnam but elsewhere, notably Eastern Europe, might be very serious. Like Khrushchev, however, Brezhnev and Kosygin were unwilling to take any action that was perceived as creating a serious risk of war with the United States. Soviet policy toward the crisis in Vietnam had to be designed with this limiting factor in mind and accordingly consisted mainly of extensive military aid and advice for the North Vietnamese, but not direct involvement in the fighting to any significant extent.

The American action in Vietnam unwittingly reinforced a decision already taken in Moscow, in the aftermath of the Cuban missile crisis and the resulting Soviet humiliation, to build up the Soviet Union's strategic nuclear forces to a level of at least approximate parity with those of the United States, in order to avoid having to back down in any similar confrontations in the future. During the second half of the 1960s this was done with remarkable speed, although at the cost of serious strains on the Soviet economy, with transforming effects on Soviet-American relations and international politics in general.

These effects took time to make themselves felt, however. In the meantime, the Soviet leadership developed a highly uncomfortable feeling that the United States, emboldened by its own behavior in Vietnam, was inflicting a series of setbacks by proxy on the Communist cause in the Third World. In Africa, in particular, there was a series of military coups against leftist civilian leaderships in 1965–66; to Moscow the most traumatic of these was the one against President Kwame Nkrumah of Ghana, in whom the Soviets had invested a great deal of aid and political capital in the hope that his socialist regime could eventually be transformed into a Communist one without a civil war or an international crisis. The Brezhnev leadership evidently decided that it would be desirable, for psychological and political reasons, to inflict a compensating setback by proxy on the United States in the Third World.

The target chosen was an obvious one, Israel. The idea was to allege that Israel was about to attack Syria, to convince Nasser that this was the case, and then to manage the ensuing Israeli-Egyptian crisis so as to avoid an actual war, weaken the Israeli position, and enhance the reputation of Soviet statesmanship especially among the Arabs. The plan proceeded approximately on schedule until U Thant unexpectedly panicked and withdrew the United Nations Emergency Force from between the Israeli and Egyptian armies, whereupon what had been envisaged as a phoney crisis turned suddenly into a real war, even if a short one. It took Israel only six days to win the June War (1967). Instead of a success, Moscow had suffered another setback, this time self-inflicted.*

Still looking for a success, the Soviets selected the following year an area within their own sphere of influence, where the risks accordingly were more controllable. It was furthermore an area in which strong liberalizing tendencies were at work that seemed likely in Moscow, if unchecked, to have adverse effects on the Soviet leadership's position and interests not only in Eastern

---

* Cf. Adam B. Ulam, *Expansion and Coexistence: Soviet Foreign Policy, 1917–1973*, 2nd ed. (New York: Praeger, 1974), pp. 732-733.

Europe but in the Soviet Union itself. This was Czechoslovakia. Among the many aspects of the complex crisis that culminated in the invasion of Czechoslovakia in August 1968 by forces of the Soviet Union and four other Warsaw Pact states (East Germany, Poland, Hungary, and Bulgaria), the one most directly relevant to the Cold War was Soviet concern over the possible American reaction; if it had been perceived as sufficiently adverse, there would probably have been no invasion of Czechoslovakia. But it was an election year in the United States, and President Johnson was eager before leaving office to have a summit meeting with Kosygin and if possible reach an agreement on limiting strategic arms. Furthermore, Secretary of State Dean Rusk had a strong bias against the Czechs because they had been sending aid to North Vietnam. Accordingly, public statements by high American officials during this period made it clear that the United States still regarded Czechoslovakia as falling within the Soviet sphere of influence and indicated that it would take no strong action in the undesired and seemingly unlikely event that Czechoslovakia were invaded. When it was, Johnson felt compelled to cancel his meeting with Kosygin and thereby neatly got the worst of both worlds. He warned Moscow publicly against attacking Romania, which appeared to be another likely target, and this warning probably had something to do with the fact that Romania escaped the fate of Czechoslovakia.

By demonstrating its political resolution and military power, in short its machismo, through invading Czechoslovakia, Moscow had gone far toward restoring its self-confidence, reasserting its hegemony over Eastern Europe, increasing its influence on European affairs in general, and improving its position in the Cold War. To put it mildly, this was hardly good news for the United States. As for what the United States could and should have done, an eminent European remarked at the time that "You could at least have observed a decent silence."

CHAPTER IV

The Sino-Soviet Alliance

THE ROOTS of the Sino-Soviet relationship of the early 1950s, which was sufficiently close to be perceived in Washington as "monolithic," go back into the history of Chinese Communism, which therefore needs to be briefly discussed.

The Chinese Communist Movement

The Communist Party of China (CPC) was founded in 1921, under the auspices of Lenin's Communist International (Comintern), by Chinese who believed that Marxism-Leninism and Soviet support could eliminate China's backwardness and oppression at the hands of the "imperialist" powers. In 1922 they were ordered by the Comintern to ally themselves with Sun Yat-sen's stronger party, the Kuomintang (Chinese Nationalist Party). The reason was that the Comintern had decided to support the "national bourgeois" Sun as the best hope of combatting "imperialist" influence (mainly Japanese and British) and ultimately revolutionizing China. The problem was that the latter objective obviously required strengthening the Kuomintang, but if this were done the Communists would have great difficulty in taking control over it as the Comintern intended. In 1927 Sun's successor Chiang Kai-shek, who had been greatly strengthened by Soviet political advice and military aid, but who distrusted the Comintern and feared the social revolution that the CPC was working to bring about, turned against his leftist allies.

The CPC was nearly but not quite destroyed as a result of Stalin's excessive trust in Chiang Kai-shek and Stalin's confidence in his own ability to manage the turbulent situation in China by remote control. For the time being, however, Stalin and the Comintern retained their domination over the central leadership of the CPC, while the emergence of Communist-controlled rural bases in the interior of Central and South China initiated a process over which he could exert almost no control at all. The most successful of the bases was one in Kiangsi created by Mao Tse-tung, who proved remarkably effective in combining organizational work among peasants with revolutionary warfare by Red Army troops so as to expand the base. His control over it was badly eroded after 1932 by a combination of pro-Comintern elements and the able organizer Chou En-lai, who for a time acquired control over the Red Army. This combination had the misfortune to be in charge when mounting Nationalist military pressures dislodged the CPC from its bases in Central and South China, including the one in Kiangsi, in 1934 and set them in motion toward Northwest China in the famous Long March. During this epic trek Mao exploited his adversaries' setbacks and alleged errors to achieve control over the Party's military machinery, as well as a political position that was "more equal" than that of his colleagues. He refrained, however, from assuming formal Party leadership at that time, probably in order to avoid a possible choice between subservience to Stalin (nominally, the Comintern) and a break with him; Mao assumed the title of Chairman of the Central Committee in June 1943, the month after Stalin dissolved the Comintern. In spite of Mao's rise, the extraordinarily adaptable Chou En-lai remained an important figure in the Party leadership, in some ways second only to Mao.

Mao and his colleagues took advantage of the Sino-Japanese War (1937–45) to increase the Party's power and to enlarge its autonomy with respect to Stalin. For two years before the war Stalin showed his belief that only Chiang Kai-shek could lead a Chinese national resistance to Japanese aggression, negotiated a substantial program of military aid to the Chiang government, and put pressure on the Chinese Communists to accept Chiang's leadership in connection with the war with Japan. Mao outwardly deferred to Stalin and Chiang, as well as to Chinese public opinion, but in reality insisted on operating politically and militarily against the Nationalists as well as against the Japanese, as the opportunity presented itself. As a result of this strategy, but probably still more as a result of the damage inflicted on the Nationalists' position by the Japanese invasion, the CPC emerged from the war in 1945 much stronger than at the beginning. Corresponding to this growth, and to a large extent flowing from it, occurred a further decrease in Stalin's ability to influence the CPC and an increase in Mao's power within the party to virtually unchallengeable proportions.

Nevertheless, Stalin tried to use the Soviet invasion of Manchuria in 1945, in connection with the collapse of Japan, as a lever to reestablish control over the CPC and push it into another coalition with the Nationalists so as to minimize the chances of a civil war and a Soviet-American confrontation in and over China. He was unsuccessful regarding the first but not the second, since the United States government was as eager to avoid such a confrontation as he was. Once the Soviet Union and the United States withdrew their forces from Manchuria and China proper, respectively, in the late spring of 1946, their Chinese partners went at each other in full-scale civil war. Weakened by its own shortcomings, by the effects of the Japanese invasion, and by a falling off in American aid to levels lower than had been hoped for, the Nationalists lost by 1949 to the politico-military strategy that the Communists under Mao Tse-tung's leadership had developed during the two previous decades.

"We Lean to One Side"

Although Mao made a few overtures to the United States during the years from 1945 to 1949, it is very unlikely that anything the United States could reasonably have done would have prevented an accommodation between Mao and Stalin as the Chinese civil war drew to a close. They were linked by a common ideology— somewhat differently interpreted to be sure and later to become a source of disunity between them—a mutual historical relationship, a desire not to repeat the disaster of the Stalin-Tito controversy, and a common fear and dislike of American "imperialism." The Chinese were probably afraid that Stalin would put pressure on their Inner Asian territories (Manchuria, Sinkiang, or even Tibet) unless they conciliated him. Fearful of the United States and of a possibly resurgent Japan under American patronage, they saw in the Soviet Union the only possible source of needed aid, support, and protection. With something close to this in mind, Mao announced in mid-1949 that his party would "lean to one side," Stalin's, in the Cold War. Stalin, for his part, regarded the People's Republic of China (PRC) as a major addition to the "socialist camp" (the Communist bloc), one that helped to compensate him for the setbacks he had been suffering in Europe since the takeover of Czechoslovakia.

During an important visit by Mao to Moscow (December 1949– February 1950), Stalin gave a defensive military alliance against the United States and Japan and an increment of economic aid, in return for Mao's recognition of Stalin's effective control over the Mongolian People's Republic and of certain Soviet railway and port rights in Manchuria originally acquired at the Yalta Conference. The two men discussed a number of problems relating to the rest of Asia, the outcome being roughly that Mao conceded Stalin the primary role with respect to Northeast Asia (Japan and Korea), and Stalin did the same for Mao with respect to Southeast Asia. After China's entry into the Korean War late in 1950 (see below) Peking began to receive Soviet military equipment in significant amounts. With the help of many Soviet advisers, the Chinese began to apply the Soviet model in their own economic planning and development and in many other fields, as well as praising Soviet experience and the Soviet Union in general to the skies in their domestic and foreign propaganda. Peking, in short, really believed that it was leaning to the Soviet side, although it did so in an essentially Chinese way that Moscow did not much like, and that did not amount to the subservience that Stalin would have preferred, even though he was not in a position to demand it.

The Korean War

Since its occupation by Soviet troops in August 1945, North Korea had been a Soviet satellite, although the occupying forces had withdrawn in late 1948. Kim Il Song, the leading North Korean Communist, was naturally eager to reunite his country, which had been a Japanese colony for nearly half a century before

1945, by "liberating" the South. Since various less violent ploys failed, he evidently decided after American forces left South Korea in 1949 that an invasion was both feasible and necessary.

It was probably in January 1950 that Stalin, with Mao Tse-tung's knowledge and consent, gave agreement to this idea. Stalin and Mao were almost certainly afraid that, if not "liberated" first, South Korea might later become a springboard for a later American-Japanese military adventure on the continent of Asia. For the time being, however, it appeared vulnerable because various prominent Americans, including Secretary of State Dean Acheson (on January 2, 1950), were indicating that the United States would probably not defend South Korea if it were attacked.

The time for the North Korean attack was apparently fixed for August, but if so Kim Il Song moved it up to June 25 for reasons of his own relating to the political situation in South Korea. Having been strengthened by a recent inflow of Soviet aid, his forces advanced rapidly through the weak South Korean defenses. Contrary to the Communist side's expectations, the United States government began to defend South Korea, and the United Nations over Communist opposition gave its approval to the defense.

In mid-August the Communist offensive was deep in South Korea but began to be rolled back. At that time the United States began to indicate an intent to reunify Korea by taking over the North, to the great concern of the Communist powers. Whereas Moscow confined itself to propaganda and diplomacy, Peking warned the United States through a variety of channels not to invade North Korea and began to put itself in a position to intervene if its warnings were ignored.

They were, in effect. General MacArthur routed the North Korean troops in South Korea by his amphibious landing at Inchon on September 15 and approached the 38th parallel two weeks later in a confident mood determined to invade North Korea and hand it over to President Syngman Rhee of the Republic of Korea (South Korea), whom he admired. He considered that Chinese intervention was unlikely, and that if it did occur it could be handled through American air power, for which (under more favorable conditions) he had acquired a vast respect during the Pacific War. For several reasons, he considered Soviet intervention even more unlikely.

He was right in the last of these opinions, but Stalin was

nevertheless determined to save North Korea without confronting the United States himself. He therefore urged the Chinese, as the only available proxies, to intervene, and at Mao's insistence promised them military aid and reaffirmed his commitment to fulfill his obligations under the Sino-Soviet alliance. The Chinese, in addition to being influenced by Stalin's attitude, were concerned about the threat to Manchuria posed by the American advance, interested in saving North Korea, and anxious to deflate American prestige in Asia and enhance their own. After the beginning of their intervention, they tried to use it as a means of compelling the United States to withdraw its forces from Korea and cease its protection of Taiwan, and of gaining entry to the United Nations in place of the Chinese Nationalists. Peking's strategy in pursuit of these objectives, once Chinese intervention had begun, was to try to drive American (and other non-Korean) forces beyond the 38th parallel and indeed out of Korea altogether. There are persuasive reasons, however, for believing that the minimum Chinese objective was simply to occupy and hold a buffer zone on the Korean side of the Manchurian-Korean border (marked by the Yalu River), and that a Sino-American war became inevitable only when General MacArthur insisted, apparently in ignorance of the Chinese military presence in North Korea and against the better judgment of the Joint Chiefs of Staff, on ordering his awkwardly disposed forces to march to the Yalu.

It was of course an undeclared war; in order to keep it that way and avoid American escalation, if possible, by giving the United States an excuse to pretend officially that only a "police action" was in progress, Peking labeled its troops in Korea "volunteers." This fiction also gave the Soviet Union an excuse not to involve itself on China's behalf more than it wished to do. Moscow did little more than send arms to the Chinese and give occasional warnings against American escalation of the war beyond the limits of Korea, as initial shattering Chinese military successes galvanized MacArthur into recommending a drastic program of action (American naval blockade and aerial reconnaissance of, and Chinese Nationalist operations against, the Chinese mainland) and President Truman into suggesting that nuclear weapons might be used (they were not, for military as well as political reasons). But nervousness over the Soviet reaction, which it was feared might include a Soviet move against Western Europe, was a major factor in leading Truman and the Joint Chiefs to overrule MacArthur and refrain from escalating the war beyond Korea.

Early in 1951 the American, South Korean, and other United Nations forces, now under the competent leadership of General Matthew B. Ridgway, stabilized the front south of Seoul and began to roll the Chinese and North Koreans back, but it soon became clear that President Truman did not intend to invade North Korea again. MacArthur, who was strongly opposed to this decision, publicly revived his recommendations for drastic action and precipitated his own relief from command on grounds of insubordination. Two Chinese offensives, evidently aimed at capitalizing on the crisis created by his removal, were heavily defeated in April and May 1951. The Chinese and North Koreans then agreed to armistice talks, which went on for two years (June 1951–July 1953) while the front stabilized in the vicinity of the 38th parallel.

The talks had made considerable progress, although with difficulty, when it became clear early in 1952 that a large percentage of the prisoners taken by the United Nations Command did not want to go home for various reasons, and that their captors were unwilling to compel them to do so. This development presented the Communist side with a serious political and prestige problem, to which it responded by massive riots among North Korean prisoners still loyal to their regime and by a massive propaganda campaign, alleging that the United States had been waging "germ warfare" against North Korea and in Manchuria; the purpose was presumably to soften the American stand on the prisoner question and deter the United States from escalating the war by focusing international attention on its behavior, actual or alleged.

Tension rose during 1952 as a major deadlock developed over the prisoner issue, and as Stalin entered the last months of his life in a belligerent mood marked by a plan to purge many of his colleagues and apparently by a tendency to contemplate military action against the defiant Tito and against the United States in the Far East. The Indian government, which had been decidedly "neutral in favor of" the Communist side during the Korean War, introduced an essentially pro-Communist "compromise" resolution on the prisoner issue into the United Nations General Assembly in the autumn of 1952. American and other diplomatic pressure, however, led the Indian delegation to revise the resolution in a direction much more acceptable to the United States, whereupon it was loudly rejected by the Communist powers.

The prisoner deadlock was highly frustrating to the Eisenhower administration, which came into office in January 1953 pledged to achieve an armistice in Korea by any necessary means, preferably peaceful ones. Its first move was to "unleash Chiang Kai-shek" by removing the ban imposed by President Truman in June 1950 on Nationalist military operations against the China mainland, while keeping in force his commitment to defend Taiwan against Communist attack. This move, which was virtually meaningless since the Nationalists lacked the ability to attack the mainland at that time, made no impact on Peking, although for some reason it seems to have startled Stalin. Soon afterward, shortly before his death, he and Peking had to consider a much more serious problem: a covert, explicit threat by the United States to expand the war from Korea to the mainland of China and to use nuclear weapons.* Whatever Stalin may have thought about this, his successors were in no position or mood, given their serious domestic difficulties, to confront the United States on China's behalf. Although they tried to conciliate Peking in a number of marginal ways, they told it in effect that it must not count on them for active support in forcing the United States to back down on the prisoner question. Accordingly, Peking had no real choice but to sign, on July 27, 1953, an armistice that incorporated the principle of voluntary repatriation of prisoners espoused by the United States and reflected in the revised Indian resolution.

Militarily and politically speaking, the Korean War was inconclusive from many points of view. Probably the most important outcome was the obvious one, the frustration of the Communist effort to seize South Korea by force, as well as a determination in both Peking and Washington to avoid another Sino-American war. Another significant result was the American policy of trying to contain the People's Republic of China militarily and isolate it politically, which was to last for about fifteen years. Finally, although the Korean War saw the zenith of the Sino-Soviet alliance and of cooperation between Moscow and Peking, the circumstances of its termination contributed to the beginnings of the Sino-Soviet dispute.

* Dwight D. Eisenhower, *Mandate for Change, 1953–1956* (New York: Doubleday, 1963), p. 181.

CHAPTER V

The Containment
Policy in Asia

WHEREAS the American containment policy in Europe and
the Middle East was designed to cope with what were perceived as Stalin's hostility and expansionist tendencies, American
containment efforts in Asia were aimed mainly against behavior
also perceived as hostile and threatening on the part of the People's Republic of China, which was considered to be very closely
allied with the Soviet Union.

The Origins of Sino-American Hostility

The United States was drawn into the Second World War
largely because it refused, on account of its traditional friendship
for China symbolized by the Open Door Policy and its desire to
keep Southeast Asia in friendly hands, to concede Japan the freedom of action in China and Southeast Asia that Tokyo demanded.
The support that the United States gave to Chiang Kai-shek's government in connection with the American war effort against Japan
created a considerable sense of commitment to the survival of that
government, even though its shortcomings were recognized to be
numerous and serious. Thus American support for Chiang Kai-
shek turned fairly logically after V-J Day, although not without
objections from some American officials and private citizens, into

support for Chiang Kai-shek against the Communists. This policy, which took the form mainly of economic and military aid but not the commitment of American combat forces, was limited until mid-1946 by an active American effort to mediate between the Nationalists and the Communists, and for a year after that by an embargo on American arms shipments to the Nationalists, but it was nevertheless substantial. Although obviously not sufficient to save the Nationalists, who probably could not have been saved by any action that it would realistically speaking have been within the power of the United States to take, this support was quite sufficient to antagonize the Communists. Their ideology and their orientation toward Stalin at the height of his Cold War with the United States, as well as their felt need for a proclaimed external adversary against whom Chinese popular support could be mobilized, further biased the Communists against the United States. Some indications to the contrary notwithstanding, it is unlikely that anything the United States could realistically have done would have prevented the emergence of an adversary relationship with the Chinese Communists, who openly proclaimed their support for Stalin against not only Tito but the United States as early as November 1948.

Although discouraged by these indications and by the maltreatment of some American diplomats by the Communists in late 1949, in violation of their diplomatic immunity, the State Department hoped until about the beginning of 1950 that some sort of reasonable relationship could be worked out with the new Communist regime without a complete abandonment of the Nationalists, who had taken refuge on Taiwan. With this in mind, American support for Taiwan was limited to economic aid; President Truman announced on January 5, 1950 that the United States would not try to prevent the Communists from taking the island. This stand was not changed when Mao Tse-tung concluded an alliance with Stalin on February 14, 1950, even though that action startled American officialdom and contributed heavily to bringing it to the conclusion that China was now a Soviet satellite.

Domestic American politics also played an important role in the estrangement between Peking and Washington. Conservative Republicans began to accuse the Truman administration, quite unfairly, of having "lost" China, and in the spring of 1950 Senator Joseph McCarthy offered as the explanation for the "loss" the allegation that the administration was riddled with Communists and Communist sympathizers. To this partisan furor a major contribution seems to have been made by the so-called China Lobby, a lavishly financed propaganda operation working on behalf of the Nationalists. It rapidly became a political impossibility for the State Department, which was the conservatives' main target, to go on exploring the possibility of a relationship with Peking, especially in view of the Chinese Communists' increasingly anti-American and pro-Soviet stance.

The North Korean invasion of South Korea on June 25, 1950 appeared to a startled Washington as the opening gun of some Stalinist master plan for Asia of which his presumed satellites, the North Koreans themselves and the Chinese, were the active agents. This view tended to make the administration review its stand on Taiwan. Furthermore, the conservatives and the China Lobby were demanding American support and protection for the island. It seemed unlikely that the administration would get sufficient Congressional Republican support for military operations in defense of South Korea unless Taiwan was also brought under the American wing. On June 27, accordingly, President Truman not only began to commit American forces to Korea but announced that the United States would prevent military movements across the Taiwan Strait in either direction; since the Nationalists had no capability of attacking the mainland, this meant in effect simply that Taiwan was now under American protection. This step, which Peking promptly began to denounce as an American "occupation" of Taiwan, which it regards as Chinese territory, immediately became the most serious single political issue between the Chinese Communists and the United States. The undeclared Sino-American war in Korea was even more traumatic, but it was comparatively short-lived (October 1950-July 1953). Its main significance in this context was that it generated a strong belief on the part of the political public of each adversary that the other was its principal enemy and rival in Asia. The Chinese, as the weaker party in terms of strategic military power, acquired a strong sense of the United States as a serious threat to their security and even to their survival, not only on account of the Korean War but on account of the threatening military posture assumed by the United States in Asia at that time for the purpose of containing China.

Containment and Isolation

The predominant official and public American view of Peking for about a decade after 1950 was that it was expansionist, both by its own nature and by virtue of its presumed status as a Soviet satellite. Being expansionist, it must be contained militarily and to the extent possible isolated politically, in this view.

Beginning in 1950, the United States expanded the military bases it already had in Japan (notably Okinawa) and the Philippines into a vast network that included bases and powerful combat forces in South Korea, and ultimately Indochina and Thailand as well. The main adversary against whom these forces were arrayed was of course Communist China.

Parallel with the presence of American forces in the Far East and the Western Pacific, a series of military alliances and similar pacts was negotiated by the United States with friendly Asian governments (Japan, the Republic of Korea, the Republic of China, and the Philippines) during the last few years of the Truman administration and the first few years of the Eisenhower administration. In addition, SEATO was brought into being by Secretary Dulles in 1954 as a collective security organization embracing the United States, Britain, France, Australia, New Zealand, Pakistan, Thailand, and the Philippines. Its main single purpose, at least in official American eyes, was to give Thailand some protection against possible Chinese attack or subversion. SEATO lacks NATO's joint command structure and has become increasingly ineffective as the image of a Chinese military threat to Southeast Asia has faded. The bilateral pacts lack the automatic quality of the NATO treaty; at Congressional insistence, the United States can act to meet threats to its Asian allies only in accordance with its own "constitutional processes." Accordingly, American military activities have had to be conducted to a large extent under various executive orders and agreements and Congressional resolutions, rather than pursuant to formal treaty rights and obligations. The two major relevant Congressional resolutions are the Formosa Resolution, which was adopted in 1955, had become a dead letter by about 1970, and authorized the President not only to defend Taiwan if attacked but to commit American forces to the defense of the Nationalist-held offshore islands (mainly Quemoy, opposite Amoy), if in his judgment a Communist attack on them was part of an attack on Taiwan itself; and the Tonkin Gulf Resolution, which was adopted in August 1964, repealed in 1970, and authorized the President to employ American forces in Indo-china more or less as he saw fit.

Partly, although by no means exclusively, in connection with its effort to contain China, the United States became involved in the 1950s in economic aid programs for practically every non-Communist Asian country. There were also large military aid pro-grams for the Republic of Korea, the Republic of China, and the Republic of Vietnam (South Vietnam), as well as smaller ones for Japan, the Philippines, Thailand, Laos, and Cambodia. The size of the individual programs was not made public. In addition, these countries, except for relatively prosperous Japan, received substantial amounts of a special type of economic aid known as defense support, much of which consisted of consumer goods, and the announced purpose of which was to help them support higher defense budgets than would have been possible otherwise and to combat inflation by "mopping up excess purchasing power." The actual effect was often to encourage inflation and increase the po-litical power of authoritarian governments and military elites. The latter tendency was generally regarded by the United States as an inevitable byproduct of the entire containment policy, one of whose strategies was strengthening "indigenous forces" on the principle (to use one of the Eisenhower administration's slogans) of "Let Asians fight Asians."

Parallel with containment went a far-reaching American effort to isolate the People's Republic of China from even peaceful ex-ternal contacts to the extent possible, in the hope of "hastening its passing" (Dulles's phrase) in favor of the Nationalist regime, which continued to enjoy American diplomatic recognition and political support, as well as aid and protection. The United States did not permit the Nationalists to try a major attack on the mainland, however. The United States accordingly withheld diplomatic rec-ognition from Peking and urged other countries to do the same, although with gradually diminishing success. The United States worked hard and continually, and until 1971 successfully, to keep Peking out of the United Nations and the Nationalists in. Ameri-can influence was largely responsible for the passage by the United Nations General Assembly in February 1951 of a resolution con-demning Peking as an aggressor in Korea, and in May of the same year of a resolution urging all members of the United Nations to avoid exporting strategic commodities (i.e., items considered to have military significance) to mainland China. The United States went farther and embargoed all trade with mainland China after 1949; it also persuaded its major allies, until about 1957, to apply a broader definition of the term "strategic" in the case of exports to China than was applied in the case of exports to the Soviet Union, the discrepancy being referred to in bureaucratic terminology as the "China differential."

The main exception to the containment-with-isolation policy was a series of Sino-American talks at the ambassadorial level that began in 1955, first at Geneva and then (after 1958) at Warsaw. From time to time these talks achieved useful results, such as a mutual release of civilian prisoners and the maintenance of communication during crises (notably those of 1958 and 1962 in the Taiwan Strait, and the escalated war in Vietnam after 1965). The possibility of Sino-American trade and travel was discussed; until about 1957 the Chinese side was more forthcoming on this question, but after that the reverse was usually true, because the Great Leap Forward induced a mood of overall militancy whereas the United States government came under pressure to allow American correspondents to go to China. The State Department issued passports valid for travel to China to about thirty correspondents, but Peking refused (except in one case) to grant them visas. There was a virtual deadlock on the critical question of Taiwan; the American side demanded a "renunciation of force" by Peking with respect to the island, whereas the Chinese side rejected this demand and insisted that the United States abandon its military protection of Taiwan.

The Trend toward Containment
without Isolation

During the 1960s the idea of containing possible Chinese military expansion at the expense of American allies or interests in Asia continued to find favor with official American opinion and with most sectors of American public opinion except for radicals. Peking's attack on India in 1962 seemed to demonstrate the need for a continuation of the containment policy. American military intervention in Vietnam was officially rationalized to a considerable extent on the ground that it was an indispensable act of containment of China, inasmuch as Hanoi was considered, although incorrectly, a virtual satellite of Peking. The Chinese were known to be the more militantly anti-American of the parties to the Sino-Soviet dispute, whose existence was generally conceded by official Washington after 1962.

On the other hand, Peking's militancy or apparent militancy made many American liberals believe that it would be dangerous to continue the effort to isolate China, for whose attitude increased international contact was held to be the best or even the only cure. Chinese resentment at American policies was advanced as an argument in favor of the thesis, which turned out to be too alarmist, that the two powers were on a "collision course" over Vietnam. Furthermore, isolation was not working very well; Peking's external political and economic relations had continued to expand in spite of it, and in the matter of China policy it seemed to be the United States that was in danger of becoming isolated. American public attitudes toward China were tending to mellow with the passage of time since the Korean War, the main aspect of Peking's external behavior that affected the American people as a whole. On the other hand, there remained an articulate core of conservative opinion that still strongly opposed any changes in the containment-with-isolation policy.

For the latter reason, and because of the narrowness of his electoral victory, President Kennedy felt it advisable to be very cautious about any changes in China policy, although some of his subordinates proposed relaxing the ban on trade with and travel to mainland China (over and above the travel by correspondents already authorized). Chinese behavior during this period, some aspects of which have already been noted, did little to change his mind. In 1961, at a time of food shortages in China, he offered to sell Peking grain, only to be rudely rebuffed. Nevertheless, he made it clear in June 1962 that the United States would not support a Nationalist attack on the mainland if one occurred. In December 1963, the month after Kennedy's assassination, Assistant Secretary of State Roger Hilsman made a speech indicating that the United States government regarded the Communist regime in China as more or less permanent and hoped for better relations with it as the passage of time eroded its militancy.

By the spring of 1966, concern over the possibility of a Sino-

American war over Vietnam had become fairly acute in both Washington and Peking. One result was a kind of tacit agreement, worked out at Warsaw in mid-March, to the effect that neither side would escalate the existing level of its involvement in Vietnam to the direct disadvantage of the other; as long as China did not intervene in the war the United States would not attack it, and vice versa. At the same time, liberal concern over the possibility of a Sino-American clash found an important expression in the shape of hearings on China conducted by the Senate Foreign Relations Committee under the chairmanship of Senator J. William Fulbright. The first witness, Professor A. Doak Barnett, proposed the principle of "containment without isolation" for American China policy; the phrase was echoed by Vice President Humphrey shortly afterward, and in July President Johnson spoke publicly in favor of "reconciliation" with mainland China. These developments seriously alarmed Moscow, which began to be nervous about the possibility of Sino-American "collusion" at Soviet expense. Soviet policy itself was to bring about something like this result a few years later, by virtually driving China into the arms of the United States.

In spite of all this, apart from the avoidance of war over Vietnam the idea of modifying American China policy was not translated into action during the Johnson administration. Preoccupation with Vietnam tended to blot out possible initiatives in other aspects of foreign policy. In spite of a continuing decline in the effectiveness and credibility of isolation, containment remained the actual official policy.

CHAPTER VI

Peking's Foreign Policy and the Sino-Soviet Dispute

CHINA'S emergence since 1949 as a major Asian power, for the first time since the eighteenth century, has inevitably exerted a profound effect on the international politics of the region. The effect has perhaps been most powerful on the Soviet Union, which is linked to China by a uniquely long frontier and a common ideology, however differently it has come to be interpreted. Rarely has any country's external behavior been so differently described by its supporters and by its opponents; Chinese foreign policy is either principled and defensive, or expansionist and adventurous, depending upon the point of view. There is considerable agreement that in either case it is mysterious. Actually, both of these value judgments are so oversimplified as to be misleading and almost meaningless, and the mysteriousness exists only for those who prefer to believe in it.

Peking's External Objectives and Strategies

Like any other state, the People's Republic of China is concerned to preserve its own security. Unlike some others, it has usually believed since 1949 that its security was being actively threatened. From 1950 to the mid- or late 1960s the threat was perceived as being the United States, and for the first half of that period the Sino-Soviet alliance was seriously counted on as a necessary and, it was hoped, an adequate shield. During the second half, Peking's confidence in Soviet protection decreased rapidly as the Sino-Soviet dispute escalated, and it began to create its own nuclear deterrent with the help of substantial Soviet technical assistance. After the Soviet invasion of Czechoslovakia in 1968, Moscow was perceived by Peking as a serious threat to itself, and the United States, which was showing an interest in improving its relations with China, came to be regarded as an important source of political, although not military, support, to be supplemented by other political means and by accelerated modernization of Peking's conventional and nuclear forces.

At a lower level of threat, Peking has been concerned when foreign forces it regarded as hostile approached its borders. The classic reaction of Mao Tse-tung to such a threat, since the guerrilla days of the early 1930s, has been to "lure the enemy in deep" and then destroy him on one's own territory. Always objectionable in the eyes of Chinese Communist professional military commanders, this approach has never been applied since 1949, in spite of occasional bouts of Maoist propaganda (especially during the Vietnam War) claiming to welcome the idea of a foreign invasion of or attack on China. In two major cases (the Korean War, and the Sino-Indian border war of 1962), Chinese forces took preemptive, or forestalling, action against foreign forces perceived as both hostile and uncomfortably close to the Chinese border, although Peking's aims in both cases included political ones as well. During the Vietnam War the problem never actually arose, because American forces kept well away from the Chinese frontier so as not to provoke Peking dangerously. The most serious problem to date has been the presence of massive, hostile, Soviet forces near Chinese territory since 1969, both in Soviet Asia and in the Mongolian People's Republic. In view of Soviet strategic superiority and the absence of reliable American military support, the People's Republic of China is obviously not in a position to do much about this situation by purely military means. Nor can Peking formally deny the right of the Soviet Union to maintain troops on its own soil, even if they are near the Chinese border, although Peking does demand openly that Soviet troops be withdrawn from the Mongolian People's Republic. But in its private negotiations with Moscow since 1969, Peking has apparently indicated that a full normalization of Sino-Soviet relations would require, among other things, the removal of most Soviet forces from the Soviet Far East and the greater part of Siberia. The Chinese leadership, of course, remembers and resents the Japanese invasion of China between 1937 and 1945, and it is aware that Japan has the industrial strength to become a threat again, but (a loud burst of Chinese anti-Japanese propaganda in 1970–71 notwithstanding) it also knows that Japan is not a major military power and has no current plans to become one.

China is a divided country, since Taiwan is inhabited by people the vast majority of whom are ethnically Chinese, and yet Taiwan and the mainland of China are of course under two different political systems. Peking feels very strongly that Taiwan belongs to it by right and is only prevented from belonging to it in fact by American military protection. While that protection continues, and while Peking is, therefore, not in a position to "liberate" Taiwan by military means, the possibility of "liberation" by political means, or in other words through some sort of agreement with the Nationalist leadership, remains the only course realistically open to Peking. This has been tried, but without any visible success to date. The reunification of China as one of Peking's external objectives is a concept that really applies only to Nationalist-held territory, notably Taiwan. Peking claims, usually with some basis in Chinese history, that various adjacent parts of Asia once formed part of the Chinese empire in some sense but were taken from the "Chinese people" by one "imperialist" power or another. But these statements have been made mainly for domestic effect and have not been used as the basis for serious claims on other countries' territory, except in the case of fairly limited areas actively in dispute with neighboring states. Most of these disputes were settled in the early 1960s, usually on terms that were fairly reasonable from the standpoint of the other party, mainly in order to isolate on this question the two main adversaries, the Soviet Union and India, whose border disputes with China have not been settled on account of the bad general relations between China and those countries.

Although it rarely talks in these terms, Peking unquestionably aspires to a position of major influence in Asia. It knows that it cannot dominate Asia or exclude external powers from it, now or in the future, but it would like to exercise as much influence as can be acquired without undue risk or cost. China's size, geographic location, population, cultural heritage, current dynamism, and growing power create a mystique and an ability to exert influence on Asian affairs that are very great and likely to increase. Peking's main concern in Asia is to compete or cope with the other leading powers: the United States, the Soviet Union, and Japan. At present Peking apparently prefers a multilateral Asian balance involving all four of the major powers to a bipolar situation in which China confronted only one of the others, as it once did the United States, and as it fears it might some day have to confront the Soviet Union. One of the corollaries of this attitude is that Peking does not want further American military withdrawals from the region, except probably from Taiwan. The promotion of Peking's policy toward Asia requires the full deployment of China's formidable foreign policy resources, consisting mainly of a capacity for skillful diplomacy and intensive propaganda aimed primarily at the states of the region, which are the next most important objects of Peking's concern. Last, but not insignificant if only because the commitment to it of the Maoists among the Chinese leadership, comes support (through propaganda, political guidance, arms, funds, etc.) of leftist armed revolutionary movements, or "people's wars." The one in Indochina is obviously the most important of these; other, lesser, ones in which Peking has been involved to varying degrees in recent years have occurred along the Sino-Burmese border, in northern Thailand, along the Thai-Malaysian border, and in Sarawak (in East Malaysia).

China has analogous aspirations for influence in the Third World in general, but the limitations on its resources and obvious problems of distance and cultural differences tend to render it considerably less effective outside Asia than in Asia. Apart from aid programs in carefully selected countries—at the present time the largest is in Tanzania— and propaganda, China's main strategy has been to cultivate resentment toward the United States (and since the early 1960s toward the other superpower, the Soviet Union, as well) and portray Peking as a friend of the interests of the local peoples as against Washington and Moscow. In addition, Peking has in some cases given support (arms, etc.) to insurgencies of the "people's war" variety, for example the Arab guerrilla movements.

Until about 1959 Mao Tse-tung tried to bring the Soviet leadership around to his way of thinking on the growing list of issues between them, which are discussed later in this chapter. He then gave this approach up as hopeless and began to conduct an open ideological and political struggle against the Soviet leadership, not only in the international Communist movement but in other areas as well. Mao and his colleagues realize that neither the Soviet party nor their own can dominate the international Communist movement, but they are determined to reduce Soviet influence on it and increase their own as much as possible; they have been only moderately successful, partly because some other aspects of their foreign policy (such as the recent accommodation with the United States) have tended to contradict the pose of ideological purity and lofty principle that Mao has chosen to adopt.

China aspires to be a major power (although not a superpower, a term that it interprets to include a tendency to oppress other states and peoples) and has already made significant strides in that direction. It acquired China's permanent seat (with a veto) in the United Nations Security Council in 1971. It has made progress, especially since 1969, toward winning universal diplomatic recognition while allowing no other country to have full diplomatic relations with itself and with the Nationalists at the same time. It has played a role, or tried to, in an increasing number of international issues, crises, etc. It is creating a thermonuclear weapons capability complete with ICBMs. Economic and technological limitations, on the other hand, will probably prevent China from ever acquiring a level of power and influence equivalent to those of the United States and the Soviet Union.

Peking and "Peaceful Coexistence" in Asia

After 1951 Peking, and even Stalin, moved gradually away from the view that the independence and nonalignment in the Cold War of the new states of Asia were a fraud and that their governments could and should be overthrown in the fairly near future through armed Communist revolutions. The two most important reasons for this shift were that the revolutions of this kind that had actually been attempted were not doing well, except, of course, for the one in Vietnam, and that the tensions of the Korean War and the pressure of American containment of both the major Communist powers made the cultivation of the new states in the hope of diplomatic support seem more sensible than the continuation of unpromising efforts to subvert them.

From both the Soviet perspective and the Chinese, the key country among the Asian neutrals was India on account of its political and moral influence on the others. Nehru and his government accordingly became, after about 1953, the object of wooing by both Peking and Moscow, a wooing that contained the seeds of rivalry from the beginning. The rivalry was inevitable partly because the Soviet Union possessed three important advantages over China in seeking rapport with Nehru. It had no specific quarrel with the United States, in Asia at any rate, comparable to Peking's grievance over Taiwan, and its views on international politics and the Cold War therefore tended to seem more compatible with the concept of "peaceful coexistence" than did Peking's relative militancy where the United States was concerned. The Soviet Union obviously had a capacity superior to China's for giving economic aid, and it began to do so on a large scale to Nehru's government as early as 1954; Peking has never given such aid (as distinct from trade) to India, although it has to other smaller states. Moscow had no serious bilateral quarrels with Nehru once it stopped hoping for his imminent overthrow, whereas in China's case, there were serious problems in the shape of the status of Tibet and a Sino-Indian boundary dispute. Consequently Khrushchev gave enthusiastic public approval to Nehru in 1955 as against both the Indian Communists and Pakistan, in the latter case by endorsing the Indian claim to Kashmir. Peking, on the other hand, showed greater reserve on both scores, by cultivating some segments of the Indian Communist movement and by preserving neutrality on the Kashmir issue. A major reason for the limited nature of Peking's cultivation of Nehru was a belief that India was a serious rival of China's for influence in Asia, and to some extent the Third World as a whole.

Nehru believed at first that proper handling could keep his problems with China manageable and that cooperation could be maintained between them instead of rivalry. Accordingly, he reached an agreement with Peking in the spring of 1954 under which India recognized China's claim to Tibet, with the understanding that the Chinese would respect Tibetan autonomy, in return for a clear though implicit pledge (the so-called Five Principles of Peaceful Coexistence) that Peking would not commit aggression in Asia and would not try to manipulate the overseas Chinese communities in Southeast Asia for subversive purposes. Nehru also went out of his way at the Bandung Conference to introduce Chou En-lai to non-Communist Third World statesmen.

By that time, however, Nehru was already aware that Peking took a more bellicose line toward the United States than he or Khrushchev did, that it was not keeping its pledge of more than token autonomy for Tibet, and that its version of the Sino-Indian border differed significantly from India's. Peking was publishing maps, mainly although not exclusively for domestic consumption, indicating a version of several sections of the Chinese frontier, especially the southern frontier, that did not jibe with the versions of the other states concerned. These Sino-Indian issues simmered until 1958 and then began to come to a boil. In 1957–58, for reasons explained in the next section, Peking's entire foreign policy veered in the direction of greater militancy, with inevitably adverse effects on its relationship with India. Furthermore, a revolt in Tibet, with which most Indians sympathized, gathered strength after the mid-1950s and in March 1959 became a crisis of such proportions that the Dalai Lama fled to India and thousands of insurgents took refuge in India and Nepal, from where they occasionally mounted raids back into Tibet. As Peking moved troops forward to seal the border and denounced Nehru publicly, for the first time, for his sympathy with the Tibetans and his general attitude, tension rose. There were Sino-Indian firefights, though not very large ones, in each of the two major areas in dispute between China and India. One of these was Aksai Chin, at the northeastern corner of Kashmir, across which the Chinese had built a military road to link western Tibet and western Sinkiang, and which Peking held. The other was the North East Frontier Agency, to the east of Bhutan, which Peking claimed but had left in Indian possession inasmuch as it lies to the south of the main Himalayan ridgeline. A reasonable outsider's view of the merits of the dispute would be that neither side has a clearly superior claim to either of the contested areas.

For reasons already indicated, Chinese policy in the mid-1950s toward all the uncommitted Asian countries, and not toward India alone, had been predominantly one of conciliation. Even Thailand, which joined SEATO in 1954 out of fear of Chinese subversion, was treated in a way calculated to impress it with the advantages of neutrality and accommodation with Peking, and the neutrals were treated with still greater outward consideration (flattery, diplomatic support, economic aid in some cases, etc.). After 1957, the Chinese line hardened somewhat, for reasons just suggested, but it softened again in 1960 in an effort to avoid driving the smaller Asian neutrals into the arms of India or the Soviet Union. As part of this effort, Peking concluded boundary treaties on reasonable terms in 1960–63 with almost all of its neighbors with which it had border disputes, except for India and the Soviet Union—to be specific, with Burma, Nepal, Pakistan, Afghanistan, and the Mongolian People's Republic. Conciliatory gestures of this kind, as well as Peking's power to cause trouble if provoked, did help to prevent the other Asian states from following India and the Soviet Union into a state of confrontation with China. In fact, Indonesia under President Sukarno, who was moving to the left in both his domestic and his foreign policy, concluded what amounted to an informal alliance with China in 1960–61 on the basis of common and militant opposition to Western influence in Southeast Asia; Peking gave support in various forms to Sukarno in his struggle (successful in 1962) with the Netherlands over West Irian (Dutch New Guinea) and his unsuccessful "confrontation" with Britain and Malaysia after 1963.

In the spring of 1962 Peking felt its external security to be in a state of crisis requiring some sort of response, and Mao Tse-tung wanted to dramatize his effort to regain revolutionary momentum at home, after the collapse of the Great Leap Forward in 1960, through an external initiative. What Peking interpreted as crises in the Taiwan Strait, on the border between Sinkiang and Soviet Central Asia, and in Laos and Thailand more or less evaporated about the middle of the year, but a problem with India remained. Sino-Indian negotiations on the border question had broken down, and the Indian Army had begun to build outposts in parts of Aksai Chin in order to acquire control over the whole of it. When Chinese warnings to stop had no effect, Peking sent its forces into action on October 20, 1962, in both the disputed sectors of the border region. The Chinese were aware that their behavior on the territorial question had contributed to a closer relationship between India and the Soviet Union since about 1959, and Peking may very well have timed its border offensive to coincide approximately with the Cuban missile crisis, which would inevitably tend to distract Khrushchev from taking any effective role on India's side in a Sino-Indian border war. In two brief bouts of sharp fighting (October 20–25, November 18–21) Chinese forces inflicted serious defeats on their Indian opponents. Peking then stopped fighting unilaterally, both because it had already achieved a strong and not entirely advantageous political effect and because continuation of the war would have created serious problems, including probable increasing Soviet and American involvement on the Indian side. To this day the Sino-Indian boundary dispute remains unresolved, and since the early 1960s China has had what amounts to an informal alliance with Pakistan on the basis of common hostility to India. Peking accordingly gave loud propaganda support to Pakistan during the Indo-Pakistani war of 1965 over Kashmir but for a number of reasons, including fear of possible American or Soviet action, was able to do little more, apart from initiating a program of substantial military aid to Pakistan after the war.

Peking and the Taiwan Question

Peking and its Nationalist adversaries agree that Taiwan is a part of China—a view for which a very strong case can be made— and that the Chinese civil war is not over as long as the Nationalists make their headquarters on the island. Since June 1950, when American military protection was extended to Taiwan, Peking has believed with much justification that it was prevented from "liberating" Taiwan, through some combination of political and military pressures leading to a conditional Nationalist surrender in exchange for some sort of "autonomous" status, solely by the United States. Its Taiwan policy, accordingly, has amounted to a search for leverage on both the United States and the Nationalists.

For a time after Peking intervened in the Korean War it hoped to use its intervention as a lever to compel the withdrawal of American protection from Taiwan, but its military setbacks frustrated this effort. In late 1954 and early 1955, it tried to gain leverage, as well as security from suspected Nationalist plans for offensive action against the mainland, through a military crisis in the Taiwan Strait. But the main result was to drive the United States to conclude a security treaty, or alliance, with the Nationalists that seemed to render the "liberation" of Taiwan by Peking more remote than ever. Khrushchev gave Peking no support during this crisis, and Chinese irritation at this was compounded in ensuing years as Moscow continued to show no enthusiasm for Peking's pleas for increased political support in connection with its efforts to "liberate" Taiwan.

Peking's next ploy was foreshadowed as early as April 1955 in Chou En-lai's concluding speech to the Bandung Conference. Later that year, Sino-American talks at the ambassadorial level on Taiwan and other issues began at Geneva, but the results were unsatisfactory to Peking since the Chinese demand for the withdrawal of American protection from Taiwan was countered by American insistence on a "renunciation of force" by Peking with respect to Taiwan. Peking accordingly began to make propaganda appeals for a deal to the Nationalist leadership in 1956, but without visible result.

Discouraged by the failure of these approaches and all the more in need of an external success because of the unexpectedly severe criticism of the regime that greeted Mao's Hundred Flowers campaign (for free public discussion) in the spring of 1957, the Chinese leadership decided in the following autumn to try to gain leverage from the Soviet Union, in the form of military aid, political support, and the like, in connection with the prospective "liberation" of Taiwan. The moment seemed favorable, because Khrushchev had just won a major victory over his leading political opponents, who tended to be more cautious in foreign policy than he and whose restraining influence was now removed. Furthermore, the Chinese leadership was in the process of launching a major, militant, domestic campaign, to be known as the Great Leap Forward, and in Mao's view this called for a more activist foreign policy by way of accompaniment. Khrushchev, however, was not much impressed by Mao's argument that, on account of recent Soviet successes in space and missile technology, notably the orbiting of the first earth satellite by the Soviet Union on October 4, 1957, Moscow now had the opportunity and the obligation to apply increased pressure, short of war, to the United States on such issues as Taiwan. Khrushchev was so embarrassed by Mao's arguments that he made an unparalleled commitment, in October-November 1957, to give China substantial aid with a nuclear weapons program, including MRBMs. This program, which was cancelled in 1959 on account of growing Sino-Soviet differences, provided the basis for China's subsequent entry into the nuclear club.

For both domestic and external reasons, including a desire to stiffen Khrushchev's spine or at least smoke him out on the Taiwan question, Mao decided in mid-1958 to initiate a politico-military crisis in the Taiwan Strait. He hoped to drive a wedge between the Nationalists and the United States by demonstrating the vulnerability of the Nationalist-held offshore islands just off the China coast (notably Quemoy, the largest of them) to Communist military pressures, as well as the presumed inability or unwillingness of the American "paper tigers" to render effective help to their allies in such situations. Brushing aside Khrushchev's objections, which were reflected in the fact that his support for Peking in the ensuing crisis was purely verbal, Peking began to shell Quemoy on August 23, without attempting an amphibious landing. Both the Nationalists and the United States responded with reasonable firmness, and the crisis accordingly died away in October. The United States had made it clear that although it would defend Taiwan, and probably the offshore islands, from a Communist attack, it did not favor a Nationalist landing on the mainland.

The result was a continued stalemate. The Nationalist presence on the offshore islands was (and is) agreeable to both sides because it prevented them from being separated by the full width of the Taiwan Strait and therefore from being in effect "two Chinas," an outcome that neither wants since each insists that there is only one China, of which it is the legitimate government.

In the spring of 1962, as the mainland was beginning to recover from the economic disaster inflicted by the Great Leap Forward, the Nationalists gave some signs of intending to attack the mainland at what must have seemed a favorable opportunity. Peking accordingly doubled its troop strength in the area opposite Taiwan in June and tried to smoke out American intentions by loudly accusing the United States of inciting a Nationalist attack on the mainland. The Kennedy administration, which was actually trying with little success to establish a less hostile relationship with Peking, denied the charge and insisted that it would not support a Nationalist attack if one should occur. This assurance relaxed Peking considerably but did little to advance the "liberation" of Taiwan, except perhaps indirectly by helping to undermine the Nationalists' faith in an eventual triumphant "return to the mainland."

Peking and Moscow:
The Accumulation of Issues (1953–59)

With Stalin's death in early 1953, Mao Tse-tung began to consider himself the leading figure in the Communist world, far senior to Stalin's quarreling successors. This posture irritated them increasingly, although Khrushchev was able to gain a degree of Chinese approval and support for his own position in 1954 by posing as more Stalinist at home and more militant in his foreign policy than his chief rival, Malenkov. As Khrushchev gained ascendancy over Malenkov in 1955–57, however, he increasingly moderated his views so that they came to resemble those of his defeated rival. Less geopolitically minded than Stalin, he placed less value on his Chinese neighbor and ally and liked to conduct his anti-American struggle by operating in a free-wheeling fashion through diplomatic maneuvers, aid programs, and the like in relatively remote non-Communist countries such as Egypt and India. As already indicated, he showed little enthusiasm for helping Peking to "liberate" Taiwan.

At his party's Twentieth Congress (February 1956), from which Peking officially dates the beginning of the Sino-Soviet dispute, Khrushchev expounded in a public report two propositions that profoundly troubled the Chinese by implying Soviet unwillingness to risk a military confrontation with the United States, on behalf of the Chinese ally or for any other reason. One was that war was not "fatally inevitable," meaning that another World War must be avoided at virtually any cost, because it might destroy all the gains and prospects of Communism. The other was that both local Communist Parties and Moscow itself must be cautious about promoting revolution in non-Communist countries by means more violent than political struggle, because the result of an attempt at armed revolution might be a Soviet-American confrontation. In his secret speech on Stalin, furthermore, Khrushchev outraged Mao by attacking Stalin, whom Mao respected, and by giving Mao's own colleagues a lever with which to reduce his political position to a more modest scale, something that they proceeded to do later in that same year. Mao's personal political initiatives of that period, notably the Hundred Flowers campaign and the Great Leap Forward, were in part efforts to regain lost ground and assert his own continuing creativity as a statesman.

These efforts, the Great Leap Forward above all, placed serious strains on his relationship with Khrushchev, whose growing reservations about Mao's erratic behavior and whose general attitude led Mao increasingly to hold him guilty of "revisionism," or ideological deviation in the direction of undue moderation. Mao's conviction was strengthened by Khrushchev's performance during the Taiwan Strait crisis of 1958, his withdrawal of nuclear aid to China in 1959, his sympathy for India during the Sino-Indian border crisis of the same year, and above all his quest for détente with the United States after the death of John Foster Dulles in the spring of 1959.

Whether as a result of a conscious decision or not, Mao embarked in the second half of 1959 on what can be called a dual adversary strategy, one of simultaneous ideological and political struggle, with military overtones but short of war, against both American "imperialism" and Soviet "revisionism." This important shift coincided with, and was reflected in, the appointment of Mao's principal military colleague Lin Piao as Defense Minister in September 1959. Lin succeeded P'eng Te-huai, who had been purged for his objections to the Great Leap Forward and to the harm inflicted by Mao's policies on Sino-Soviet relations. Lin himself was a militant Maoist, whether out of conviction or opportunism or a mixture of the two, and he was a leading exponent of the dual adversary strategy. Shortly after taking over the Defense Ministry, he began to organize violations of the Soviet border by parties of Chinese military personnel, presumably as an expression of contempt and defiance of Soviet "revisionism," which he evidently thought of as a paper bear. Although the Soviet response to these provocations was remarkably restrained at first, the effect on Sino-Soviet relations was bound to be serious sooner or later, inasmuch as Moscow is not in reality a paper bear.

Peking and Moscow:
The Surfacing of the Dispute (1960–64)

One of the last straws from Mao's point of view was an indication by Khrushchev that he hoped not only to reduce his conventional forces, under cover of détente with the United States, but to reach an agreement with the United States that would tend to bind China to reduce its own conventional forces as well.

By the spring of 1960, Mao could no longer keep silent. He chose the ninetieth anniversary of Lenin's birth (April 22) as the occasion for publishing a strong editorial denouncing Khrushchev, although not by name, for insufficient resolution in opposing the United States and promoting revolution on account of fear of another world war. Mao had maintained for several years that the Soviet-American strategic balance was sufficiently stable so that the likelihood of such a war was slight, and its consequences if it occurred could even be portrayed for propaganda purposes as beneficial to the Communist cause. Khrushchev regarded this attitude as irresponsible and bellicose.

Peking also denounced Khrushchev much more explicitly, at some private meetings held in the spring of 1960. His reaction, or rather overreaction, was to cancel all industrial and technical aid to China during the ensuing summer. The two sides agreed to submit their cases to an international meeting of Communist parties, which met at Moscow in November-December 1960. Before an astounded audience, the two sides stated their positions in vituperative language, along lines already indicated. Since the opposing positions could not really be compromised, the outcome was a published statement that incorporated some features of each while adopting consciously vague formulas on the really difficult issues.

The two sides then suspended the dispute in order to take the measure of the incoming Kennedy administration. Peking felt more concern than Moscow over that administration's alleged tendency to practice "special warfare" (counterinsurgency) against leftist "national liberation movements," because the area mainly affected was Indochina. In 1958–60, the United States had provoked a crisis in Laos by trying unsuccessfully to bring a pro-American government into existence; the result of this effort was an agreement of 1962 under which Laos was to remain neutral in the Cold War and governed by a coalition government with Communist participation. In the autumn of 1961, the Kennedy administration began to try to strengthen the non-Communist government of President Ngo Dinh Diem in South Vietnam, in the face of growing Communist insurgency directed from North Vietnam, through increased economic and military aid. These moves on the part of the United States were due in part to a belief that Peking, the more militantly anti-American party to the Sino-

Soviet dispute, was inciting Hanoi to escalate the struggle in Indochina.

In 1961 Khrushchev developed an explosive quarrel with Albania, whose leaders had attitudes and policies comparable to the Chinese and sympathized with Peking in its confrontation with Moscow. Peking promptly stepped in with aid and political support for Albania and rejected Khrushchev's public plea (at his party's Twenty-second Congress in October 1961) to cease and desist. Khrushchev's problem was seriously complicated by the fact that his leading domestic rival, Frol Kozlov, was less anti-Chinese than he and was accusing him of being too tough with Peking. Under this pressure, Khrushchev appears to have gone rather far in 1962 in trying to patch up his quarrel with Peking. During the summer he backed away, at Chinese insistence, from a nuclear test ban agreement with the United States that had seemed imminent (see Chapter III). There are reasons to believe that Khrushchev not only informed the Chinese in advance of his intent to install offensive missiles in Cuba but intended to use the leverage gained in this way partly to force a withdrawal of American protection from Taiwan and thereby promote the "liberation" of Taiwan and an improvement in Sino-Soviet relations.

But Khrushchev had underestimated the toughness of the Kennedy administration and had to agree on November 27, 1962 to withdraw his missiles and bombers from Cuba in the face of what amounted to an American ultimatum. His entire plan of course came unstuck at that point, and Peking began in early November to attack him for having perpetrated "another Munich" on Castro and the Cuban people. Infuriated, Khrushchev promptly shifted his support from China to India in the Sino-Indian border war of October-November 1962. Peking was trying to inflict a political humiliation on the Nehru government and to push its border troops back from the vicinity of the Chinese-controlled highway across Aksai Chin, toward which the Indians had begun to advance. China's brilliant, although limited, military victory drove India closer to the Soviet Union than ever before, and Khrushchev's sympathy for India combined with his fiasco in Cuba produced a sharp escalation of the Sino-Soviet dispute.

Early in 1963 Peking took a dangerous step by reminding the world that tsarist Russia had taken territory from China, and in

June 1964 Mao aggravated the provocation by stating publicly that the Soviet Union had done the same from China and several other countries as well, during the Second World War. Since Peking was obviously about to acquire a nuclear weapons capability, Khrushchev became alarmed and by the time of his fall (in October 1964) may have been contemplating some form of military pressure on China. In the summer of 1963 he outraged the Chinese by signing a partial nuclear test ban treaty with the United States and Britain, which Peking regarded as almost the ultimate in Soviet betrayal of China and collusion with "imperialism." Peking responded by a drastic escalation of the ideological polemic that it had been waging against Khrushchev. By this time Khrushchev was trying to organize another international meeting of Communist parties like the one of 1960, in the hope of maneuvering some kind of condemnation of the Chinese; this ploy failed, because it was resisted not only by the pro-Chinese parties but by others as well, such as the Romanian. Peking for its part was trying to bring pro-Chinese "Marxist-Leninist" splinter parties into existence in some of the countries (ultimately about thirty) where the orthodox Communist Party was firmly pro-Soviet.

By the time of Khrushchev's fall in 1964, in short, Sino-Soviet relations were in a state of dangerous confrontation. Khrushchev's heavyhandedness in bringing things to such an impasse was very probably a major although unannounced count against him in the eyes of those of his colleagues who overthrew him.

Chinese Foreign Policy after Khrushchev

Shortly after his overthrow, Khrushchev's successors offered Peking a sweeping accommodation that was to include a suspension of ideological polemics, resumption of Soviet economic and possibly military aid to China, and "united action" on Vietnam. This offer was brought to Peking by Premier Kosygin in mid-February 1965, just after the United States began to bomb North Vietnam. The offer was rejected, evidently at Mao Tse-tung's insistence and because he considered that his current militant domestic and foreign policy required the maintenance of an atmosphere of struggle against Soviet "revisionism." This approach was made easier and more plausible by Soviet insistence on reviving Khrushchev's plan for another international Communist Party conference like the one of 1960, which was anathema to the Chinese leadership.

The escalation of the Vietnam war in 1965 raised serious political and military problems for Peking and started a strategic
debate that lasted for about six months and probably postponed
for that length of time the onset of Mao's favorite project, the
Cultural Revolution (see Chapter VIII). The view that prevailed
was that of Defense Minister Lin Piao, and presumably of Mao
himself, that China should avoid both the risk of a clash with the
United States that would be generated by direct Chinese intervention in Vietnam and the political humiliation of an accommodation with the Soviet Union; in effect, the dual adversary strategy
was reaffirmed.

Mao and Lin had a tendency to assume that Chinese militancy,
contrasted with the "imperialism" of the Americans as demonstrated anew in Vietnam and with the "revisionism" of the Soviets,
would evoke a widespread positive response around the world.
This happened to only a small extent, partly because the United
States and the Soviet Union continued to be major sources of
economic aid for Third World countries and the latter were
therefore usually reluctant to antagonize them unnecessarily. In
fact, Chinese militancy tended to be counterproductive. It contributed heavily to the collapse of the Afro-Asian Conference
scheduled to meet in Algiers in June 1965 (see Chapter II).
Chinese involvement in subversion in Africa contributed to a
number of military coups that occurred south of the Sahara in
1965–66. Worse still for Peking were some setbacks suffered at
that time in Asia. Chinese influence in Indonesia contributed to a
radicalization of President Sukarno's domestic and foreign policies
and increasingly close cooperation between him and the Indonesian Communists. In this atmosphere, although not necessarily
with direct Chinese incitement, Sukarno and the Chinese leadership attempted a coup against the anti-Communist army leadership
at the end of September 1965. It was unsuccessful, and the result
was a military takeover that deposed Sukarno, inflicted heavy
casualties on the Communists, and reduced Chinese influence to
zero. Chinese incitement probably contributed to Ayub Khan's
decision to use force in Kashmir in 1965 (see Chapter XII). When
the effort began to fail, Peking tried without success to keep
Pakistan in the war and to intimidate India by issuing a phoney
ultimatum seeming to threaten another attack on India like the
one of 1962. The outcome was a setback for Pakistan and a diplo-

matic triumph for the Soviet Union, which acted as a mediator in the conflict.

A sense of frustration in foreign policy probably contributed to Mao's decision to launch the Cultural Revolution, on the theory that China's international influence would increase in proportion as its domestic ideological and political stance became truly Maoist. It is interesting, however, that he did not launch the Cultural Revolution in earnest until Peking and the United States had reached a tacit understanding in March 1966 that seemed to guarantee against an American attack on China in the context of the Vietnam War (see Chapter V). Probably Mao and Lin, and perhaps others as well, were reluctant to push China into a major political upheaval as long as they perceived a genuine risk of war.

The main sources of the Cultural Revolution, however, were domestic rather than foreign. Mao was concerned about what he considered to be the influence of Soviet "revisionism" on some of his colleagues and on China's youth. In the latter case, he was worried about the future of China's revolutionary momentum. In the former case, he had been engaged in a gradually intensifying power struggle with the leaders of the Communist Party apparatus, whom he regarded as "revisionist" and bureaucratically inclined, since the mid-1950s. He was also uncomfortably conscious of considerable opposition among the intellectuals to his "cult of personality" and militant policies. He was determined to launch a mass movement that would sweep away "revisionist" tendencies and generate more or less permanent revolutionary momentum. Given the lack of enthusiasm of the party apparatus leadership for this idea, which turned to outright opposition under Mao's pressures, this was a difficult task. Its accomplishment required the extreme measure of forming in the spring of 1966, with the cooperation of the Army, units composed of millions of Red Guards, the radical elements of the student population. They easily put the party apparatus at the national level out of action in the autumn of 1966 but were then stymied by the much more effective resistance offered by the regional and provincial elements of the party apparatus. Mao and Lin then ordered the Army to intervene in support of the Red Guards, in January 1967. There ensued a year and a half of difficulties between the radical Red Guards, whose activities often generated serious disorder, and the essentially stability-oriented provincial military commanders.

Finally in July 1968 Mao reluctantly gave the Army a mandate to suppress the Red Guards, which it proceeded to do. The Cultural Revolution was over, after doing considerable damage to the fabric of normal Chinese life. But many radicals did not regard it as a failure and hoped to revive its spirit, if not its actual programs, at some future time. Meanwhile, the political system began to return to normal at the national level as bureaucratic tendencies reasserted themselves under the guidance of Premier Chou En-lai, while at the provincial level the military were effectively in power and engaged in a complex process of bargaining with the center.

The domestic militancy of the Cultural Revolution was accompanied by a comparable militancy in foreign relations. Red Guards and other militants besieged most of the foreign embassies in Peking and even staged demonstrations outside the country, in Hong Kong in particular. Chinese propaganda exhorted radicals everywhere to launch their own Cultural Revolutions. The impact of all this abroad was mostly negative. In fact, China's international influence was reduced to a very low level. This was only a temporary situation, however. All that was required to end it was the termination of the Cultural Revolution and a diplomatic campaign by Chou En-lai to restore China's international influence. Such a campaign got under way in 1969, under the stimulus of Soviet pressures.

CHAPTER VII

The Indochina War

SINCE its emergence under Ho Chi Minh's leadership about 1930, the Vietnamese Communist movement has sought to dominate the whole of Indochina, Vietnam directly and the rest through Laotian and Cambodian junior partners. This effort would probably have succeeded, at least in Vietnam and Laos, after the Japanese collapse in 1945, in view of the Communists' superiority in organization to their local rivals, their militant ideology, and their ruthless use of terror, if the northern part of Indochina had not been occupied by Chinese Nationalist troops and the southern part by British forces, under arrangements worked out at the Potsdam Conference. This was only the first of a series of foreign interventions and initiatives that have checked the Vietnamese Communists short of their goal, but the termination of each has left them closer to it than before.

The French Defeat

The French, badly weakened by their ordeal in the Second World War, were nevertheless determined to regain their empire in Indochina. The British gave way readily to them in the south, but the Chinese Nationalists had to be maneuvered out through tacit cooperation between the French and Ho Chi Minh, who regarded them as the lesser and more short-lived evil. Furthermore, Stalin at that time had high hopes for the political future of the French Communist Party and was reluctant to antagonize French public opinion by encouraging insurgency on the part of the Vietnamese Communists. Ho accordingly showed a willingness to keep the Democratic Republic of Vietnam (DRV), as he called the regime he had established in North Vietnam at the time of the Japanese surrender, within the French Union, provided it were given control over South Vietnam as well. But this the French were unwilling to do, and fighting broke out between the two sides in Hanoi at the end of 1946. The more powerfully armed French soon pushed their adversaries back into the jungle and mountains and settled down to fight what promised to be a prolonged counterinsurgency campaign, one for which their commanders were rather poorly prepared.

The war was a serious drain on the French, but they were able to get American aid and support for it after the formation of NATO, of which France was a key member, in April 1949. But American aid was conditioned on greater freedom for the Indochinese states, to which accordingly France granted limited degrees of self-government at intervals between 1949 and 1953. On the other hand, the French resisted an American effort to provide training and equipment directly to a non-Communist Vietnamese national army and insisted on performing this role themselves. They did it badly on the whole, as their poor colonial record predicted. Their indifferent success in what later came to be called Vietnamization, political as well as military, helped to ensure their defeat and to make Ho Chi Minh a great national hero in the eyes of most Vietnamese, including many non-Communists.

Another important cause of the French defeat was the Communist victory in China, even though it enhanced American willingness to support the French effort in Indochina. For ideological reasons, Peking desired the victory of its Vietnamese colleagues in Vietnam itself, although not necessarily in Laos and Cambodia, where China has ambitions of its own. Peking recognized the DRV in January 1950, and later that year Ho Chi Minh's forces opened the Sino-Vietnamese border to Chinese aid by clearing it of French outposts. The actual flow of aid, however, was limited by Peking's preoccupation with the Korean War. At the end of 1950 Ho Chi Minh's forces launched a premature and disastrous offensive against the Hanoi area. This defeat apparently enhanced

Chinese political influence, one possible manifestation of which was the foundation of the Vietnam Workers Party (Lao Dong), in reality a Communist Party, in the spring of 1951. On the other hand, like all Vietnamese Ho Chi Minh was strongly determined to remain free from Chinese control.

In 1953 the end of the Korean War made possible a considerable increase in the flow of Chinese military aid to the DRV. This development helped to convince the French, who in any case were tiring of the losses and strains imposed by the Indochina War, that they could not win and must withdraw. They were also influenced by a desire to concentrate their resources on holding Algeria, which had begun to be threatened by Egyptian support for nationalist insurgents. They hoped to leave behind a viable non-Communist Vietnamese state and to strengthen its position by some final military initiatives. One of these, aimed at preventing a repetition of earlier Vietnamese Communist thrusts into Laos, was the occupation at the end of 1953 of Dienbienphu, a post in northwestern Vietnam on a road into Laos and unfortunately surrounded by hills that the French did not control and did not reconnoiter adequately. With equipment specifically supplied by the Chinese, Ho's forces besieged Dienbienphu in March 1954 and took it after heavy fighting on May 7, the day before a major international conference at Geneva began to negotiate a settlement of the Indochinese conflict.

The Geneva Settlement

The conference had been decided on in February at a meeting of the Big Four foreign ministers (the United States, the Soviet Union, Britain, and France). Its convening and proceedings were considerably complicated by two preoccupations of Secretary of State John Foster Dulles. One was his determination to remain on good terms with the powerful Republican right wing in Congress. This led him to veto the People's Republic of China as one of the convening powers of the conference, a status that would have allowed the chairman of its delegation to chair sessions of the conference in rotation with delegation chairmen of the other convening powers. Dulles would tolerate Peking only as one of the participating powers, and the chairmanship alternated between the British and Soviet delegation chairmen. The other preoccupation was Dulles' determination to use the Indochina crisis as a springboard to facilitate the formation of a new anti-Communist alliance, SEATO (see Chapter V), which would be his equivalent achievement to NATO, the creation of his predecessor Dean Acheson. As a means of stampeding Britain, France, and the anti-Communist states of Southeast Asia into the prospective new alliance, Dulles in April 1954 let it be thought that he was contemplating American military intervention to save Dienbienphu, although in reality he appears to have been considering nothing of the kind even if some of his colleagues in Washington were. In addition, Dulles had made his "massive retaliation" speech in January, which even though the label is misleading (it actually espoused the concept of "flexible response") made a considerable impact on the leaders of the Communist world as well as others. Occasionally, during the spring of 1954 and last months of 1953, he threatened American military intervention in Indochina. His behavior, as well as a series of colossal thermonuclear tests conducted by the United States in the Pacific in March 1954, gave the United States and the entire non-Communist side considerably enhanced leverage at the Geneva Conference. An additional concern for the Soviet Union was a desire not to be so tough with France as to push it into adhering to the European Defense Community, a proposed integrated West European army that was anathema in Moscow because there would be West German participation.

During the first stage of the conference, however, the Soviet and Chinese representatives (Molotov and Chou En-lai, respectively) gave full support to the DRV's demands for prompt political settlements (including elections) in all three of the Indochina countries on a virtual package deal basis, so that military victory in Vietnam could be translated into political triumph in the entire region. The result was a deadlock at Geneva and the fall of the French government. The new Premier, the energetic and able Pierre Mendès-France, increased his leverage significantly by saying that he would resign if a settlement were not reached within six weeks; no other party to the conference, apparently, wanted to risk the uncertain consequences of his resignation. After his coming into office and another round of threats from Dulles, the deadlock was broken, mainly through a reduction in the level of Soviet and Chinese diplomatic support for the DRV, which was understandably infuriated. Chou En-lai agreed that the three Indochina countries should be treated separately, each on the basis of its individual situation. Molotov agreed that Vietnam, the major prize, should be partitioned at the 17th parallel pending elections, rather than farther south as the DRV had been demanding.

The agreements signed on July 21, just before Mendès-France's deadline, gave Peking something it wanted very much, in that the Indochina states were prohibited from entering into military alliances, having foreign troops or bases on their soil, or receiving arms from external sources at more than replacement levels; these provisions tended to guarantee against an American military presence in Indochina that might threaten China. Peking failed in another of its objectives, to get an American signature on the main political agreement; for the reason already indicated, the United States would not sign a document also signed by a Chinese Communist representative, and accordingly the main political agreement was not signed by anybody. The essence of it and the other agreements reached at the conference was that there should be no legal Communist presence in Cambodia; that in Laos the local Communist front (the Pathet Lao) should have two provinces bordering on North Vietnam into which to "regroup" its political cadres and military personnel pending the working out of an agreement to hold national elections and install a coalition government reflecting their outcome; and that Vietnam should be divided temporarily near the 17th parallel for purposes of "regrouping," the DRV's zone being in the north and the non-Communist Vietnamese government's zone being in the south, pending national elections to be held within two years to unify the country, presumably under a coalition government. The conference also created an International Control Commission for each country, with an Indian chairman, a Polish member, and a Canadian member, to verify the observance of the military aspects of the settlement; the International Control Commission for Vietnam was to operate in the North as well as in the South.

Although the DRV was distressed over several aspects of the settlement, notably the postponement of elections in Vietnam for two years, it soon came to realize that the Communist ticket would not only sweep the North (given Communist skill at manipulating the semblance of support from people under their control) but do very well in the South, given Ho Chi Minh's prestige. The result presumably would be a nation-wide Communist victory. The DRV began to count heavily on achieving in this way what it had not quite been able to achieve by force of arms, control over the whole of Vietnam.

Socialism in Half a Country

The DRV proceeded rapidly and effectively to establish control over the North. Its leadership's penchant for terror and a tendency at that time to imitate the Chinese Communist example produced a bloody "land reform" campaign in 1954–55, in the course of which many thousands of innocent people were killed. In 1956 Hanoi realized it had gone too far and eased the pressure on the rural population considerably, but much irreparable damage had been done. In November a serious peasant revolt, which was suppressed by North Vietnamese troops, broke out in the southernmost province of the DRV.

The time-table established at Geneva called for certain preliminaries to the elections of 1956 to be set in motion as early as July 1955. Anxious that the elections be held, Hanoi tried to get these preliminaries started, only to encounter firm opposition from South Vietnam and the United States. This situation obviously created the difficult problem of deciding what to do next; Hanoi's inclination in all probability was to revert to force in one way or another, but a decision of such importance could not be made without some reference to the views of its allies.

As they had already demonstrated at Geneva, the Soviet Union and China were none too reliable from Hanoi's point of view. Their strong distaste for becoming involved in a crunch with the strategically superior United States, at any rate over an area as remote as Indochina, persisted, and it was clear that the United States was involving itself increasingly in aid and support for the South Vietnamese government.

With seeming appropriateness, Moscow and Peking began to do the same for Hanoi; in the second half of 1955 major commitments to give economic aid to the DRV were made by the Soviet Union and China, and their fulfillment in due course gave North Vietnam the most advanced industrial system in Southeast Asia. The International Control Commission was unable to observe, let alone interrupt, the military aid that also flowed in from the

Soviet Union and China. It is also very likely, although it cannot be proved, that Moscow and Peking were consciously encouraging Hanoi in effect to build socialism in half a country and to refrain from stirring up a crisis by putting military pressure on South Vietnam. At any rate, Soviet and Chinese reluctance to see such a crisis occur, and their preference for preserving the status quo for at least a while longer, are reasonably clear. In 1957 the Soviet government proposed, although unsuccessfully, that both Hanoi and Saigon be admitted to the United Nations.

In 1960 the DRV felt itself sufficiently stabilized to introduce a new state constitution strongly resembling that of the People's Republic of China. Like Mao Tse-tung, Ho Chi Minh was to occupy a special and prestigious position, that of President of the Republic. Communist control was preserved behind a semi-democratic façade. Support for national unification through the "liberation" of South Vietnam from alleged American domination, the leadership's main objective, was demanded of the people as well. The DRV's policy toward its *montagnards* (mountaineer minorities), although firm, has been the typically Comunist one of granting them at least the semblance of autonomy and has probably been less repressive in practice than that of some non-Communist Southeast Asian governments.

The Emergence of Diem

During the Geneva Conference the post of Premier of the Republic of Vietnam (South Vietnam), which seemed to have little if any future, was bestowed by President Bao Dai on Ngo Dinh Diem. His family, to which he was very close and to whose leading members he gave a variety of important posts, was Catholic, whereas most of the population was non-Catholic, Buddhist for the most part. The Ngo family, partly isolated from the people by religion, tended to lean on other Catholics for support, and many of these were Northerners (and hence aliens to the Southerners) drawn from the 800,000 Catholics who moved to South Vietnam in 1954 to get away from the Communists. Although personally honest, Diem was conservative and narrow-minded; his brother Nhu, on whom he depended heavily, had much less integrity and was apparently not of sound mind. All in all, it was an unhealthy and unpromising situation from the start, even apart from the

Communist problem, and the United States government tended to believe that Diem and his government would not survive and should not be supported on a large scale.

But since he was not under attack from the Communists, who were waiting for the 1956 elections, Diem in an astonishing burst of courage and energy succeeded in 1955 in winning over his Army leadership and in crushing his main non-Communist adversaries. At this point the United States came to the conclusion that he had been underestimated and that he stood a chance of surviving as long as he was not forced to sign his own death warrant by agreeing to the elections prescribed at Geneva. American aid, economic and military, began to flow to him on a large scale.

Under these circumstances, Diem was able to make his refusal to hold the elections envisaged at Geneva stick. This success emboldened him, unfortunately, to set up later in 1956 what increasingly became a dictatorship under himself and his family. At the local level, this policy involved serious restrictions on the traditional autonomy of the village, and police pressures aimed at eliminating actual, suspected, and alleged Communists. Although the Diem government was never quite as bad, at least in comparison with some other Asian governments, as the American press came to portray it after 1960, there is no question that it grew increasingly repressive, ineffective, and unpopular. To a large extent, it dug its own grave.

Insurgency in South Vietnam

In violation of the Geneva Agreements, several thousand Communist cadres of southern origin remained south of the 17th parallel after 1954. They stayed underground, presumably with the mission of getting into position to influence the elections. But when the July 1956 deadline passed without elections, peasants began in some cases to inform on the Communist cadres to Diem's police and troops, who made life very difficult for them. They began, about the spring of 1957, to engage in acts of terror and sabotage. Hanoi, however, while keeping in touch with them and determined to preserve them as the nucleus of a probable "people's war" in the future, still withheld its consent to the actual launching of such a war. As already suggested, the main reason was probably Moscow's and Peking's attitude.

But in 1957–58 Peking's general policy, foreign as well as domestic, shifted in a more militant direction, and Hanoi's difficulty was eased to some extent. A probably more important influence, in the same direction, was a crisis that arose in Laos in 1959. The agreement for that country envisaged at Geneva had been reached in 1957. The ensuing elections, held in the spring of 1958, gave a strong bloc of thirteen seats in the National Assembly to the Pathet Lao and their allies. With a threat to suspend its aid, which is vital to the survival of a non-Communist government in Laos, the alarmed United States government then forced the neutralist Premier, Prince Souvanna Phouma, out of office and attempted with some success, and in violation of the Geneva Agreements, to encourage the emergence of a more Western-oriented government that would be willing to appeal to SEATO for support if necessary. As a result of this a crisis broke out in the spring of 1959, in the course of which both Peking and Hanoi made it clear that they would not tolerate such a situation. Accordingly, American intervention eased off for a time, and a neutralist coup restored Souvanna Phouma to power in the summer of 1960.

Parallel with the Laotian crisis, and presumably emboldened by a more sympathetic attitude in Peking, Hanoi began in the spring of 1959 to send Communist cadres of southern origin who had been in the North since 1954 into South Vietnam, with arms, funds, etc., to start an insurgency in earnest. This they proceeded to do, with increasing effect.

The Beginnings of Direct American Involvement

Although the Eisenhower administration had continued to assume complacently that Diem was a good man and had things under reasonable control, it was obvious to the Kennedy administration almost from the time it took office that such was not the case. Worse still, the situation in South Vietnam threatened to deteriorate rapidly on account of developments in Laos.

At the time of his restoration to power in the summer of 1960, Souvanna Phouma was still not acceptable to the United States government. Accordingly, the Central Intelligence Agency engineered his overthrow by a right-wing army. He fled to Cambodia and appealed for Soviet support, which soon began to arrive by air. The arms involved were intended for Souvanna Phouma's "neutralist"' forces, but a high percentage actually got into the hands of the Pathet Lao and the North Vietnamese. Taking advantage of the general confusion and the lame duck period between American administrations, North Vietnamese troops occupied most of the highlands of eastern Laos in force at the beginning of 1961, never to be dislodged. Through this wilderness they then began to construct the so-called Ho Chi Minh Trail, actually a complex of trails leading from North Vietnam into South Vietnam via Laos. Together with its subsequent extension via Cambodia, the so-called Sihanouk Trail, these routes posed a mortal threat first to the highlands of South Vietnam, and ultimately to the lowlands, including the Mekong Delta.

The impact of these developments on Laos itself was also serious. President Kennedy rejected the idea of American military intervention and promptly abandoned the Eisenhower administration's efforts to create an anti-Communist government in Laos; he considered that the best that he could get would be a neutral Laos. To cope with the onward advance of the Pathet Lao and their North Vietnamese patrons, as well as to deter possible Soviet and Chinese support for them, he indulged in early 1961 in a number of threatening gestures ("coercive diplomacy"), while pressing vigorously for negotiations. The outcome was another international conference at Geneva in 1961–62, similar in some ways to the one held in 1954 but confined to Laos. The external powers participating agreed that Laos should be neutral, under the supervision of a revived but still weak International Control Commission. It was to have a coalition government under a neutral premier (obviously Souvanna Phouma), a Pathet Lao vice premier, and an anti-Communist vice premier, any of whom was to have a veto over any major proposed act of the government; this formula, clearly designed to produce a deadlock and prevent interference from Vientiane with the advance of the left-wing forces on the ground, was essentially a Soviet invention, and its acceptance was hardly a triumph for American diplomacy.

In reality, this machinery worked as intended for only a brief period. Encouraged by the fact that most of the North Vietnamese forces that had entered Laos remained there in violation of the agreement, the Pathet Lao soon began to exert pressure on Souvanna Phouma's neutralists to win over as many as possible. The main result was to polarize the political scene into two elements (rather than three), drive Souvanna Phouma closer to the United States and vice versa, and produce the breakdown of the projected tripartite ("troika") government. Without violating the agreement to the extent of maintaining a formal military presence in Laos, the United States began to support (through the Central Intelligence Agency) an effective anti-Communist irregular army composed of Meo tribesmen from the vicinity of the Plain of Jars (a strategic area in northern Laos) under the redoutable General Vang Pao.

Laos was important to the United States (and to the North Vietnamese) mainly on account of its relevance to South Vietnam, and the situation there seemed serious enough so that the Kennedy administration sent a high-level mission under General Maxwell D. Taylor in October 1961 to take stock and make recommendations. It urged a policy of pressing reforms and aid simultaneously on Diem as the best means of keeping South Vietnam out of Hanoi's hands. The reforms never came but the aid did. A rapidly growing number of American military advisers and technicians, although not yet full-fledged combat units, began to appear in South Vietnam during the next few years. Given the Diem government's shortcomings, the results were not encouraging, and it appears that if President Kennedy had survived to be re-elected in 1964 he would then have begun to eliminate the American involvement in support of Saigon.

Diem and Nhu were barely aware of the seriousness of their problems, of the nature of the needed countermeasures, or of the means of putting the latter into effect. They insisted on treating intellectuals, opposition politicians, and other critics as subversives. In the early 1960s Nhu inaugurated an alleged effort to give security to the rural population by reconcentrating much of it in "strategic hamlets." But the program was undercapitalized and aimed to a large extent at building a personal political base for Nhu; this it failed to do, and the entire effort was probably countereffective from Saigon's standpoint. The Communist insurgency continued to grow more serious.

In the spring of 1963 the Diem government became involved in a violent dispute with a large percentage of the Buddhist population. This triggered a series of student demonstrations, and the Army leadership began to show increasing reluctance to support a government whose political base was obviously crumbling. The situation was all the worse because Nhu was in secret contact with the National Liberation Front (or "Viet Cong"), the South Vietnamese Communist organization. These developments, taken as a whole, completed the process of souring the Kennedy administration on the Diem government and leading it to look favorably on an emerging conspiracy within the South Vietnamese military leadership to overthrow it. The coup took place on November 1, and Diem and Nhu were killed on the following day (contrary to Washington's wishes).

Bad as the Diem government had become, its overthrow was probably a serious mistake, at least in the sense that the political and military situations began to deteriorate at an even faster rate. The United States would have preferred, and tried to foster, a truly democratic civilian government as the successor to the Diem dictatorship. But the latter had so effectively prevented the emergence of a loyal opposition (as contrasted with the thoroughly disloyal Communist opposition) that there was no alternative but rule by the only force strong enough to overthrow Diem, the Army of course. Increased military involvement in politics after November 1963 tended to distract the Army from fighting the Communists and to produce further successes for the latter.

The year 1964 was a tense one that saw a further American build-up in South Vietnam, especially in the field of tactical airpower, and American bombing of the Ho Chi Minh Trail in Laos and of some North Vietnamese naval shore installations following the so-called Tonkin Gulf Incident of early August, which President Johnson used to get a joint Congressional resolution authorizing him to use American forces in Southeast Asia virtually as he saw fit. On the other hand, during the American election campaign President Johnson took a rather dovish line in public on Vietnam, although this was mainly in order to contrast his own apparent reasonableness with the hawkishness of his Republican opponent, Senator Barry Goldwater. Hanoi apparently took Johnson's remarks too literally and drew great encouragement from his overwhelming electoral victory. In addition, the North Vietnamese may have feared that a victory for the Viet Cong, which appeared fairly imminent as long as there was no further American intervention, would lead to an overly independent (of Hanoi) Communist regime in South Vietnam, unless North Vietnamese forces were also on the scene.

Escalation

Probably for these reasons, at the end of 1964 Hanoi began to introduce regular North Vietnamese Army units into South Vietnam for the first time. Their apparent mission was to establish bases in the highlands from which the lowlands could be seized with the support of the Viet Cong. Hanoi had great expectations of victory in 1965. Moscow, more experienced and sophisticated at interpreting American motivation, seems to have realized that the United States was not likely to accept this outcome without counterintervention, and that its actions would probably include air strikes against North Vietnam. Accordingly, during a visit to Hanoi in February 1965 Premier Kosygin offered to provide substantial air defense equipment (surface-to-air-missiles, etc.). The timing could not have been better, since the United States inaugurated air strikes against North Vietnam and against Communist forces in South Vietnam during his visit. In the spring the United States sent in Marine combat units and, beginning in the middle of the year, Army units as well. A reason often given for this step was the need to take reprisals against Viet Cong attacks on American military personnel already in South Vietnam. The actual reason was to prevent the fall of Saigon. Whatever the legitimacy of this objective—the arguments pro and con are familiar and in many cases go far beyond Vietnam—the United States government had the mistaken impression that Hanoi was acting as a virtual agent of Peking, much as Washington had believed earlier, also mistakenly, that Peking was acting as a virtual agent of Moscow. Thus the American escalation, or more accurately counterescalation, in Vietnam was officially viewed, until about 1967, as a critical aspect of the containment of China.

And yet to a large extent because of an exaggerated fear of another war with China, this time over Vietnam, as well as for other reasons such as a regard for domestic and international opinion, the Johnson administration publicly repudiated any intent to use measures likely to bring about the collapse of the North Vietnamese state. It therefore refrained from invading the North and from systematically bombing population centers or the dikes containing the Red River. Mainly in order to avoid a confrontation with the Soviet Union, it also refrained from mining or blockading Haiphong, the port through which flowed most of those Soviet supplies for North Vietnam that did not move across China by rail. Given the absence of any serious threat to its survival, North Vietnam was able to send virtually as much of its Army as it pleased into South Vietnam, subject to the none-too-effective if energetic American efforts at interdiction through air strikes. To cope with this large North Vietnamese military presence in South Vietnam, the United States felt compelled to engage in massive "search and destroy" operations, which inflicted not only heavy losses on the combatants but also substantial damage on the countryside and civilian population of South Vietnam.

The United States ended by waging something that resembled a regular war more closely than a counterinsurgency, that generated serious strains in its domestic politics and foreign relations, that compelled the Soviet Union and China to increase the level of their aid to North Vietnam by way of response, and that had almost no advantages apart from giving career American military men a chance to try out their latest weapons and win promotions. In this way a well-intentioned decision, to refrain from threatening North Vietnam with destruction, produced results so bad that the United States was able to accept them for only a limited time and had to withdraw from the war (after 1969) without having achieved a decisive result in compensation for its effort and sacrifices; furthermore, the United States government was not even given credit for good intentions. It would perhaps have been more humane and fruitful as to result, even though less obviously well-intentioned, if the United States government had posed a credible threat to invade North Vietnam—without actually invading it—by some such means as occasional demonstrations by an amphibious landing force in the Gulf of Tonkin, and in this way kept most of the North Vietnamese Army pinned where it presumably belonged, in North Vietnam. It has been said that God writes straight with crooked lines; in Vietnam the Johnson administration wrote crookedly with straight lines.

It is also true that the American overmilitarization of the war in South Vietnam after 1965 flowed from the virtual physical impossibility of isolating the battlefield, as the United States had been able to do in the case of Japanese-held islands in the Pacific during the Second World War and as the British had been able to do during the Emergency in Malaya. The enemy could not be denied, even by intensive bombing, the ability to receive reinforcements and supplies in significant amounts from his base in North Vietnam and from his Soviet and Chinese patrons. The enemy was too numerous and well organized, and the terrain too difficult, to permit the American and South Vietnamese forces to isolate and defeat him within the limits of time, casualties, and expenditure that American and world opinion would accept.

Nevertheless, at vast cost, considerable if not decisive progress was made. The North Vietnamese Army suffered far heavier losses than it inflicted on its American adversaries. The Saigon government survived and even began to stabilize itself somewhat, although still under the essentially military rule of President Nguyen Van Thieu. It was far from a democracy, but it did make some slow and uneven progress toward "pacification," or in other words the elimination of the Viet Cong "infrastructure" (cadres, paramilitary units, etc.) in the rural areas. In 1967, Hanoi evidently made an "agonizing reappraisal" of its position and concluded that it was gradaully losing the war in South Vietnam, in addition to suffering serious although not crippling damage at home from American bombing. Peking's advice to de-escalate to the level of a protracted "people's war" and imitate China's Cultural Revolution in order to regenerate public morale was rejected, and another approach was decided on. This was to launch major simultaneous offensives by the North Vietnamese Army and the Viet Cong aimed at producing some American military defeats along the lines of Dienbienphu, seizing and holding some important South Vietnamese cities, and producing a collapse of the Saigon government and the creation of a leftist alternative oriented toward Hanoi. One reason for the obvious sense of urgency was that Ho Chi Minh's life was running out, and he unquestionably wanted to see South Vietnam "liberated" before he died.

From these causes flowed the famous Tet Offensive, which began at the end of January 1968. After some spectacular initial successes achieved through surprise, it turned into a disaster. The North Vietnamese units suffered heavy losses, and the Viet Cong organization, which necessarily surfaced and exposed itself in the process of playing its assigned part in the offensive, was reduced almost to ineffectiveness by hostile action. On the other hand, the psychological impact on American opinion, via the television screen in particular, of the galvanic Communist effort was sufficient to crystalize a determination in influential circles to de-escalate. The futility of competitive escalation in a war that, realistically speaking, neither side could win in the conventional sense, was driven home to both the major adversaries. Hanoi decided to seek by diplomatic means, and while Ho still lived, the goal that had eluded its commanders. The door to an exit via negotiations, at least for the United States, began to open.

PART TWO

Asia in the Era of Soviet-American Parity

CHAPTER VIII

The Sino-Soviet
Confrontation

T HERE are a number of reasons why the emergence of strategic parity between the United States and the Soviet Union
is a sensible theme for an analysis of Asian international politics
since 1969. The Soviet-American relationship is clearly the dominant one in international politics as a whole, in spite of the gap
between the two superpowers' enormous economic and military
power and their much more limited ability to translate that power
into concrete political influence on particular situations. Since
about the time of the invasion of Czechoslovakia, the Soviet Union
has been considerably more assertive in world politics than it
generally was before, although (as shown in Chapter X) this trend
has been subject to fluctuations. This Soviet assertiveness has been
displayed in Asia, where Moscow has sensed opportunities in the
British withdrawal from "east of Suez," the American disengagement from Vietnam, and the weakening and destabilizing effects
of the Cultural Revolution in China.

The cutting edge of Soviet assertiveness in Asia as elsewhere,
however, is not local and possibly temporary situations, but the
fact that for the first time in its history the Soviet Union no longer
suffers from marked strategic (and therefore psychological) in-

feriority to its main adversary or potential adversary. Traumatized by the necessity for "blinking first" in the Cuban missile crisis, the Soviet leadership decided to avoid such experiences in the future by building up their strategic forces, at enormous cost to the civilian economy, to a level of approximate parity with those of the United States; this was achieved by the end of the 1960s. It is probably fortunate for the world that the current Soviet leadership is not as adventurous as Khrushchev showed himself to be when he tried to smuggle offensive missiles into Cuba in 1962, and that the United States retains a retaliatory capability against a possible Soviet nuclear attack.

China, of course, is in a much less favorable strategic position than is the United States. With the exception of the tendency toward American military withdrawal from Asia, no recent development has had a greater impact on the international politics of Asia than the confrontation that has arisen between the Soviet Union and China since the fall of Khrushchev. There is a great deal of irony in this situation, inasmuch as there is a strong possibility that Khrushchev was overthrown in part for the excesses of his China policy, and inasmuch as Moscow by its recent treatment of China has virtually made a self-fulfilling prophecy of its charges (since 1966) of Sino-American collusion against it.

Soviet Perception of a Chinese Threat

It was evidently in 1965–66 that Moscow began to perceive China, for the first time, as a possible military threat in the fairly near future. Among the aspects of Sino-Soviet relations that troubled Moscow at that time, two appear to have been particularly important. One is that China began to construct an ICBM testing range in 1965 and in this way gave notice that it intended to become a major nuclear power. The other is that Premier Sato announced in August 1965 that he intended to recover Okinawa in the reasonably near future, a move that would inevitably reduce the island's utility as a key American base for regional containment of China and that might open the way to Chinese expansion in non-Communist Asia as the American presence declined sooner or later. Since most Soviet leaders had begun by that time to come to the conclusion that the Chinese were adventurous and expansionist, the outlook appeared ominous from their point of view.

There were other, less military, reasons for increased Soviet concern over China in the mid-1960s. In early February 1965, immediately after the United States began to bomb North Vietnam, Premier Kosygin proposed a campaign of "united action" on behalf of Hanoi and the Viet Cong. Mao rejected this proposal, both because of his belief that acceptance would be politically advantageous to Moscow and because of his ideological conviction that the Soviet leadership was incurably "revisionist," a view strengthened by the Soviet revival in early March of Khrushchev's plan for an international conference of Communist Parties. In addition, Kosygin proposed a suspension of public polemics and a normalization of Sino-Soviet intergovernmental relations to include an increase of trade and a resumption of Soviet economic aid to China; this was also rejected at Mao's insistence. The Chinese turned down shortly afterward a Soviet request for overflight rights and for facilities in Southwest China to permit air supply of the North Vietnamese. Instead, Peking agreed at the end of April to cooperate in transshipment of Soviet equipment to North Vietnam by rail. This agreement was not very faithfully observed, but it is not clear to what extent the fault lay with decisions taken in Peking, disruption of the rail system by the Cultural Revolution, seizure of equipment from the trains by rival Red Guard units, or some combination of these.

The escalation of early 1965 in Vietnam, which resulted from the injection for the first time of regular North Vietnamese military units into the South being countered first by American bombing and then by the introduction of American ground forces, came as an even greater shock to Peking than to Moscow for obvious geographic reasons. Furthermore, Mao had gone on record in January with a prediction that the United States would not escalate, and he was apparently badly shaken by the subsequent realization of his error. He soon saw his current favorite project, the Cultural Revolution, postponed for several months while the Chinese leadership debated what the escalation in Vietnam meant for China and what should be done about it. Probably speaking for many of the professional military, Chief of Staff Lo Jui-ch'ing argued publicly in May that North Vietnam was acting correctly in sending its troops into South Vietnam, that China should give active logistical support (including full cooperation in transshipping Soviet equipment) to this step, that such a policy would create a serious risk of an American strategic attack on China, and that accordingly China should reestablish cooperation with the Soviet Union at least in the military field. Although he subsequently modified this position, which was stated so strongly as to be positively anti-Maoist, he was purged early in 1966, probably in part because his views on Vietnam were considered dangerously hawkish.

It was Defense Minister Lin Piao who put his name on the main statement of the Maoist position on Vietnam, a tract entitled *Long Live the Victory of People's War* (September 3, 1965). In contradiction to Lo, he insisted that the war in South Vietnam should be fought primarily by the Viet Cong on a "self-reliant" basis, that Chinese support for North Vietnam should be kept at a correspondingly low level, that if there was an American threat to China it would take the form of an invasion that could be defeated in a "people's war," and that there was no need and no justification for "united action" of any kind with the "revisionist" Russians. Indeed, Lin made what is probably the classic statement of the dual adversary strategy. Projecting the experience of the Chinese revolution on a global scale, he also argued that the "world countryside" (the developing countries) would encircle and defeat the "world city" (the developed countries, especially the "imperialist" ones) by fighting "people's wars" against their alleged tendency to invade the developing countries as the Japanese had invaded China. This last concept was especially irritating to the Soviets, who considered it a racist effort to promote antagonism between themselves, as well as others, and the countries of the Third World.

The Maoist view on Vietnam, as expressed by Lin, prevailed in Peking, especially after the purge of Lo Jui-ch'ing. Support for Hanoi was confined largely to logistical support of a kind unlikely to encourage escalation above the "people's war" level. Peking gave North Vietnam and the Viet Cong loud propaganda support, urged them to fight a "people's war" indefinitely and avoid negotiating with the "imperialist" adversary, and exhorted Hanoi unsuccessfully after 1966 to have a Cultural Revolution of its own as the indispensable means to victory. In addition, some 30–50,000 Chinese military railway personnel entered North Vietnam to help keep the rail lines to China open under American bombing.

In spite of this essentially cautious policy, Peking felt considerable nervousness over the possibility of a direct clash with the United States. This was fully reciprocated, since the United States government was convinced that Hanoi was acting as an agent of Peking. There was fear on both sides of another Sino-American war in Vietnam along the lines of the Korean War, although in fact there was little analogy between the two situations since North Vietnam did not need or want Chinese intervention, Peking's logistical problems would have been much greater than in Korea, and the Sino-Soviet alliance had lost most of whatever vitality it had possessed in 1950. Furthermore, even assuming identical Chinese behavior in Korea and Vietnam, Peking would have sent troops into North Vietnam to set up a buffer zone next to the Chinese border if the United States had invaded North Vietnam, but would have actually fought only if American forces had moved far enough north to penetrate the buffer.

This common concern over the possibility of a Sino-American war, which was strongly felt by influential congressional and public figures in the United States, produced its own partial corrective. In mid-March 1966, at a Sino-American ambassadorial conversation in Warsaw, the two sides agreed in effect that neither would be the first to escalate the war in Vietnam to the direct disadvantage of the other. After that Peking's nervousness subsided considerably, except for a brief interval in early 1967 when the United States began to base B-52s in Thailand for use in the Vietnam War.

From the spring of 1966, the Soviet leadership became extremely nervous over what it regarded as Sino-American "collusion" over Vietnam, which it thought was bound to be anti-Soviet in effect if not necessarily in purpose and was the exact opposite of the "united action" proposed earlier by Moscow to Peking. Although greatly exaggerated at first, this fear turned into a virtual self-fulfilling prophecy during the next few years, as Moscow built up its strategic forces to a level of approximate parity with the United States and put pressure on China in order to cope with the threat it was thought to present and to exert political influence on it. In the spring of 1966, the Soviet Union moved significant offensive forces into the Mongolian People's Republic, where they were only a few hundred miles from Peking. It also appears that Moscow considered military intervention in China at that time, but if so it obviously decided to refrain, presumably because no adequate political justification, and no prospect of political cooperation from within China, existed.

The Cultural Revolution and Sino-Soviet Relations

Since the mid-1950s, and especially since the early 1960s, Mao Tse-tung had increasingly come to view some of his own colleagues as infected with Soviet "revisionism." Mao believed profoundly that the youth of China needed to be rescued from and immunized against "revisionist" influences through a synthetic revolutionary experience as similar as possible to the genuine one that he and his colleagues had undergone. In this concept lay the germ of the Cultural Revolution and the Red Guard movement, in which militant youths were used in 1966–67 to destroy the power of the party apparatus. This extraordinary episode, which began only after Peking felt reasonably certain that it would not have to cope with an attack by the United States, aroused the profoundest concern in Moscow, coming as it did on the heels of the developments already discussed. The Soviet party apparatus, solidly in control of its own country and regarding this situation as the only one appropriate to a Communist state, was greatly upset at seeing its Chinese opposite number nearly put out of action by the Red Guards. The atmosphere on both sides was worsened by some events that occurred early in 1966: Mao vetoed a Japanese Communist Party proposal for a form of "united action" with the Soviet Union, Moscow addressed a "secret" letter complaining about Chinese behavior to some of the European parties, and Peking cited this letter as its reason for refusing an invitation to send a delegation to the Soviet party's Twenty-third Congress.

During the Cultural Revolution, Peking's external behavior was almost as obnoxious to Moscow as its domestic politics. The aspects that bore most directly on the Soviet Union were an intensification of anti-"revisionist" propaganda, extremely provocative incidents staged along the Sino-Soviet border, and a siege of the Soviet Embassy in Peking by Red Guards in January-February 1967. In December 1966, after the anti-"revisionist" mood of the Cultural Revolution had become clear and the Red Guards had begun to assault the party apparatus in the provinces, where it was more powerful than at the center, the Soviet party held a Central Committee meeting that appears to have been devoted in large part to the Chinese situation and to have discussed once more the pros and cons of intervention; again the decision was negative, presumably for the same reason as before. The injection of the Regional Forces (but not to any great extent the Main Forces, whose mission remained essentially military) of the Chinese Army into the Cultural Revolution in January 1967, in order to overcome the resistance of the Party apparatus to the Red Guards, did nothing to quiet Moscow's apprehensions. Soviet propaganda began to picture China as an expansionist militant country run by a coalition of Maoists, military leaders, and bureaucrats typified by Chou En-lai; what was most distressing, obviously, was the absence of the Party apparatus from this lineup.

Czechoslovakia

In the spring of 1968, the Soviet ideological press (as distinct from the party and government propaganda organs) began a series of long and bitter attacks on the Chinese for their ideology, party history, political system, foreign policy, etc. Ideological matters in the Soviet Union are under the general supervision of Mikhail Suslov, the elder statesman of the Politburo, who appears to detest the Chinese not only as ideological deviants but as disrupters of the unity (under Soviet hegemony, by implication) of the international Communist movement, a unity which in the current era finds its main, if limited, expression in occasional international meetings. By contrast, Suslov appears to have been opposed to coercing the Dubcek regime in Czechoslovakia, whose "socialism with a human face" began to attract the unfavorable attention of a majority of the Soviet leadership in April 1968. One of the reasons for Suslov's attitude was probably a correct perception that pressure on Czechoslovakia would disrupt his plans for another international conference by antagonizing most of the European Communist Parties, whereas pressure on the Chinese would produce less serious complications since most of the more or less pro-Chinese parties (the North Koreans and North Vietnamese, for example), as well as the Chinese themselves, would not attend the conference in any case.

It might be thought that under these circumstances Peking would be relieved at the Soviet invasion of Czechoslovakia on August 21, 1968; such was not the case, however. Except perhaps for militant Maoists like Lin Piao, any Chinese leader who had regarded the Soviet Union as a paper bear now felt compelled to change his mind and regard it as an imminent threat. One reason for this shift was the so-called Brezhnev Doctrine, which was announced in the months following the invasion and in effect claimed a right for the Soviet Union to intervene in any Communist country where it judged the cause of "socialism" to be in danger, and not merely in Czechoslovakia. The tension created in Peking by the invasion of Czechoslovakia probably accelerated the effective termination of the Cultural Revolution through the suppression of the Red Guards, although this important step had been decided on already for essentially domestic reasons. Chou En-lai, although no doubt genuinely alarmed at the implications for the rest of Eastern Europe (especially Albania) and for China of the invasion of Czechoslovakia, seems to have sensed an opportunity to begin moving away from the risky and untenable dual adversary strategy in the direction of a limited accommodation with the United States, to be rationalized on the basis of the threat (real or alleged) from the Soviet Union. The dual adversary strategy was still sacred to Lin Piao and other Maoists, if not necessarily to Mao himself, however, and Chou had to move carefully. He waited until Mao had gone on winter vacation and then, on November 25, invited the incoming Nixon administration to resume the currently suspended ambassadorial talks at Warsaw on February 20, 1969; this move, which was bound to be controversial, was rationalized by the republication of a tract written by Mao in 1945 and saying that on occasion negotiations with the adversary were justified and necessary.

Drums along the Ussuri

During the next several weeks, however, Mao was evidently influenced by some other colleagues, probably including Lin Piao, to cancel the invitation (on February 19), launch a propaganda campaign against the Nixon administration, and authorize a more or less parallel blow at the Soviet Union as seemingly required by the dual adversary strategy. This latter blow, which was designed like the first to help create an appropriate atmosphere for Lin's proclamation as Mao's heir at the forthcoming Ninth Party Congress, was probably struck in the incorrect belief that Moscow would be prevented from retaliating by a crisis over West Berlin in which it then appeared to be involved, but which turned out to be short-lived. Lin's anti-Soviet move took the form of an ambush of a Soviet patrol on a disputed island in the Ussuri River (between Manchuria and the Soviet Far East) on March 2, 1969. The Soviet response, which was unexpectedly violent, included a massive anti-Chinese propaganda campaign, a demonstration against the Chinese Embassy in Moscow, an attempt to exploit the Chinese issue to rally the Warsaw Pact countries under Moscow's leadership, and a larger and more devastating ambush of a Chinese unit on the same island on March 15. Peking postponed its party congress in alarm and did not open it until April 1, by which time dovish voices in Moscow, probably concerned over the possibility of driving the Chinese into the arms of the United States, had prevailed to the extent that Kosygin invited Peking on March 29 to negotiate the border dispute. Peking's intensely anti-Soviet mood prevented acceptance of this offer. On the other hand, it was thought wise for Lin Piao to include in his report to the Ninth Party Congress a statement implying that Peking did not seriously claim any significant amount of Soviet Asian territory, provided a new boundary treaty were signed on a footing of equality and recognizing that the old tsarist treaties were "unequal" (i.e., unethical because imposed by force), and provided some minor adjustments of the border were made in China's favor.

Moscow has never admitted publicly to a realization that this is Peking's position, probably because to do so would hamper propaganda exploitation of the border issue. On the other hand, the Soviet attitude contains genuine, if exaggerated, elements of concern. These are based partly on racial feelings, but also on a belief that Peking is adventurous, and that as it becomes a major nuclear power it is likely either to expand into non-Communist Asia as the United States disengages, or to reach an understanding with the United States to facilitate an attempt at expansion into Soviet Asia. In either case, a strong Soviet military presence near the Chinese border is considered a necessary deterrent. Although this estimate of Peking's expansionist propensities is unduly alarmist, it is true that Soviet pressures along the border have contributed to a less assertive Chinese policy toward Asia, as well as to Peking's celebrated diplomatic approaches to the United States. The Soviet leadership also appears to be interested in being in a position to exert pressure on China, for political effect, probably after Mao's death.

With these considerations, or something like them, in mind, the Soviet Union began a rapid buildup of its forces near the Chinese border in the spring of 1969, gave Peking a virtual ultimatum to begin negotiating the border dispute by September 13, and backed up this demand with a succession of warnings and threats. Early in September, at North Vietnam's urgent request, the Chinese agreed to let Kosygin talk with Chou En-lai in Peking on September 11, and on October 7, after some further Soviet pressures had been applied, both sides agreed to hold negotiations in Peking in the near future. In this way the tension along the border was partly defused, although the Soviet military build-up continued at least into 1972 and rose to a level of some fifty divisions (including an estimated eight in the Mongolian People's Republic) backed by nuclear weapons.

The Border Negotiations

The border talks began in Peking on October 20, 1969, and promptly became deadlocked, although they were not suspended. Neither side was in a position to make major concessions, if only for reasons of domestic politics, and neither was realistically speaking in a position to make war if its demands were not met or if no agreement were reached. On the Chinese side, strategic inferiority alone is a sufficient argument against starting a war. On the other side, in spite of Soviet strategic superiority there are powerful reasons why Moscow should and does hesitate to attack China. One is China's formidable defensive potential and its growing retaliatory capabilities, nuclear and conventional; Chinese forces could probably cut the Trans-Siberian Railway and damage or destroy several Soviet cities with nuclear-armed missiles. The Soviet Union's external relations with both Communist and non-Communist countries would be severely harmed if it attacked China; the United States, although it probably would not intervene militarily, has indicated strong opposition to such an attack and would presumably find some way short of war of punishing Moscow for it. Finally, the Soviet Union's political and social systems, which suffer from serious internal tensions, would experience severe strains in the event of a war with China, or any other major power.

The Chinese position at the talks has been essentially that there should be a prompt agreement on a cease-fire and a mutual withdrawal of troops from the common border. Peking demands publicly that Moscow withdraw its forces from foreign territory (i.e., from the Mongolian People's Republic, where they are closer to Peking than anywhere else), and privately that as part of a long-term accommodation the forces in Soviet Asia near the Chinese border be pulled back to Western Siberia. China still insists on a new boundary treaty that, while branding the previous treaties as "unequal," does not necessarily make any changes in China's favor in the existing border, except for minor ones in areas where Peking insists that the Soviet Union is in occupation of territory somewhat in excess of what was conceded under the "unequal" treaties.

The Soviet position amounts to a rejection of these demands, in the case of the first because acceptance would remove a major source of leverage on Peking. The exception is that there can be a new treaty that reaffirms the boundary established by the "unequal" treaties, which Moscow is unwilling to label as such, and that makes some minor adjustments in Peking's favor.

The basic deadlock in the border negotiations has not prevented, and may even have stimulated, a limited improvement of Sino-Soviet intergovernmental relations in other fields. In October-November 1970, ambassadors were exchanged (their predecessors had been withdrawn in 1966), and a new trade agreement was signed.

Continued Tension

In mid-December 1969, Peking became worried that the Soviet Union might be about to break off the border negotiations and therefore began to show an interest in resuming Sino-American ambassadorial talks. Moscow resumed the negotiations in Peking early in 1970, however, and in the spring of 1970 the tentative trend toward an improvement in Sino-American relations was badly disrupted by the overthrow of Prince Sihanouk and the subsequent entry of American ground forces into Cambodia, which led Peking to break off the ambassadorial talks and denounce the United States loudly. About the middle of the year there occurred a major, although unpublicized, Sino-Soviet military clash in Central Asia. The responsibility is unclear; the Soviet side may have started it in the hope of pressuring Peking into concessions now that the latter seemingly had no American card to play, or the Chinese side may have started it as another validation of the dual adversary strategy (a slap for the "imperialists," a slap for the "revisionists" or "social imperialists."). Whatever the truth, Moscow approached the United States privately at the SALT talks in early July with a proposal for joint action against aggressive third countries, obviously meaning China. Although the United States declined, Peking was certainly becoming worried by the situation in which it found itself and was impressed by President Nixon's withdrawal of American troops from Cambodia at the end of June as he had originally promised and by his continued expressions of interest in an improved relationship with China, in part as a means of increasing American leverage on the Soviet Union.

There is little doubt that the resulting resumption of Sino-American contacts contributed to moderating Soviet policy toward China. It may have had something to do with the exchange of ambassadors already mentioned. It is even more likely to have contributed to Brezhnev's private offer, made in February 1971, of a nonaggression pact with China. Peking, by then in a bolder mood and probably regarding the offer as meaningless as long as the other issues in Sino-Soviet relations were left unresolved, refused.

Peking's conduct of its relations with Moscow continued to be strongly influenced by Maoist ideology and domestic politics. In spite of the suppression of the Red Guards by the Army and the effective end of the Cultural Revolution in late 1968, extreme Maoists like Lin Piao and Chiang Ching (Mme. Mao Tse-tung) still exercised considerable influence on Mao himself, and therefore on Chinese domestic politics and foreign policy. This remained true even though Lin's personal political fortunes began to decline long before his fall in September 1971, and perhaps from as early as March 1969. Chou En-lai accordingly found it wise to avoid trouble by injecting some Maoist elements into his conduct of foreign relations. His statement of October 7, 1969, announcing the decision to open border negotiations with the Soviet Union, for example, contained a bow to the Maoists in the form of a statement that "irreconcilable differences of principle," or in other words of ideology, separated the two sides, a proposition probably not of intense concern to Chou himself. Presumably to demonstrate to everyone, especially the Russians, that the opening of the border talks in October 1969 did not indicate any lessening of the Maoist faith in "people's war" as the best deterrent to attack, an extensive campaign of "war preparations" (tunnel digging, etc.) was launched at about the same time. Also at that time, the texts of the famous Maoist "revolutionary operas" associated with the Cultural Revolution were revised somewhat, and the commentaries on the revised versions sometimes mentioned the Soviet Union among the adversaries against whom viewers of the operas should remember to struggle.

Over and above the genuine detestation of Soviet "revisionism" and "social imperialism" by the Maoists and the serious concern felt by Chou En-lai and others (probably including some Maoists) over the Soviet military threat, the Soviet demon image was consciously manipulated to some extent for political effect. In particular Chou appears to have been exploiting the Soviet threat, while trying not to provoke Moscow beyond endurance, in order to promote his military policy. Whereas Lin's conception stressed loud publicity for the nuclear weapons program, rapid development of an ICBM, and training of the conventional forces for "people's war," Chou's is both more rational and less assertive; it emphasizes IRBMs and MRBMs (which are useful as a deterrent to Soviet attack, but do not alarm the United States to the same degree as an ICBM would), minimal publicity for the nuclear weapons program, the gradual withdrawal of the Regional Forces from the dominant political role that they assumed in the provinces during the Cultural Revolution on the plea of military necessity created by Soviet pressures, and improvement of the capabilities of the entire People's Liberation Army (both the Main Forces and the Regional Forces) for conventional warfare.

Complex political forces are at work on the Soviet side as well. Brezhnev has clearly committed himself to a strong anti-Chinese line and has been implicitly accused by one of his most important junior colleagues, Shelepin, who appears to be less anti-Chinese, of exploiting the China issue for personal political purposes. One reason for Brezhnev's attitude is probably his close ties with the Soviet military, some elements of which still want revenge for the

Ussuri clash of March 2, 1969, regard China as a threat, and might advocate an attack if favorable conditions should materialize. Suslov, although genuinely and strongly hostile to Chinese ideology and behavior, appears to find Peking useful as an adversary against whom to try to rally the essentially pro-Soviet Communist Parties under Moscow's leadership, and he evidently does not favor the use of force against the Chinese or anyone else. To some extent, Soviet propaganda exploits the controversy with China in an effort to make Moscow more acceptable in Western eyes.

Thus the Sino-Soviet confrontation remains a process in which each adversary displays a concern that is partly real and partly exaggerated and seeks advantage over the other in a variety of ways. Among the latter are a number of Soviet gestures, informal and often covert, toward Taiwan since 1968; one of the most interesting was the passage of four Soviet naval vessels through the Taiwan Strait, apparently without advance notification to Taipei, on May 12, 1973, two days before the arrival of David Bruce in Peking as Chief of the United States Liaison Office there, as though to suggest that the developing relationship between the United States and the People's Republic of China might be countered by one between the Soviet Union and the Republic of China. In spite of occasional reports of armed clashes along the Sino-Soviet frontier and suggestions from time to time in the Soviet press that the stability of Inner Asia requires the transfer of all territory north of the Great Wall from Chinese control to Soviet influence, Peking seems somewhat less nervous than it once did and apparently believes that its growing military strength and improving international position will be enough to deter a Soviet attack. On the Soviet side, anti-Chinese statements and moves are evidently designed in many cases to put Peking in the worst possible light in connection with an apparently projected international conference of Communist Parties, rather than as serious threats; on the other hand Soviet concern is growing, at least in some quarters, in proportion as the strength of Peking's position increases.

The existence of apparent elements of gamesmanship in the Sino-Soviet confrontation does not cancel out a strong tendency for each side to regard the other as capable of extreme irrationality and therefore as requiring to be restrained by virtually any available means. In such a situation there is always the danger that the stronger party will take action to destroy the other, or at least to teach him an unforgettable lesson. There was an apparent increase of Sino-Soviet tension in the early months of 1974, probably as a reflection of Soviet concern over the approach of a Chinese capability of hitting Moscow with missiles emplaced near the Central Asian sector of the border, a Soviet belief that the Sino-American relationship had lost some of its vigor, and an effort by Chou En-lai to exploit an atmosphere of tension in Sino-Soviet relations as a means of helping to restore elite harmony in China after several months of political turmoil.

The Chinese and Soviet "Tilts" toward the United States

It is obvious that one of the most promising moves on the part of either adversary in the Sino-Soviet confrontation would be to improve its relations with the United States, ideally to the point of gaining effective American support against the other, and that the recent decline of Cold War attitudes in the United States has increased the apparent feasibility of such an approach.

On the Chinese side, even the Soviet threat was not considered as eliminating certain prerequisites for a détente with the United States. The two most important were that the United States must be perceived as no longer a serious threat to China, or at any rate as a significantly less serious threat than the Soviet Union, and that the United States must end its military involvement in Indochina, which Peking viewed as wrong in principle as well as dangerous to itself and others. The first of these conditions evidently began to materialize in 1966, when official American statements about China took on a more conciliatory tone and it became clear to Peking that the United States was not likely to escalate the war in Vietnam to the level of an attack on China. The second began to materialize in 1968, when President Johnson halted the bombing of North Vietnam. In these ways the United States qualified itself in Peking's eyes for Chou En-lai's invitation of November 25, 1968, issued under the impact of the invasion of Czechoslovakia and the Brezhnev Doctrine, to the incoming Nixon administration to resume the Sino-American ambassadorial talks at Warsaw on February 20, 1969. As compared with the massive Soviet threat that arose in 1969, the Nixon administration appeared to Peking as no threat to itself and in fact as anxious to improve its relations with China. Furthermore, in spite of the American incursion into Cambodia in the spring of 1970 and occasional bombing offensives against North Vietnam, the Nixon administration appeared in Chinese eyes to be genuinely committed to ending direct American military involvement in the Indochina war, and in fact to reducing substantially the American military presence in the Far East and the Western Pacific.

Above and beyond these prerequisites, there was reason to believe that the Nixon administration could be maneuvered, by virtue of its felt need for a better relationship with Peking, into greater flexibility on the Taiwan question, although probably not into an outright abandonment of the Republic of China. It was unlikely that President Nixon's desire for improved relations with Peking and his rather hostile attitude toward the Soviet Union (as indicated for example in a statement he made on July 1, 1970) would eventuate in actual American military support for China, but the mere possibility that they might would be a valuable, and perhaps decisive, deterrent to a Soviet attack. An interesting, although not necessarily very important, example of the benefits to Peking, in its confrontation with Moscow, of a better relationship with the United States is Brezhnev's public acceptance in March 1972, after ten years of rejection, of the Chinese and Albanian contention that the vague concept of "peaceful coexistence" was applicable to relations among "socialist" (i.e., Communist) states; the reason was almost certainly the fact that in the Shanghai Communiqué, signed the previous month, the United States had endorsed the Chinese variant, the Five Principles of Peaceful Coexistence.

On the Soviet side, the need for improved relations with the United States, in the context of the Sino-Soviet confrontation, was less urgent, inasmuch as the Soviet Union was militarily far stronger than China. An improvement was also more difficult, in view of American concern over the build-up of Soviet strategic weapons and over occasional Soviet forward moves in the Middle East. Moscow was also inhibited by a reluctance to appear in the eyes of the international left as conciliatory toward the United States while bullying China; it is interesting that the Soviet Union did not begin the long-discussed SALT talks with the United States until November 1969, a month after it had initiated the border negotiations in Peking, the sequence suggesting an implicit denial that Moscow found it easier to deal with the "imperialist" Americans than with the Chinese. Such in fact was increasingly the case, however, and fortunately so for Moscow, since it would have been unwise and even dangerous for it to leave Soviet-American relations as they were while Sino-American relations improved. Other powerful considerations were the need to ease the heavy burden of the arms race on the Soviet economy and a desire to strengthen the latter through increased trade and technological contact with the United States and other advanced industrial countries.

The outcome was what amounted to a competitive wooing of the United States. To be effective, this had to include a more moderate policy on Indochina, the area of most acute concern to the United States. Both Moscow and Peking have considered since about 1971, when the reality of the Sino-American détente became apparent, that the United States was more important than the troublesome North Vietnamese ally, with the qualification that neither Moscow nor Peking has wanted to act on this priority so vigorously as to drive Hanoi into the arms of the other. Moscow demonstrated its sense of priorities in May 1972 by deciding to go ahead with the summit conference with President Nixon in spite of the U.S. bombing and mining campaign in North Vietnam, and Peking later that year by threatening to cut off aid if Hanoi did not sign an agreement with the United States. More generally, Peking's relatively quiescent policy in Asia as a whole since 1969 and Brezhnev's personal détente diplomacy with the United States have clearly been motivated to a high degree by the compulsions of competitive wooing.

The "tilt" toward the United States has not been universally popular in either Moscow or Peking. One of the hard-line Soviet opponents of American "imperialism," the Ukrainian boss Pyotr Shelest, evidently favored cancelling the Moscow summit in May 1972 on account of the American bombing and mining of North Vietnam, only to be outvoted in the Politburo and demoted.

But it is on the Chinese, not the Soviet, side that the most serious objections to an improvement of relations with the United States have materialized, essentially because ideological and military fundamentalism are at a higher level in Peking than in Moscow. The radical Maoists have opposed, with decreasing effectiveness on the whole, the opening to the United States, which

Chou En-lai favors and Mao himself considers unavoidable under present circumstances. In fact, the opening was not assured until after the fall of the most powerful and radical of the Maoists, Defense Minister Lin Piao. Peking's official account of his fall, which is to the effect that he tried to assassinate Mao and was so pro-Soviet that he then tried to defect to the Soviet Union only to die in a plane crash in the Mongolian People's Republic on the night of September 12-13, 1971, is almost certainly consciously misleading and designed to make a good impression on American (as well as Chinese) opinion by bracketing the Soviet adversary with a Chinese villain.

In reality, as far as his attitude on foreign affairs was concerned, Lin appears to have remained the convinced advocate of the dual adversary strategy that he had shown himself to be in 1965 (in *Long Live the Victory of People's War*) and 1969 (on the Ussuri River). He probably interpreted Brezhnev's offer of a non-aggression pact in February 1971 as showing that the Russians were paper bears after all and that there was therefore no need to "tilt" toward the United States in order to cope with the Soviet threat, as Chou En-lai insisted there was. His opposition to the opening to the United States made him a source of danger to his colleagues, as did his personal unacceptability in Moscow; he was especially disliked there not only as a radical Maoist but as a "Bonapartist" military man trying to succeed Mao as China's leader, as the principal exponent of the allegedly racist concept of "people's war" (the "world countryside" against the "world city"), and as the architect of the first of the two clashes on the Ussuri River.

The announcement on July 15, 1971 in Peking and Washington that Dr. Henry Kissinger had just visited China and that President Nixon had been invited to do the same set in motion an increase in the apparent Soviet threat to China that contributed powerfully to the purge of Lin Piao as, among other things, a particular target of Moscow's wrath and an obstacle to the best available source of enhanced security against it, an improved relationship with the United States. The late summer of 1971 saw a series of especially strong anti-Chinese statements in the Soviet press and a number of important Soviet diplomatic moves. Among the latter, the two with the strongest impact on Peking were probably the Soviet-Indian friendship treaty of August 9, 1971 (Articles

8 and 9 of which say by clear implication that the Soviet Union will take any necessary military action against China if it should intervene in an Indo-Pakistani war), and the four-power agreement of September 3, 1971 on West Berlin (which had the effect of helping to free Moscow's hands in Europe the better to cope with China and was all the more meaningful in Peking because signed on the anniversary of the publication of Lin Piao's *Long Live the Victory of People's War*). Accordingly, Lin was purged and killed on September 11 or September 12, quite possibly after attempting a coup against Chou En-lai; the crash of a Chinese aircraft in the Mongolian People's Republic the following night was probably staged in order to discredit Lin by providing the basis for subsequent unproven and implausible charges that he had died while trying to flee to the country where his true loyalties lay.

Lin's fall removed the most powerful Chinese opponent of the "tilt" toward the United States and opened the way to the announcement on October 5 of a second visit by Kissinger to Peking, which occurred later that month. After that the Nixon visit, and at least a considerable improvement in Sino-American relations, were probably irreversible, although they remained far from completely acceptable to many radical Maoists at all levels of the political system. During the months before the presidential visit, cadres were extensively briefed to the effect that Nixon had shown a friendly attitude toward China and asked to come, and that it therefore made sense to invite him and see what he had to say. At the higher levels, objections were kept under control only through personal action by Mao himself, notably his receiving Nixon on the first day of the presidential visit (February 22, 1972), probably at Chou En-lai's strong request.

All this was immensely upsetting in Moscow, but fortunately from the Soviet viewpoint the Nixon administration claimed to be following a policy of "equidistance" with respect to the two major Communist powers. The implication was that, while discouraging a Soviet attack on China both directly and in various indirect ways, and while pursuing the normalization of its own relations with Peking, the United States was strongly interested in improving its relations with the Soviet Union as well. The major reasons included a desire to stabilize the Soviet strategic weapons build-up through an arms control agreement and a desire to increase the level of Soviet-American trade. Furthermore, it was obvious that President Nixon was determined for personal political reasons to visit both Peking and Moscow in 1972, an election year. This determination gave both Communist powers considerable leverage in dealing with him; it also meant that neither was, realistically speaking, in a position to cancel the summit or otherwise jeopardize its own détente with the United States while the other's continued to progress.

The Asian "Collective Security" Issue

Brezhnev seems to have made his brief, vague proposal at the international conference of Communist Parties in June 1969 for a "collective security" system in Asia after failing in his maneuvers to get the conference to pass some sort of anti-Chinese resolution. Accordingly, as Peking perceived from the beginning, the proposal had an anti-Chinese flavor, even though subsequent Soviet comment indicated that Moscow hoped to see China included in the system. As in the case of the "united action" proposal of 1965, Peking sensed an effort to enhance Soviet influence at Chinese expense and denounced the idea accordingly.

Chinese opposition, expressed at a time when Peking was rapidly increasing its international influence through a diplomatic normalization campaign following the end of the Cultural Revolution, was one major reason why the Soviet "collective security" proposal was received without enthusiasm by the other Asian states, whose governments had no desire to become involved in the Sino-Soviet dispute. Many of them preached nonalignment, furthermore, and regarded the Soviet proposal as only doubtfully consistent with this principle. In any case, the Soviet Union has rather limited contacts, a poor image, and little influence to date in some parts of Asia, although many Asians realize with varying degrees of approval that Moscow is likely to play an increasing role in the affairs of the region in the future. China probably has greater influence, actual and potential, in Asia as a whole, for reasons that can be summed up in the obvious statement that it is not only a much more authentically Asian power than the Soviet Union but the largest of the Asian states. It appears that this will hold true as long as Peking refrains from asserting its desire for influence so aggressively as to drive other Asian states into the arms of a rival, such as the Soviet Union.

After two years of futility, the Soviet Union began to revive its "collective security" proposal in 1971. The most important reason was probably the striking success achieved by Peking in establishing its diplomatic opening to the United States. A second was very likely the appearance of a competing idea in the form of a proposal from Prime Minister Razak of Malaysia in July 1971 that Southeast Asia be neutralized (i.e., be without foreign troops, bases, and military ties) under the guarantee of the great powers, which he specified as China, the Soviet Union, and the United States (note the order, and the omission of Japan); this proposal was endorsed by ASEAN (the Association of Southeast Asian Nations: Thailand, Malaysia, Singapore, Indonesia, and the Philippines) the following November. Since Moscow has tended to claim that its plan must operate without competition, Soviet comment on the Razak proposal has been only minimally polite; Peking has been considerably more cordial.

The Soviet proposal has become considerably more explicit in its revised form, as elaborated for example in an important speech by Brezhnev on March 20, 1972, than it was originally. It has obvious similarities with the standard Communist slogan of peaceful coexistence and with its Chinese variant, the Five Principles of Peaceful Coexistence. It specifies the nonuse of force among Asian nations (of which the Soviet Union, of course, claims to be one), the "inviolability" of frontiers (an obvious attempted defense against Chinese and Japanese territorial claims on the Soviet Union); noninterference in the internal affairs of other states (not a guarantee against revolutionary activity by local Communist Parties), and economic and political cooperation. The proposal is rationalized on the ground, sometimes very strongly put, that Asian security is currently threatened by China, the United States, and Japan. To date Iran is the only state to have endorsed the Soviet idea.

Soviet propaganda, nevertheless, often cites the Soviet-Indian friendship treaty of August 1971, which was signed at the time when Moscow was reviving its efforts to lend some reality to "collective security," and Soviet-Indian relations in general as the major and exemplary achievement in the field of Asian "collective security" to date. The treaty and the relationship were certainly one of the factors that deterred Chinese intervention on Pakistan's side in the Indo-Pakistani War of November-December 1971 over the Bangla Desh issue; the others were the six Indian divisions stationed along the Sino-Indian frontier and logistical problems (including snow-filled passes). The best that Peking felt it could do, apart from propaganda, was to give Pakistan more economic and military aid and to postpone recognizing Bangla Desh or improving relations with India at least until Pakistan should do so. Peking fears, fairly reasonably, that the Soviet Union may try to play the role of policeman in the Indian Ocean through an expanded naval presence, something in which China is no position to compete.

Logically enough, Soviet propaganda does not stress Soviet-Mongolian relations as an example of "collective security" in action even though the Mongols themselves praise that slogan in the course of their slowly increasing but still rather limited contacts with Asian countries. For the Mongolian People's Republic is essentially a Soviet satellite, and has been one since the 1920s. Its pro-Soviet stand in the Sino-Soviet dispute, one manifestation of which is the presence on Mongolian soil of several Soviet divisions threatening China, is the result both of the massive Soviet presence in the country and of a fear of China heightened by the spectacle of the domination of the Mongols of Inner Mongolia by Peking's officials and by Chinese colonists.

Historic and recent Soviet heavy-handedness toward Japan, as well as Soviet resentment of past Japanese behavior, have made Soviet-Japanese relations tense and difficult. Moscow greatly fears the possibility of a close Sino-Japanese relationship and tries to prevent it, but is prevented by its obsession with China, among other things, from conciliating Japan effectively. A Soviet-Japanese peace treaty is being delayed mainly by Moscow's objections, on account of the possible effect on China and others of the Soviet Union's neighbors, to giving back any of the Northern Territories (the Japanese terms for four small islands lying at the southern end of the Kuriles) as demanded by all political elements in Japan. Moscow has been more than normally difficult about giving effect to its desire for large-scale Japanese capital and technical assistance in the economic development of Siberia and the Soviet Far East and especially in the construction of a pipeline eastward from Irkutsk to Nakhodka on the Pacific to carry oil from the vast Tiumen fields in Western Siberia, apparently because of Soviet annoyance at Japan's policy of improving its relations with China.

Peking's objections to the pipeline project, on the ground that it would serve Soviet forces in the Far East as well as the Japanese economy, have eased somewhat recently, probably on account of a realization that the project is not likely to be completed in the near future and that American as well as Japanese firms will probably be involved in it. Premier Tanaka's visit to Moscow in October 1973 produced no perceptible progress on the Northern Territories, a peace treaty, or the pipeline. The Japanese government has shown no enthusiasm for the Soviet "collective security" proposal, largely because of its overriding concern for its security relationship with the United States.

Peking regards the Soviet proposal as aimed at "encircling" China and is extremely anxious that Japan not participate. Peking like Tokyo regards the Japanese-American security treaty as a vastly preferable alternative to the Soviet scheme and to unilateral Japanese rearmament and has therefore begun to indicate informally that it no longer has any serious objection to the former or to the modest Japanese military establishment, as currently maintained and projected. No matter how desirable an improvement in Sino-Japanese relations may have been from Peking's viewpoint (as well as Tokyo's), however, it was postponed until 1972 by two main obstacles. One was the survival in office until that year of Premier Eisaku Sato, whom Peking regarded as unacceptably pro-American and as likely to try to fill any power vacuum in Asia created by American military disengagement under the Nixon Doctrine. Peking's unique psychological, cultural, and political leverage on Japanese elite opinion, which it maximized through a massive anti-Japanese propaganda campaign in 1970–71, is such that Peking was able to contribute to the selection of a relatively pro-Chinese successor to Sato—Kakuei Tanaka, as it turned out.

The other obstacle, and another apparent reason for the Chinese anti-Japanese propaganda campaign just mentioned, was the objections of some Chinese leaders, Lin Piao in particular, to the proposed opening to the United States. By portraying the familiar enemy Japan as the real threat to China and Asia, Chou En-lai tried to rationalize the invitation to President Nixon as the best means of splitting Japan from its main source of support, the United States, an especially promising plan in a year when Japanese-American relations were reeling under the impact of the "Nixon shocks." A particularly loud aspect of the Chinese anti-

Japanese propaganda offensive related to a dispute over a group of small islands (Tiao-yü-t'ai in Chinese, Senkaku in Japanese) located on the continental shelf about one hundred miles northeast of Taiwan and in an area that may be very rich in oil. The fall of Lin Piao in September 1971 removed the main obstacle to the Nixon visit and therefore also the main reason for the anti-Japanese propaganda campaign, and accordingly the latter, including the aspect relating to the islands, began to die away almost immediately. As soon as the Tanaka cabinet was formed in early July 1972, Chou invited Tanaka to visit China. He did so at the end of September 1972 and succeeded in initiating substantial normalization of Sino-Japanese relations, including the establishment of diplomatic relations at Taiwan's expense. Even though the relationship has not progressed much since then, Peking apparently feels satisfied that Tokyo is not likely to "tilt" toward the Soviet Union.

For a variety of reasons including ideological ones, it would be a major triumph for the Soviet Union to bring North Vietnam into its "collective security" system. But Hanoi is too wary of Soviet ambitions, and too vulnerable to Chinese pressures by virtue of a common border, to antagonize Peking to that extent, at least under present conditions. On the other hand the Soviet Union has fewer basic serious disputes with the United States in Asia than China has and therefore is paradoxically in a somewhat better position to displease the United States by political support for Hanoi in its struggle for domination of Indochina. Furthermore, the Soviet Union is better able than China to provide North Vietnam with large-scale economic aid (neither appears to be providing much military aid since the signing of the January 27, 1973 agreement on Vietnam, and especially since the supplementary agreement of June 13, 1973).

In view of the unremarkable progress of its "collective security" proposal to date, Moscow has begun to supplement its formal diplomacy on this subject with parallel activity conducted through the leftist front organizations that it dominates, such as the Afro-Asian People's Solidarity Organization. Another ploy is a call, such as Brezhnev gave while in India in November 1973, for an international conference on Asian security, analogous to Soviet overtures in recent years for a conference and an agreement on European security. The Soviet Union obviously has some claim to be regarded as an Asian as well as a European power. In Asia, as in Europe, its "security" campaign is in reality a campaign to increase its influence.

Sino-Soviet Competition outside Asia

Of the non-Asian areas in which Soviet and Chinese interests find themselves in rivalry or conflict, Europe is almost certainly the most important. This is mainly due to the fact that Europe is the principal area (apart from the Sino-Soviet border region) where Soviet troops are stationed or that is threatened by military dispositions on Soviet soil, and away from which Soviet forces could be transferred, if conditions there permitted, in order to strengthen the anti-Chinese build-up. Peking accordingly considers that it is emphatically in China's interest that conditions in Europe be such that no such transfer is possible. But since the situations in Eastern and Western Europe obviously differ greatly from one another, so do Peking's policies toward them. In Eastern Europe, China's behavior is almost purely anti-Soviet; in Western Europe, it is also pro-American to an astonishing degree.

In the Northern Tier countries (Poland, East Germany, and Czechoslovakia) Soviet influence, actual and potential, is so great that there is little opportunity for Chinese activity, and Peking tends to estimate Soviet influence as being even greater than it is. Czechoslovakia has not only been dominated politically by the Soviet Union since the invasion of 1968, but has been subjected to Soviet military occupation; accordingly, Czechoslovakia was one of the last two Communist countries to be sent a Chinese ambassador after the end of the Cultural Revolution, the other being the Mongolian People's Republic, which Peking also considers to be occupied by Soviet troops. Peking misinterpreted, at least in its propaganda, the Polish risings leading to the fall of the Gomulka regime in December 1970 as the result of Soviet intervention and accordingly is on chilly terms with the successor Gierek regime. The replacement of the aged Walter Ulbricht by Erich Honecker in May 1971 resulted in an East German regime even more dependably receptive to Soviet guidance than before.

Hungary, under Janos Kadar's leadership, has been purchasing immunity from Soviet wrath at its rather experimental economic policy by closely following Moscow's lead in its foreign policy.

Farther south, however, the Communist countries of the Balkans all have quarrels with Moscow that have provided political openings for Peking to varying degrees. In the case of Albania, the quarrel goes back to 1960 and led to a very close Sino-Albanian relationship for about a decade. Perhaps the high point was Peking's obvious nervousness when Albania defied the Soviet Union to the extent of withdrawing from the Warsaw Pact in September 1968, in response to the invasion of Czechoslovakia. Growing Chinese flexibility in foreign policy in recent years, however, and in particular Peking's détente with the United States and its contacts with right-wing anti-Soviet Communist Parties, such as the Spanish, have cooled the Sino-Albanian relationship considerably. The invasion of Czechoslovakia led to a period of tension in Soviet-Yugoslav relations that led in turn to a warming trend between Belgrade and Peking, which for a decade had been loudly denouncing Tito as a "revisionist." The main result, however, has been at least a temporary improvement of Soviet-Yugoslav relations; Moscow having few levers it can use against Belgrade, unless and until Tito's death or retirement removes most of the cement holding his country together, conciliation has seemed the only effective Soviet response to Belgrade's improvement of its relations with China. Romania and China have encouraged each other for the past decade in their pursuit of policies that have been independent of Moscow's and in Peking's case downright anti-Soviet. Romania is in a weaker position than China to maintain this independence of action, however. It has remained in the Warsaw Pact, even though it interprets its military obligations as not including one to fight China, as Moscow tries to insist its allies are bound to do if necessary under the revised versions of their bilateral security treaties with the Soviet Union. The Romanian economy occasionally develops a need for Soviet aid. Accordingly, when President Ceausescu was strongly rebuked by Moscow in 1971 after carrying a message from Peking to Washington (in October 1970) and another in the opposite direction (in June 1971), he relapsed into behavior that was considerably less independent of the Soviet Union. Peking is well aware that there are limits beyond which the Balkan countries cannot defy the Soviet Union, and that there is little China can do for them if they do; in August 1971, Chou En-lai told a Yugoslav journalist in this connection that "Distant water cannot quench fire."

Peking's activities in Western Europe are complicated, not of course by Soviet control, but by the generally positive response to Moscow's overtures since 1967 for an agreement on European security, even though there is a widespread and justified suspicion that the Soviet Union's main objective is the enhancement of its own influence. Chinese diplomacy and propaganda have been doing their best to encourage the United States to maintain a strong military presence in Western Europe and the countries of the region to take a strong pro-NATO and pro-Common Market line. Except perhaps in the last respect, Peking is obviously trying to swim upstream, and its efforts have been greeted in the capitals of Western Europe mainly with puzzlement and amusement.

Peking's main success in Western Europe has not been in combatting Moscow's efforts to secure its rear through a security agreement and then perhaps turn more forcefully against China, but simply in expanding its diplomatic relations; by now, it has them with every West European country but Portugal, which (at least until the change of government in 1974) has been ideologically unacceptable to Peking on account of its role in Africa. About half these relationships were established shortly after 1949, and the other half since the end of the Cultural Revolution. In the case of both groups the motives of the West European governments usually related more to expanding trade with China than to hampering or even irritating the Soviet Union. In the most important recent case, West Germany, which established diplomatic relations with Peking in October 1972, the Willy Brandt government had been so pro-Soviet that Moscow gave its consent in private, even though a few years earlier Soviet propaganda had been falsely alleging the existence of an anti-Soviet "Bonn-Peking axis." Peking can count on some French sympathy for its public opposition to both "superpowers," but not on any sort of French support that would be more than marginally effective in strengthening China's hand against the Soviet Union.

In the Middle East, Peking has little direct influence or responsibility apart from its intermittent support for Arab guerrilla movements. It is in no position to buy Middle Eastern oil. Accordingly, its behavior is ideologically based to a high degree. Its propaganda curries favor with the Arabs by denouncing Israel and tries to convince them that the two superpowers, both of which have far greater influence in the region than China has, are their other principal enemies. Peking's role during the Middle Eastern War of October 1973 was limited substantially to this sort of propaganda, which apparently reflected a sense that it had no handle on the situation and that no outcome would be particularly favorable to its interests. By its own encouragement of the Arab attack on Israel, the Soviet Union achieved among other things a setback for the developing Sino-American relationship; Peking was forced to take a loudly anti-American and anti-Israel line in order to avoid alienating the Arabs, and Secretary of State Kissinger was predictably compelled to postpone his scheduled visit to China until mid-November. One thing that Peking almost certainly does not want to see is an Arab-Israeli settlement sufficient to produce the reopening of the Suez Canal, which would help the Soviet Union to increase its naval strength in the Indian Ocean. In the non-Arab countries of the Middle East (apart from Israel), Peking's problems have been simpler. Its recent success in establishing diplomatic relations with Turkey and Iran was due to a considerable extent to those countries' interest in acquiring a counterweight to the Soviet Union, a traditional problem for them even when not an actual threat.

Sino-Soviet rivalry in Africa and Latin America is a rather amorphous subject. Both Moscow and Peking are of course active in these regions. Each tries to promote its own influence through diplomacy, aid, propaganda, and the like, and to denigrate the other whenever possible. But the stakes are not as high as in regions closer to the centers from which the Sino-Soviet dispute is conducted. The Communist Parties of Latin America are almost all bureaucratized and solidly pro-Soviet, and the radical movements tend to look to Cuba more than to China for guidance.

On the whole, the fact that the Soviet Union is a superpower and China is not, even by Peking's standards, is reflected in greater Soviet overall influence in the world outside Asia. But Peking's challenge to Moscow in this vast arena is impressive, even though it has not been truly successful to date and is not likely to succeed in the near future.

CHAPTER IX

The Nixon Doctrine and the Sino-American Détente

THE AMERICAN presidential election of 1968 was fought out in the shadow of Vietnam, although not quite to the extent that the election of 1952 had been dominated by Korea. Vietnam had become a major, perhaps the major, issue of American politics and foreign policy and had acquired a symbolic significance going far beyond its actual relevance.

The American Predicament

The power with which Vietnam made itself felt on the American scene and in American foreign relations after 1965 resulted from the convergence of two processes. One was the emergence of a new generation born since the Second World War, much of it scornful of the logic under which the elite of the older generation had been rationalizing the employment of American military power abroad and committed to quite different values and behavior patterns. The other was a predictable (because typically American) pendulum swing, on the part of much of the population and of Congress, away from acceptance of the executive branch's domination of foreign policy and its overinvolvement of the United States, not only militarily but politically and economically as well, in far-flung operations in many parts of the world.

The first of these processes reflected, in addition to inevitable generational change, the increasing urbanization of the population and a rising educational level—in short, greater sophistication, although not necessarily greater wisdom. The resurgence of radicalism among American intellectuals and on American campuses that began about 1960 owed much to the civil rights movement that had begun several years earlier, to the coming to power of Fidel Castro, to ferment in the Third World and Africa in particular, to the stimulating atmosphere of the Kennedy years, and to a sense of alienation from an increasingly technological and supposedly impersonal society.

The second process reflected a belief, at the elite level at any rate, that a succession of presidents had overstrained the country's resources and relations with its friends by committing it to too many "police actions," confrontations, aid programs, etc. Congress, which tended to be less interventionist and had once been regarded by most American intellectuals as unenlightened and obstructionist, came to be looked on as the best available counterweight to an overambitious and overextended executive. A more thoroughgoing remedy, the adoption of a parliamentary system under which executive and legislature would be in closer harmony rather than in balanced opposition, was favored in principle by some academic political scientists but was advocated by no major public figure.

To both these ways of thinking, the American escalation in Vietnam came as the last straw, or pile of bricks. It was a predominantly unpopular war from the beginning. The enemy and the objective were never defined by the executive for the public in a way that commanded assent and support on a nation-wide scale. Among the major reasons for this were Vietnam's geographic remoteness and the fact that the other side's efforts bore just enough of the character of an insurgency to make its forces difficult to identify and hate and to give its cause the image of a revolution. These effects were reinforced by the media (especially television), which were irked by the administration's and the military's efforts at managing the news on Vietnam and unavoidably conveyed to the public a more vivid sense of the violence committed by the South Vietnamese and American side. The perception of excessive costs and casualties expended on an unwinnable war grew to almost overwhelming proportions after the Tet offensive of 1968.

The better informed segment of the educated public was also troubled by the knowledge that the country's foreign relations were being adversely affected in many quarters by its involvement in Vietnam. If some of the French criticism could be attributed to sour grapes at the thought that the United States might possibly succeed where France had failed, the objections from other NATO countries could not be so easily dismissed; some West Germans, for example, believed that the United States was permitting itself to be distracted to a dangerous degree from the defense of Western interests in Berlin and Germany. The Japanese right believed to some extent, and with some measure of correctness, that the United States was contributing to international stability in Asia through its role in Vietnam, but this view was less articulate than that of the left (including the press), which was to the effect that the United States was waging a counterrevolutionary war in Vietnam with inhuman methods. The American involvement in Vietnam was clearly helping to push the Soviet Union ahead faster in its strategic weapons build-up and to make it more difficult to deal with in a variety of ways. Peking was perceived, plausibly although incorrectly, as perhaps being goaded into some massive act of irrationality outside its borders by the insult it was suffering by proxy in Vietnam.

The Johnsonian Turnaround

The shock of the Tet offensive convinced a critical grouping within the United States government that it would be senseless to continue pumping troops into Vietnam, and that a process of de-escalation and disengagement must be initiated. Accordingly, President Johnson rejected a proposal by the Joint Chiefs of Staff for sending another 200,000 men to Vietnam. For some time, furthermore, he had had personal reasons, including a realization that his political stock was declining, for not wanting to run for re-election. In a speech on March 31, 1968, therefore, he coupled an announcement of his decision not to be a candidate again with a statement that he was denying the request for more troops, was suspending bombing operations against North Vietnam north of the 20th parallel, and was renewing his invitation of three years' standing to Hanoi to come to the conference table.

For reasons already indicated (in Chapter VII), Hanoi proved unprecedentedly willing to do exactly that even though the two conditions for negotiations that it had been posing, a prompt and complete bombing cessation and a prompt and complete American military withdrawal from South Vietnam, were being met to only a very limited extent, and even though Peking, not yet recovered from the militant mood engendered by the Cultural Revolution, clearly disapproved. In mid-May, accordingly, negotiations began at Paris between high-level American and North Vietnamese delegations, and in October they were joined by delegations from the Saigon government and the National Liberation Front. Just before the American presidential election, and presumably in an effort—unsuccessful, of course—to influence its outcome, President Johnson suspended the bombing of North Vietnam entirely, something that Vice President Humphrey had promised to do if elected. The talks at Paris were making a little progress, but not much. The Vietnamese quagmire bedeviled the Johnson administration until its last day in office.

The Nixonian View of Asia

After returning from an extended trip to Asia in the spring of 1967, Richard Nixon, who was not then an avowed presidential candidate, published an article in *Foreign Affairs* giving his findings. In retrospect at least, the most important of these was that the United States had overinvolved itself in Vietnam and in Asia as a whole and must cut its liabilities judiciously. He portrayed China as still a serious threat to non-Communist Asia. He advocated involving China increasingly in peaceful international contacts (a process he described as "dynamic detoxification") and continuing to contain it through "creative counter-pressure" exerted mainly by the Asian nations themselves, "backed by the ultimate power of the United States." For this role he especially favored a substantially rearmed Japan and the rather somnolent anti-Communist regional organization ASPAC (the Asian and Pacific Council). He praised Indonesia for having coped with a major Communist coup in 1965, partly under the inspiration (as he said erroneously) of the American role in Vietnam, but by implication without the help of an American military presence.

His actual views went somewhat beyond his published ones. On the basis of the Indonesian case, he had become convinced, or claimed to have been convinced, that other Asian countries could also cope with Communist subversion without the help of American combat forces, or at any rate ground forces. This proposition was clearly sound when applied to a large self-confident country not threatened from abroad, like Indonesia, but had the defect of all generalizations: there were significant exceptions, the most obvious of which were the relatively small and vulnerable countries of Indochina. In addition, Mr. Nixon's views on the People's Republic of China were, or soon became, much more conciliatory than suggested in his article. He wanted to go to Peking and make a major contribution to improved Sino-American relations. One of his motives undoubtedly was to give Peking an effective incentive not to try to expand in Asia as the United States disengaged, American disengagement to one degree or another being obviously inevitable. Another flowed from his longstanding and well-known aversion to the Soviet Union, now enhanced by concern over Moscow's strategic weapons build-up and its growing role in the Middle East; as he said to the correspondent Howard K. Smith on July 1, 1970, a closer Sino-American relationship could render these problems more nearly manageable.

The main early byproduct of this line of thinking was the Nixon (or Guam) Doctrine, announced in July 1969. It proclaimed in general terms that the United States would honor its treaty commitments, which it seemed to imply were too well known to require elaboration. The United States would provide a "shield" (not otherwise defined, but presumably referring mainly to air cover) to any ally (although the frame of reference was Asian), and to any country regarded by the United States as vital to its own security or to that of the region, if threatened by a nuclear power (a term evidently meant to cover the People's Republic of China). Military and economic aid could be provided on its government's request to a country threatened by a non-nuclear power, but the threatened country was to "assume the primary responsibility of providing the manpower [i.e., essentially, ground forces] for its defense."

Some leftist critics have maintained that the Nixon Doctrine rationalizes a strategy of reliance on nuclear weapons, presumably tactical. A more reasonable criticism would be that in reality it implies a genuine and probably irreversible American military disengagement from Asia and the Western Pacific, and that this process has been proceeding too rapidly for the stability of the region and the survival of American influence in it. Another relevant comment is that the trend toward disengagement did not cancel out President Nixon's long-standing tendency to react vigorously—many would say overreact—to real or imagined crises.

Before taking office as the President's Special Assistant for National Security Affairs, Dr. Henry A. Kissinger had relatively little knowledge of or contact with Asian affairs, apart from some experience as a consultant on the Vietnamese problem. His unquestionably brilliant mind had wrestled mainly with European questions. He strongly favored a multilateral balance of power, such as had existed in Europe between the Congress of Vienna (1814–15) and the formation of the two hostile alliance systems toward the end of the nineteenth century. He evidently hoped to see the same situation emerge in contemporary Europe, in lieu of a Soviet-American confrontation, and in Asia, in lieu of a Sino-American confrontation. In general, he tended to take his lead in Asian matters from the President. Soon after coming into office, he formed from contacts with American "China-watchers," official and unofficial, the essentially correct impression that previous administrations had considerably exaggerated China's propensity to expand, and that Peking would probably not try to take significant advantage of American disengagement from Asia; a major reason for the latter conclusion was the limitations on China's freedom of action imposed by its confrontation with the Soviet Union.

Approaches to Peking

As early as March 1969, President Nixon began to convey to Peking through French channels his genuine interest in improving Sino-American relations, as well as in ending direct American military involvement in Indochina. He had sensibly refused to be unduly discouraged by Peking's withdrawal on February 19 of its invitation to resume the Sino-American ambassadorial talks at Warsaw. He almost certainly counted on the crisis of that period in Sino-Soviet relations to soften Peking's attitude toward the United States, and it is probably significant that the Nixon Doctrine was not announced until the seriousness of that crisis had become clear. Subsequently intermediaries from other third countries, including Presidents Ceausescu of Romania and Yahya Kahn of Pakistan, and other channels as well, were used by both sides to transmit messages between Washington and Peking.

There were encouraging signs in early 1970, when two Sino-American ambassadorial conversations were held at Stockholm (January 20, February 20); at the second of these the Chinese expressed some interest in the idea of a visit by President Nixon to China. This promising trend was interrupted by the Cambodian crisis in the spring of 1970, which caused Peking to cancel a Sino-American ambassadorial conversation scheduled for May 20 and to issue a statement in Mao's name loudly denouncing the United States on the same day. For reasons already indicated (in Chapter VIII), however, the interruption proved to be short-lived. Progress was resumed in July and became increasingly rapid after October. On December 18, in an interview with Edgar Snow (published on April 30, 1971, in *Life*), Mao himself issued a seemingly casual invitation to President Nixon to visit China.

Meanwhile, the President had been withdrawing American forces from Vietnam fairly rapidly and had been taking steps aimed directly at conciliating Peking, as well as Americans eager for contact with it, by progressively reducing the restrictions on travel to and trade with the People's Republic of China by Americans. By April 1971, the trade restrictions were nearly gone, and the travel restrictions entirely so. Peking, which had always regarded these restrictions as insulting even though it had seldom wanted such contact until recently, was sufficiently impressed, and sufficiently anxious for improved relations with the United States, so that in that month it invited an American table tennis team then in Japan to visit China, which it did. Soon a trickle of teams and unofficial delegations began to flow in both directions, and American travelers (mainly individuals of Chinese descent and leftists, at first), journalists, and businessmen began to be given visas to China in limited numbers. Apart from their obvious value at the "people to people" level, these contacts helped Chou En-lai to defend his policy of "tilting" toward the United States by enabling his more radical colleagues to believe that American public opinion was being encouraged by the contacts to press the government for a still more conciliatory China policy.

In reality, Washington needed no such pressure. The desirability of the approach to Peking was rated so high in the White House that other government agencies, including the State Department and the Pentagon, were largely excluded from the planning of it so as to minimize bureaucratic objections and preserve secrecy. The nongovernmental China-watching community was almost totally excluded. Accordingly, it was with the greatest possible secrecy that Dr. Kissinger flew to Peking from Pakistan on July 9, 1971, for two days of talks with Chou En-lai. Secrecy was earnestly desired by Chou, who wanted to tip his hand neither to the domestic opponents of his opening to the United States nor to Moscow, whose reaction was bound to be a strong one. On the American side, secrecy was desired for the reasons already indicated and because advance notification to the ally most directly affected (apart from the Republic of China), Japan, would be risky since Tokyo was notoriously leaky where interesting secrets were concerned. On the American side, there may have been an additional incentive to secrecy, as a result of the recent publication of the so-called Pentagon Papers, which were classified documents on American Vietnam policy released to *The New York Times* without authorization by Dr. Daniel Ellsberg of the RAND Corporation; after that Washington was on its mettle to prove that it could maintain security at least on occasion. Consequently, the world was startled to learn on July 15, from announcements made in both capitals, that Kissinger had visited Peking, and that his hosts had invited President Nixon to do the same at some time in 1972. The presidential visit was still in some doubt owing to objections by Lin Piao and other radicals, and Washington did not breathe easy on this score until it was announced on October 5, after Lin's fall, that Kissinger would visit Peking again later that month. The main purpose and result of his trip were to develop the planning for the Nixon visit.

"Partnership" and Conflict with Japan

There was a tendency on the part of Americans, the Nixon administration included, to expect gratitude from Japan for American aid and protection, and compensation in the form of a contribution through aid to the economic development of Asia. As already indicated the Nixon administration initially hoped for an increased Japanese contribution to Asian security, an idea that clearly implied a measure of Japanese rearmament. The fact that such a policy would produce very serious repercussions both in

Japan and in the rest of Asia seems to have been largely over-looked, perhaps because the White House staff never included an authentic Japan specialist of high rank.

The first major Nixonian effort to give effect to the adminis-tration's slogan of "partnership" with Japan was an important meeting between President Nixon and Premier Sato in November 1969. The resulting Nixon-Sato Declaration stated (at American, not Japanese initiative) that Japan had an interest in the security of the Republic of Korea (South Korea) and of Taiwan; the real meaning of this was that Japan would not interfere with the use of existing American bases in Japan to defend these areas if they should be attacked, but the Communist powers concluded or at least claimed that Japan was admitting to predatory designs on South Korea and Taiwan. It was agreed that civil jurisdiction in Okinawa, and responsibility for its external security, should revert to Japan in 1972; there was a clear implication that after that the United States would not base nuclear weapons on the island any more than in Japan proper (apart from brief transiting of airfields and ports by weapons aboard American aircraft or naval vessels). The Japanese government agreed to liberalize its restrictions on American investment and reduce its tariffs on American goods.

In spite of the implicit prohibition on American nuclear weapons in Okinawa after "reversion," Secretary of Defense Mel-vin Laird, during an important visit to Tokyo in July 1971, re-fused a Japanese request for procedures designed to verify the removal of nuclear weapons from the island prior to reversion. Laird also appears to have urged the Japanese to increase their conventional forces somewhat beyond the level envisaged in the Fourth Five-Year Defense Build-up Plan (published in the spring of 1970), but probably not to acquire nuclear weapons. By that time, however, Japanese-American "partnership" was already little more than a myth.

President Nixon's Southern strategy had created a partial de-pendence on the support of some Southern Senators, certain of whom were seriously concerned about the damage inflicted by competing imports from Japan on the textile industries of their states. The President thought that he had gotten an informal pledge from Premier Sato in November 1969 to do something about this problem and was incensed by what he interpreted as Sato's failure to make good on this promise. In the spring of

1971, President Nixon began to support legislation to impose quotas on imports of Japanese textiles and rejected some more conciliatory alternatives, notably one proposed by Congressman Wilbur Mills. For a time it appeared that the textile issue might prevent Senate approval of the Japanese-American treaty on the reversion of Okinawa, but it was ultimately approved in November.

The tension in Japanese-American relations created by the textile issue, which was very great, was vastly increased by the White House's decision not to inform Tokyo in advance of the impending Kissinger visit to Peking even though a pledge had been given privately to the Japanese government a few years earlier that it would be notified in advance of any major change in American China policy. It is possible that the Nixon administration was not aware that this promise had been made. In any case, the announcement of July 15 hit Tokyo like a thunderbolt. At about the same time, the United States rubbed salt in the wound by working out a new approach to the problem of China's representation in the United Nations—the idea was that Peking should be admitted but Taipei should not be expelled—and blandly assuming that Tokyo would cosponsor the proposal when the time came. This actually happened without success (Peking was admitted and Taipei expelled on October 25), even though the Japanese government deeply resented not having been consulted in advance on this departure any more than on the other.

Although the textile issue was extremely irritating to the Nixon administration, an even more serious problem was the massive deficit ($3-4 billion per year) in the American balance of payments with Japan. To help eliminate it, as well as for other reasons, President Nixon announced on August 15 a program of wage and price controls, suspension of the convertibility of the dollar, and a ten percent surcharge on import duties. The atmosphere in Japanese-American relations created by this move, coming as it did on the heels of the China initiatives, was sometimes compared in Japan to the atmosphere preceding the attack on Pearl Harbor. Later in the year, the August 15 restrictions were eased, and in mid-October an agreement was reached with Tokyo under which the United States removed the surcharge and Japan agreed to limit the growth in the export of man-made fibers to the United States for three years to five percent a year and of wool to one percent a year. The crisis in Japanese-American relations was over, but the effects lingered on both sides. The White House had paid a high price in its relations with a major ally for the sake of its domestic political and economic concerns and its anxiety to improve relations with a major former adversary.

The Peking Summit

The motives on the Chinese side for wishing a Sino-American summit conference have already been discussed (in Chapter VIII). On the American side, the most urgent motive, as the White House's insistence on maximum television coverage indicated, was the greatest possible impact on the American public and on the coming presidential election campaign. Second, and related, was a strong desire for some Chinese help, or at least an absence of obstruction, with a Vietnam settlement, something that would obviously help the President's domestic political position in addition to serving other ends as well. Third was the hope of rendering Moscow more manageable through the approach to Peking. The White House's thinking on this score was heavily influenced by its conviction, or at least its repeated statements off the record, that fear of the Soviet Union was the sole sufficient cause for Peking's diplomatic opening to the United States; this was a seriously over-simplified but conveniently self-serving theory, since it relieved the architects of American China policy of any imputation that they were being used by the Chinese, whereas in fact they were. Fourth, the White House hoped that the summit conference would help Chou En-lai to stabilize and institutionalize his essentially pragmatic domestic and foreign policies in the teeth of opposition from Maoist radicals. Fifth, the White House was necessarily influenced somewhat by the eagerness of substantial numbers of Americans for easier access to China, and of many American firms for a clearer shot at the China market. There was furthermore a belief that the United States had pressed too hard on the People's Republic of China in the past and owed it restitution in the form of a friendlier general policy and some concessions, short of an abandonment of the Republic of China (Taiwan).

The week-long summit (February 22-28, 1972) was marked by good chemistry on both sides. Each was eager to get to know the other better and regarded the success of the talks as highly desirable; failure would have been a domestic political disaster for both sides. Sino-American relations at the personal level tend to be good, and they certainly were on this occasion. Superb Chinese hospitality, much of it visible on television, made a major contribution to the success of the occasion. The Chinese welcome for President Nixon was subdued at first, because of the controversial nature of his visit in the eyes of the Chinese radicals, but he performed with sufficient effect to justify Chou En-lai in asking Mao Tse-tung to receive him on the first day, rather than on the last day as had been anticipated. This audience predictably quieted any remaining radical objections and gave Chou a freer hand to proceed with the negotiations. No American interpreters were present during the Mao-Nixon talks; in fact, Chinese-speaking foreigners have generally not attended Mao's audiences for visiting dignitaries since the one for Emperor Haile Selassie in October 1971, when the Chairman made the embarrassing mistake, in the presence of a Chinese-speaking Ethopian, of confusing his guest with ex-President Kwame Nkrumah of Ghana.

Much of the negotiations consisted in mutual probing and reflected the usual Chinese interest in reaching agreement on things regarded by Peking as matters of principle, questions of detail being left for later discussion. The widespread expectations of a Taiwan-for-Vietnam deal, in which the United States would make major concessions on Taiwan in return for Chinese help with a Vietnam settlement, proved to be oversimplified. Peking gave a private and implicit pledge not to use force to "liberate" Taiwan, and the United States agreed in effect not to obstruct a peaceful or political "liberation." The Chinese side would not agree to give active help toward a Vietnam settlement, for example, by putting pressure on Hanoi; on the other hand, it did not make much of an issue of American policy on Vietnam and did not press for further American military withdrawals from it, or for that matter from anywhere else except Taiwan.

The Shanghai Communiqué

The most tangible diplomatic result of the visit was the joint communiqué (the so-called Shanghai Communiqué) issued at its close. Like all such documents, it contained statements on which both sides agreed. It was unusual, however, in that it also contained a statement of positions held by each side with which the other did not necessarily agree, although it was a statement in a moderate form relatively unoffensive to the other; offensive propositions, such as the American commitment to recognize and defend the Republic of China, were omitted or vetoed by the other side.

The agreed portion of the communiqué included a restatement of the (Chinese) Five Principles of Peaceful Coexistence, without use of that term. The United States had previously rejected these as propaganda, and acceptance of them now obviously represented an American concession. This was especially true since the third principle is "noninterference in the internal affairs of other states," a proposition that the United States knows Peking considers to rule out the American relationship to Taiwan, even though the United States government holds that its Taiwan policy does not constitute such interference. The agreed portion also pledged the two parties to work toward "normalization" (not necessarily including full diplomatic relations) of their relations with one another, not to seek "hegemony" in Asia and the Pacific, to oppose "the efforts by any other country or group of countries to establish such hegemony," and not to negotiate on behalf of any third party (for example, Peking on behalf of Hanoi). The two sides agreed to increase cultural exchange and trade between them and to "stay in contact through various channels, including the sending of a senior U.S. representative to Peking from time to time."

The unilateral American statement stressed the desirability of peace and improved international communications. The "peoples of Indochina should be allowed to determine their destiny without outside interference." Provided this outcome was not threatened, the United States envisaged the "ultimate withdrawal of all U.S. forces from the region" even in the absence of a negotiated settlement. The United States expressed support for its allies the Republic of Vietnam (South Vietnam) and the Republic of Korea (South Korea), although not the Republic of China. The United States said that it "places the highest value on its friendly relations with Japan." On the crucial question (in the context of Sino-American relations) of Taiwan, the United States stated that it did not "challenge" the proposition, which it attributed to "all Chinese on either side of the Taiwan Strait" (thereby ignoring the Taiwan independence movement) that "there is but one China and that Taiwan is part of China." As long as the Taiwan question was approached peacefully by the parties concerned, the United States would ultimately withdraw its military personnel from Taiwan (about 8,500 in number), who were concerned mainly with logistical support for the effort in Vietnam rather than the defense of Taiwan and were therefore redundant in proportion as disengagement from Vietnam progressed. Meanwhile, the United States would "progressively reduce its forces and military installations on Taiwan as the tension in the area diminishes." (The United States has interpreted "the area" as referring to the three traditional trouble spots—Korea, the Taiwan Strait, and Indochina—whereas Peking has insisted that it covers only Indochina.)

The unilateral Chinese statement stressed revolution and liberation from oppression (rather than international stability), the equality of all nations regardless of size, and China's determination never to be a superpower (in Peking's definition of that term, of course). "All foreign troops should be withdrawn to their own countries," a demand that Peking intends to cover Soviet forces in the Mongolian People's Republic as well as American forces abroad (which in fact, as distinct from propaganda, Peking is not eager to see withdrawn, as will be shown later). The Chinese statement expressed support (again mainly for the record) of the Communist revolutionary movements in South Vietnam, Laos, and Cambodia. The political demands of North Korea, the Japanese left, and Pakistan received a brief endorsement. Taiwan was reaffirmed to be a "province of China" and the "crucial question obstructing the normalization of relations between China and the United States"; American military installations must be withdrawn from the island, and there must be no more American interference with the "liberation" of Taiwan and the unification of China under Peking.

The communiqué of course did not reflect the full content of the negotiations, which brought out a rather more conciliatory Chinese attitude than Peking was willing, for reasons of "face" and domestic politics, to display in public. The Chinese gave a virtual pledge, although an informal one, not to use force with respect to Taiwan as long as the United States did not try to obstruct "liberation" by peaceful (i. e., political) means, a condition accepted by the American side. American military withdrawal from Taiwan was evidently expected by Peking to contribute to "liberation" by enhancing Taipei's sense of isolation and helplessness. The United States in turn apparently hoped that the prospect of withdrawal would encourage peaceful Chinese behavior not only toward Taiwan but toward Korea and Indochina as well, and this expectation was subsequently borne out. Peking appeared satisfied with the American position on Taiwan elaborated at the summit conference, at least as a transitional situation, even though the United States stopped short of endorsing Peking's claim that Taiwan is part of China. The Chinese side did not press for American military withdrawals (except from Taiwan) and even indicated a preference that the United States not withdraw further from Indochina, presumably because of concern that a vacuum might be created that would benefit or be filled by the Soviet Union. On the other hand, Peking declined to give any direct help in working out a settlement for Indochina.

All in all, both sides had good reason to be satisfied with the Peking summit, even if the relations of each with its allies were somewhat strained as a result of it. For the Chinese side, difficulties with North Vietnam, and to a lesser extent with North Korea, were more than offset by considerably increased leverage on Moscow, by encouraging if not spectacular progress on the Taiwan question, by the laying of the foundations for the importation of badly needed high technology equipment and food and fibre from the United States, and most of all perhaps by the establishment of the foundations for a positive relationship that could be built upon in the future. Furthermore, Chou En-lai's policies and political position were significantly enhanced, and he received some rare and valuable personal publicity in China as a result of the conference.

The American side gained at least some benefit to the President's re-election campaign, an essentially nonobstructive (if not necessarily actively helpful) Chinese attitude toward American efforts at making peace in Indochina, and somewhat more reasonable Soviet behavior as a result of Moscow's unwillingness to be odd man out with respect to a developing Sino-American relationship. The impact of the Peking summit on the United States' Asian allies was fairly serious, and in the case of the Republic of China highly traumatic, because it cast doubt on the continuing validity of the American commitment to them; in an effort to convey reassurance, an American mission under Assistant Secretary of State Marshall Green visited them shortly after the conference.

Sino-American Relations after the Summit

Probably the most striking testimonial to the vitality of the Sino-American relationship and to the importance attached to it by both sides came from the direction of Indochina. It became clear that Peking had decided that its new relationship with the United States was more important to it than its established but troublesome relationship with Hanoi. On the other hand, Peking's ability in practice to ignore or flaunt Hanoi's wishes was limited by an unwillingness to drive it into the arms of the Soviet Union. The American bombing campaign against North Vietnam and the mining of Haiphong harbor in early May 1972, in retaliation for Hanoi's invasion of South Vietnam at the end of March, produced a predictable round of propaganda attacks by Peking and a limited increase in Chinese (and Soviet) military aid to Hanoi, but no serious disruption of Sino-American relations. Such disruption was not a realistic option for Peking in view of the Soviet refusal to break off the Moscow summit conference (in May) and thereby endanger its own improving relations with the United States on account of Vietnam. Later in the year, when Hanoi first made concessions to the United States (in October) and then withdrew some of them (in December), and the United States resumed bombing, Peking evidently applied pressure in private to Hanoi, probably in the form of a threat to cut off aid, in order to push it toward a settlement, and this pressure appears to have had a great deal to do with the emergence of an agreement, at last, in January 1973. At that point, Peking expressed strong public approval for Hanoi's behavior in signing the agreement and began to reduce the level of its military aid to North Vietnam; this reduction became particularly pronounced after the signing of the supplementary agreement of June 13, 1973, by the United States and North Vietnam (see below).

At the intergovernmental level, the relationship established at the Peking summit was initially kept alive through two main channels. One was the American and Chinese embassies in Paris, which handled relatively routine matters. Questions of greater sensitivity and importance were dealt with during further visits to Peking by Dr. Kissinger.

Kissinger's visit to Peking of February 15-19, 1973 was his first after the signing of the Paris Agreement on Vietnam, and was made in an appropriately cordial atmosphere; he was received by Mao Tse-tung, and his photograph appeared on the front page of the *People's Daily* on three consecutive days. Indochina was discussed, evidently in a friendly spirit even though no observable progress was made toward a settlement for the only one of the Indochina countries for which none was in sight, Cambodia. Peking agreed to release two American prisoners and review the sentence of a third. It was decided to negotiate on the questions of blocked pre-1949 assets in the United States and American claims for pre-1949 property nationalized in China after 1949. There was to be an expansion of trade and cultural exchange. The most important form of progress toward the mutually desired "normalization" of relations made at that time was probably an agreement to establish liaison offices in both capitals. These were to be embassies in everything but name and diplomatic protocol; the reason why they could not be raised to embassies, at least for the time being, was that the United States for both domestic and external reasons was unwilling to transfer its formal diplomatic recognition from the Republic of China to the People's Republic of China, and neither of the Chinas would tolerate simultaneous diplomatic representation of the United States or any other country in both their capitals.

The liaison offices began to be set up in March. They were headed by very senior men as chiefs: in the American case, by David Bruce, a diplomat of ambassadorial rank; in the Chinese case, by Huang Chen, a former ambassador to France and a member of the Communist Party Central Committee (since 1969). Although neither mission was given full diplomatic standing, each was treated with great consideration. Huang Chen was received by President Nixon soon after his arrival, for example, and the Chinese built a new building for the American liaison office in only a few weeks.

Another Kissinger visit to Peking was scheduled for early August 1973, mainly in order to discuss Cambodia, but in late July it was postponed until some time after the August 15 deadline for the halting of American bombing in Cambodia. Another consideration was the stated unwillingness of Prince Sihanouk, who although in Peking was not entirely controlled by his Chinese hosts, and whose cooperation appeared important if not necessarily indispensable to an agreement on Cambodia, to talk with Kissinger. The visit was postponed again on account of the Middle Eastern War that began on October 6. Since this postponement was predictable, and since the Soviet Union clearly had something to do with starting the war, it seems reasonable to assume that one of the benefits to Moscow, if not one of its actual purposes, was the postponement of the Kissinger visit to Peking, and a demonstration to the Chinese that in the last analysis the Soviet Union had more leverage on the United States than they did. The American strategic alert, in response to the apparent Soviet threat (of October 24) to send troops to the Middle East, may have been warranted, or it may have been intended mainly to distract the attention of the American public from the administration's domestic predicament (Watergate, the Agnew resignation, etc.), but in either case it probably helped after a shaky start to revive Peking's confidence in the United States' ability to confront the Soviet Union when necessary.

The postponed Kissinger visit took place on November 10-14; it was his first to China as Secretary of State. The two sides naturally exchanged views on the Middle East. The American side gave assurances that its current China policy was a more or less permanent one that would not be adversely affected by domestic problems, by future changes of administration, or by Soviet-American relations (such as the recent Brezhnev visit to the United States and Soviet-American cooperation in clamping a lid on the dangerous situation in the Middle East). The American side tried, with what success is not clear, to persuade Peking to try to restrain Hanoi, whose violations of the cease-fire agreement were assuming alarming proportions. Korea was discussed; Peking may have given assurances that neither it nor North Korea would take direct advantage of the troop withdrawals from South Korea that the United States was contemplating. There was apparently an agreement to de-emphasize the Taiwan problem, and in effect to find ways around it, rather than allowing it to obstruct the progress in Sino-American relations that both sides desired. One sign of this was that the United States almost immediately began to reduce its troop strength on Taiwan; apparently the United States was satisfied with Peking's contribution to date to diminishing the "tension in the area." Both sides placed great stress on their desire for further "normalization" of their mutual relations. Since this was evidently not intended to imply full diplomatic relations in the near future, it seemed likely that intermediate measures were being contemplated: trade offices and perhaps consulates and a trade agreement, possibly most-favored-nation treatment for Chinese exports to the United States, information offices and perhaps American news bureaus in Peking, and the like. The Chinese side was clearly pleased by the visit; Kissinger was received by Mao Tse-tung for two and three-quarters hours, and the Chinese press continued to avoid making very much of the Nixon administration's domestic difficulties.

Quantitatively at least, Sino-American trade registered an even more spectacular growth than Sino-American political relations. From almost nothing two years earlier, it shot up to nearly $900 million (both ways) in 1973. The United States had become the People's Republic of China's third largest trading partner (after Japan and Hong Kong). The reasons were only partly political. The United States suited Peking well as a trading partner, since China's major import requirements fell at the opposite ends of the spectrum of technological sophistication, and at the extremes (but not in between) the United States was in a strong competitive position as an exporter. Accordingly, Peking began to import from the United States, at a level roughly ten times as high as that of its exports to the United States, high technology items (satellite communications equipment, long-range aircraft, etc.), grain, and fibre (mainly cotton).

Clearly Sino-American relations had registered an astonishing improvement. The causes lay not merely with American or Chinese diplomacy but with other factors as well, and above all with the concern of both parties to render their relations with the Soviet Union more manageable. This was a very powerful consideration, and one not likely to evaporate in the near future.

Hesitant Relaxation in Korea

A strong American commitment to the survival of South Korea in the face of the challenge from the Communist North was forged during the Korean War and took on a formal existence in a mutual security treaty (or defensive alliance) signed at the end of the war. American forces remained in South Korea after the war, not only as a deterrent to further attacks from the North, but in order to ensure the continuation of a series of American generals at the head of the United Nations Command, which formally speaking included the South Korean forces. American economic and military aid flowed to South Korea in massive amounts, although the economy limped badly on account of the after-effects of the war and the autocratic and incompetent rule of President Syngman Rhee. In these ways the United States not only protected South Korea but gave itself a veto over Rhee's occasionally proclaimed intention to "march north" (in other words, to attack North Korea).

In April 1960 Rhee was ousted by the combined action of student demonstrators and his own Army. There followed a free but rather chaotic interlude during which the idea of negotiations with North Korea on unification grew more popular in intellectual and political circles. Alarmed by this trend, the Army leadership seized power in May 1961, re-established tight political and social controls, and installed its leading figure, Park Chung Hee, as president. Since then, in spite of the existence of certain civilian and parliamentary trappings, the South Korean political system has been controlled by Park through the Army and the powerful Korean Central Intelligence Agency. This regime shortly began to do what many authoritarian regimes do in an effort to strengthen the state and distract public attention from the absence of political freedom: devote itself to economic development, an objective whose desirability few would deny. The keys to the program were incentives to Korean private enterprise to produce and export, and the establishment of diplomatic and commercial relations with Japan (in 1965) as a means of promoting trade and investment from that quarter, disliked though it was by most Koreans. These measures worked remarkably well, and the economy began to grow rapidly, but without extinguishing the desire for freedom on the part of many Koreans outside the establishment.

From wartime devastation North Korea emerged as an extraordinarily tightly controlled Communist dictatorship under the increasingly personal rule of Kim Il Song, who had been picked for this role by the Soviet occupation authorities in 1945. Far from remaining a Soviet puppet, Kim gradually purged his opponents, including some who were pro-Soviet and some who were pro-Chinese, played off Moscow against Peking while enlarging his own freedom of action with respect to both of them, and secured substantial industrial and military aid from both. He evidently feared, or pretended to fear, that the military takeover of 1961 in South Korea might be followed by a "march north," and within a few weeks of the coup he extracted military alliances from the Soviet Union and China. He was even more startled by the establishment of relations between South Korea and Japan and the sending of South Korean troops to Vietnam (at American insistence) in 1965, both of which seemed likely to enhance the strength and international stature of his hated rival, while possibly making it in the long run—in his eyes—a Japanese as well as an American puppet.

About the end of that year, accordingly, he launched a strategy of infiltrating small bodies of North Korean troops into South Korea by land and sea, evidently in the hope of touching off a "people's war" such as was going on in South Vietnam, without a recurrence of full-scale war. The people of the South, with lively memories of North Korean aggressiveness and atrocities during the war, did not respond, except negatively. In 1968–69 the North Koreans raised the level of pressure by trying an unsuccessful commando raid on President Park's residence, by seizing the American "spy ship" *Pueblo* (the crew was released after a year of captivity), and by shooting down an American reconnaissance aircraft over the Sea of Japan. The American response to this overeagerness was an impressive although temporary air and naval build-up in the region, probably made all the more menacing in Kim Il Song's eyes because the United States was beginning to disengage from Vietnam, and the construction of an electrified barrier across the peninsula below the Demilitarized Zone. He may also have feared that he might be driving South Korea into the arms of Japan, the traditional enemy and oppressor, especially since the Nixon-Sato Declaration (November 1969) stated that Japan considered itself to have an interest in the security of South Korea. He was undoubtedly troubled and puzzled by the Sino-Soviet confrontation.

For some such reasons as these, North Korean infiltration attempts fell off sharply after 1969 and gave way to a strategy designed to exploit presumed weaknesses in South Korea by political means. In the spring of 1970, Kim renewed his long-standing offer of negotiations on unification, in a somewhat more conciliatory tone than before. It is not certain whether Peking encouraged him in this shift from the beginning, as it was to do later, but there were certainly no objections from that direction, since the Chinese had been wooing him since late 1969 on account of the Sino-Soviet confrontation. Later in 1970 there came a cautious, but positive, response from Park, who apparently thought it best to begin negotiations while an American military presence and American political support were still available. The South Korean mood was, and remained, one of great uncertainty, since it was becoming clear that the Nixon Doctrine and congressional enthusiasm for reducing overseas expenditures would lead to sizable American troop withdrawals from Korea during the next several years. This prospect inevitably raised questions about the reliability and usefulness of the American security guarantee to South Korea, which had no desire to be liberated for a third time by American troops but preferred deterrence of the North through a substantial American military presence and felt itself inferior to North Korea in the air and in armor.

During 1971 the warming of Sino-American relations, quietly at first, led both parties to take steps toward removing Korea as an issue between them and to encourage their respective Korean partners to negotiate with one another. Peking continued to support the North Korean demand for the removal of the United Nations label from the American military presence in the South, if only to avoid pushing Kim Il Song too close to Moscow, but at the time of the first Kissinger visit (July 1971) it sent a delegate to take part in the proceedings of the Korean Military Armistice Commission at Panmunjom for the first time in five years. Parallel with this trend, secret contacts got under way at a high level between North and South Korea. These were announced in a remarkable joint statement dated July 4, 1972, stressing the idea of a "great national unity . . . transcending differences in ideas, ideologies, and systems." Subsequent, public, contacts quickly and predictably showed, however, that each side was still more interested in scoring points off the other than in reaching agreement. The North's program was highly political and if accepted would have spread Northern representatives throughout the South under the guise of promoting contacts between members of families divided by the Demilitarized Zone. The South rejected this approach and opted for a much more gradual and less political one. Despite the poor progress of these contacts, their mere occurrence promoted a tendency for a growing number of governments to establish and maintain diplomatic relations with both Koreas. Unlike the two Chinas, Pyongyang and Seoul tolerated this recognition of the existence of two *de facto* states.

President Park made skillful use of the exaggerated, although not entirely absurd, argument that the successful conduct of negotiations with the North and the weathering of the new international situation created by American military disengagement from the region required an increase of his personal power. In December 1971 he engineered a coup in order to assume virtually dictatorial powers, but since these had no constitutional basis beyond the end of his third presidential term (1971–75) he executed another coup in October 1972, proclaimed martial law, and extended his powers indefinitely. South Korea had the most tightly controlled political system in non-Communist Asia; North Korea had the most tightly controlled system in Communist Asia. President Park, even more than Kim Il Song, tolerated no heir apparent. Late in 1973, he purged the head of the Korean CIA, Lee Hu Rak, who had been in charge of the faltering talks with the North and whose agents had created an international scandal by kidnapping Kim Dae Jung, a prominent opposition politician, and bringing him from Japan to Korea.

The admission of North Korea to the World Health Organization in mid-1973 tended to create increased interest in the United Nations' relationship to the Korean question. Park then proposed the admission of both Koreas to the United Nations but was turned down by Pyongyang. Supporters of North Korea, notably Peking, made some progress at the fall session in 1973 toward abolishing the United Nations Command (in Korea), but Peking was noticeably less enthusiastic than Pyongyang about getting the 42,000 remaining American troops withdrawn from South Korea. The main reason was the Chinese interest in détente with the United States and in the nonappearance of a vacuum that might tempt Japan or the Soviet Union. The American plan was to modernize the Republic of Korea's armed forces over a five-year period (1971–75), within limits imposed by congressional ap-

propriations, to withdraw the remaining American troops by the
end of that period, and apparently to organize at some period an
international conference that would guarantee South Korea's
security. Meanwhile, the prospect of the abolition of the United
Nations Command posed no serious problem, since the bilateral
ties between the United States and the Republic of Korea would
not be affected and it was these that were the real external support
for South Korean security.

CHAPTER X

The Indochina Agreements

PRESIDENT Johnson's action on March 21, 1968 in suspending bombing of North Vietnam north of the 20th parallel, renewing his invitation to negotiate, and announcing that he would not be a candidate for re-election presented Hanoi with a considerable dilemma. The dramatic character of this presidential initiative made it difficult to reject, especially since the North Vietnamese forces in South Vietnam and the Viet Cong had been badly hurt during the turning back of the Tet offensive, and yet Hanoi's position was so far apart from Washington's, both in substance and in the insistence of each side that the other must make the first major move, that the Johnson offer was also very hard to accept.

As early as April 1965, the President had proclaimed that the United States was willing to negotiate without preconditions and to help rebuild North Vietnam after a settlement. The United States used its bombing of North Vietnam and the possibility of its cessation as a lever to induce negotiations; there were eight American bombing "pauses" for this purpose in 1965–67, but Hanoi's response was mainly to take advantage of them to reinforce and resupply its units in the South. Another American tactic was to promise to hold its troop strength in South Vietnam level if Hanoi would refrain from infiltrating more military units into the South; no formal agreement on this was possible since Hanoi never admitted officially that it had any troops in South Vietnam.

The North Vietnamese precondition for negotiations was that the United States must stop its bombing of the North immediately and unconditionally. In addition, Hanoi demanded that the United States withdraw its forces from Vietnam, refrain from further interference, and accept the ten-point program announced by the National Liberation Front in 1960, which called in essence for the displacement of the Saigon government by a coalition government with National Liberation Front participation and eventual unification of North and South Vietnam.

The Paris Talks

Hanoi nevertheless accepted President Johnson's offer to negotiate of March 31, 1968, and after some diplomatic maneuvering the negotiations began in Paris in May. The reason was probably a realization by both of the military failure of the Tet offensive and of its psychological impact on the United States, as well as a desire to seek gains through diplomacy before the passing of the elderly and ailing Ho Chi Minh. Hanoi's position at Paris during the first several months was that the United States must end all bombing of the North, withdraw from the South, and allow a National Liberation Front delegation to join the talks; and North Vietnamese Army units actually withdrew from South Vietnam to Laos and Cambodia during this period, but whether in order to create a better atmosphere for the negotiations is not clear. The initial American position at Paris was essentially that the North Vietnamese Army must withdraw from South Vietnam, Laos, and Cambodia and that South Vietnam must be allowed to determine its own political future without outside interference.

In September-October, a secret understanding, whose existence Hanoi was later to deny, was evidently reached.* There was to be a complete American bombing halt (although reconnaissance flights over North Vietnam would continue) on condition that the North Vietnamese Army not violate the Demilitarized Zone (by crossing it) and refrain from attacking South Vietnamese cities. The agreement had to be secret, inasmuch as Hanoi did not admit publicly to having any troops in South Vietnam and insisted on an outwardly unconditional bombing halt. In addition, it was

---

* Cf. Peter A. Poole, *The United States and Indochina from FDR to Nixon* (Hinsdale, Ill.: Dryden Press, 1973), pp. 200-201.

agreed that the Saigon government and the National Liberation Front should be admitted to the talks. Each side, however, agreed with its own junior partner that the latter should be represented by a separate delegation, to give it face, and that the other side's should be represented only as part of a single delegation. President Thieu was particularly insistent that the National Liberation Front should not be separately represented and withheld his government's participation in the talks for several weeks, until an agreement was worked out under which all participants used an intentionally ambiguous "our side, your side" formula. Nevertheless, with an eye to the approaching election and a desire to show progress on Vietnam, the Johnson administration suspended all bombing of North Vietnam (south as well as north of the 20th parallel) at the end of October.

President-elect Nixon had considerable to live up to, inasmuch as the President under whom he had served as Vice President had promised an armistice in Korea if elected and had actually achieved one six months after his inauguration. This feat proved impossible to duplicate, although Nixon had indicated during the 1968 campaign that he had an (unspecified) plan to bring peace to Vietnam. In April 1969, after his inauguration, he began to reveal what it was: the United States might withdraw unilaterally—although not necessarily unconditionally—from Vietnam and cover its withdrawal by Vietnamization, meaning the upgrading of the combat capabilities of the South Vietnamese armed forces through better training and equipment.

Although it had strong objections to Vietnamization, the other side apparently sensed an exploitable element of urgency and vulnerability in the President's position. On May 8 the National Liberation Front proclaimed a new ten-point program making the release of American prisoners of war, an outcome known to be strongly desired in the United States by the administration and the public, conditional on American military withdrawal, and calling for a coalition government in lieu of the existing Saigon government, subsequent elections, a neutral South Vietnam, and ultimate unification with the north. The National Liberation Front evidently assumed that its superior organization and discipline, compared with those of the Saigon government's following, would enable it to manage and eventually control the fluid situation that implementation of its demands would presumably create. To improve its organizational capabilities and image, the National Liberation Front established what it called the Provisional Revolutionary Government of South Vietnam in the spring of 1969.

In a major statement of May 14, President Nixon virtually accepted the National Liberation Front's ten-point program, but with the important qualification that the proposed elections be held under international supervision, presumably in order to remove the onus from the United States if anything went wrong; this condition was unacceptable to the other side. The Communist parties to the negotiations tended to become more obstructive after the death of Ho Chi Minh on September 3, 1969, probably because a major reason for serious negotiating—the desire to enable Ho to see progress toward "liberation" of the South before his death—had been removed. In spite of inevitable discouragement over this situation, the United States proceeded steadily with its troop withdrawal program and its logical concomitant, Vietnamization; during the three-year period beginning in mid-1969, American combat forces in South Vietnam were reduced from half a million almost to zero. This process, being motivated primarily by domestic political and fiscal considerations, was not affected even by the Cambodian crisis of 1970 (see below).

On October 7, 1970, President Nixon made two important concessions by dropping his demands for international supervision of the proposed elections following an agreement and for the withdrawal of North Vietnamese forces from South Vietnam. In May 1971 the United States agreed to complete its withdrawal, which was imminent in any case, in exchange for a cease-fire and the release of American prisoners of war. During this period, and through 1972, there were important although intermittent secret talks, some of them involving Henry Kissinger and Le Duc Tho, the senior North Vietnamese negotiator, in addition to the open sessions. The United States tended to prefer secret diplomacy, and Hanoi open negotiations, for the same reason: the latter gave Hanoi and the National Liberation Front a propaganda forum. On June 26, 1971, a secret nine-point North Vietnamese proposal, not published down to the present, which contained a rejection of the American statement of the previous month, was presented. On July 1, the Provisional Revolutionary Government of South Vietnam published a seven-point proposal: the United States was to stop its support of the Saigon government, including the Vietnamization program, complete its withdrawal, get its prisoners of war back only when Saigon released its civilian prisoners (including of course alleged Communists), accept a coalition government with National Liberation Front participation and eventual unification, and give reconstruction aid to North and South Vietnam. Hanoi said privately that it preferred that the United States respond to its secret nine-point proposal rather than to the public seven-point proposal and then proceeded to denounce the United States for not replying to the latter.

The fairly rapid development of a new relationship between the People's Republic of China and the United States following the first Kissinger visit to Peking (July 1971) created a different international climate for the negotiations on Vietnam, but its effect was not immediately obvious. In late January, President Nixon made a new set of public proposals, the most significant of which were probably a reintroduction of the earlier demand for international supervision of the elections to be held in South Vietnam (there was to be no displacement of the Thieu government by a coalition government with National Liberation Front participation prior to the elections, as demanded by the Communist side) and the specification that only "innocent" civilians, presumably not including political prisoners held by the Saigon government, need be released along with American and other military prisoners (an obvious effort to maintain a separation between the release of the two categories, in opposition to the Communist position). This plan was promptly rejected by North Vietnam and the National Liberation Front. In February 1972, the Communist side restated the essence of the Provisional Revolutionary Government's seven points, plus a demand that President Thieu resign, by implication after disbanding his armed forces. It may have been partly in an unsuccessful effort to soften Hanoi's stand somewhat, and as a result of a request by President Nixon at the Peking summit, that Chou En-lai secretly flew to Hanoi early in March.

This condition of deadlock was intolerable for the Nixon administration in 1972, an election year. The Communist side was obviously trying to use its American prisoners of war as its main lever on the United States, and the Nixon administration could not afford to appear to be doing less than the maximum, short of re-escalation of the war, to get the prisoners back. Accordingly, the

United States suspended the Paris talks on March 25, 1972, mainly in protest at the Communist stand on the prisoner question. Hanoi for its part evidently believed that it could repeat or improve on its performance of 1968, the previous American election year, by influencing American politics and policy in its own favor through an offensive, and perhaps that it could disrupt President Nixon's Moscow summit conference planned for May.

The Easter Offensive

Accordingly, at the end of March Hanoi launched virtually its whole army in its so-called Easter offensive against South Vietnam, with the aid of tanks and heavy artillery provided by the Soviet Union. Though it had the advantage of surprise, the offensive began to be stopped and ground down by a combination of increasingly effective South Vietnamese resistance and American air strikes, the latter being conducted mainly by aircraft based in Thailand. Furthermore, the Viet Cong forces, which had been badly weakened in the aftermath of the Tet offensive, proved unable to do anything significant in support of the Easter offensive.

Profoundly angered by the Easter offensive and convinced that it violated the 1968 understanding, President Nixon responded first by massive air strikes in South Vietnam and against North Vietnam and then (beginning on May 8) by mining Haiphong harbor, through which passed most of whatever Soviet equipment for North Vietnam did not move across China by rail, for the first time in the war. On May 8 he repeated his basic proposal calling for completion of the American withdrawal in exchange for the release of American prisoners of war, with political issues to be negotiated later between Saigon and its adversaries. The President knew that his action, taken only two weeks before the scheduled opening of the Moscow summit, posed a powerful challenge to the Soviet Union. He was outraged by the high level of Soviet logistical support for the North Vietnamese Army, and he later claimed to have considered cancelling the Moscow summit; more probably he hoped that the Soviet leadership would not only refrain from cancelling it—something that Moscow was in no position to do, in view of its need for détente with the United States —but would reduce its support for Hanoi and encourage a more conciliatory North Vietnamese attitude at Paris. If this was his calculation, he was to be successful, although both the Soviet Union and China increased their deliveries of military aid to North Vietnam somewhat for a time after May 8, 1972, in spite of the American bombing and mining. He also evidently tried with success to induce Peking to put political pressure on Hanoi; one indication of this was that on Kissinger's next visit to China, in June 1972, he took a specialist on Vietnamese affairs with him.

During this period secret talks, including some between Kissinger and Politburo member Le Duc Tho, were resumed at Paris. As in 1968, Hanoi responded to its military setbacks by reverting to diplomacy before its hand was weakened to the point of ineffectiveness. At first it insisted that the United States must withdraw its forces from Thailand, as well as from Indochina, and it continued to demand the ouster of President Thieu. By September, however, it was no longer insisting on these points, provided Thieu would deal with the National Liberation Front, the change being due according to official American sources to persuasive Soviet and Chinese pressures on North Vietnam.

On October 8, Hanoi secretly made what was to prove to be its decisive concession. While still insisting on American withdrawal and the simultaneous release of all prisoners (not merely American prisoners of war), it dropped its demand for a full-fledged coalition government with National Liberation Front participation, in succession to the Saigon government, in favor of a vaguely defined "administrative structure" to be known as the National Council of National Reconciliation and Concord, which was to operate on the basis of unanimity, in other words with a veto for any member. Hanoi had taken a step that could be interpreted as meeting the American demand for a separation of the military from the political issues, the former to be settled first and mainly between North Vietnam and the United States, the latter to be settled later between Saigon and the National Liberation Front. More precisely, the release of American prisoners of war, although still tied to Saigon's release of its civilian prisoners, was no longer linked to American cooperation in the National Liberation Front's political program through the setting up of a coalition government. It appeared for a time that an agreement could be signed by the end of October.

"Peace Is at Hand"

President Nixon was searching in effect for a way to complete the American military disengagement from the war (apart from the Vietnamization program) and to secure the release of American prisoners of war without involving the United States in the settlement of political issues, and without necessarily giving the Saigon government more than what was then known as a "decent interval" between the American withdrawal and its own possible (but not inevitable) collapse. Furthermore, the President was obviously eager for some diplomatic success at Paris, especially on the prisoner of war issue, to which he could point before the election, even though he was not prepared to ensure the signing of an agreement by election day by capitulating to Hanoi on the still contentious prisoner of war question and producing an explosion of American public wrath when the terms became known. His solution was to have Kissinger hold an important and dramatic press conference on October 26, in which he said that peace was "at hand" and minimized the remaining obstacles to its achievement. Ignoring a simultaneous public statement by Hanoi indicating that all prisoners must be released at the same time, as well as a statement by North Vietnamese Premier Pham Van Dong eight days earlier making the same point and saying that the National Council of National Reconciliation and Concord would be in effect a coalition government, Kissinger insisted that "the return of our prisoners is not conditional on the disposition of Vietnamese prisoners in Vietnamese jails on both sides of the conflict."

Kissinger dealt with another crucial question, that of Saigon's attitude on the progress toward an agreement that the United States and North Vietnam had made, not through misstatement but through vagueness. Within the next several days it became clear that President Thieu had an independent and dissenting opinion. He was still insisting on the withdrawal of North Vietnamese troops from South Vietnam, something that was no longer an issue between Hanoi and Washington; he claimed their number to be 300,000, whereas the official American estimate was 145,000. He considered Hanoi's refusal to withdraw from the South as a refusal to recognize the Demilitarized Zone, and hence the existence of South Vietnam as a separate *de facto* state. He

regarded the proposed National Council of National Reconciliation and Concord, quite reasonably in view of Pham Van Dong's
statement, as a disguised coalition government. He wanted agreements on Laos and Cambodia to be signed simultaneously with
any agreement on South Vietnam, in view of their direct relevance
to the Vietnamese conflict. While not necessarily disagreeing with
these points, Kissinger told Thieu that the United States would
sign an agreement even if Saigon did not. In fact, however, the
United States did not feel itself in a position to do so, probably
because of the unfavorable impression that would be created at
home and abroad by the spectacle of the United States taking action
on the Saigon government's fate over its explicit objections.

Furthermore, no matter what had been said just before the
election Nixon and Kissinger knew of course that they were not
yet in agreement with Hanoi. In addition to the issues already
mentioned, there was the fact that in October 1972 Hanoi had
moved a great deal of material into South Vietnam, presumably
in order to enable its forces there to take as much territory as
possible during whatever time remained before the signing of an
agreement and the beginning of a cease-fire. Presumably as a
result, at least in part, of President Thieu's vigorously expressed
views, the American attitude hardened and shifted from the "decent interval" approach to that of genuinely giving the Saigon
government a "decent chance" for survival, short of reinvolving
the United States in the political aspects of the struggle any
further, even if this meant taking action against North Vietnam.

The last straw was a new set of demands presented by Hanoi
on December 12, which included a refusal to recognize the Demilitarized Zone as a *de facto* border and an effort to ensure that the
international machinery for supervising the cease-fire should be
weak and should not be in place when the cease-fire went into
effect. On December 16, Kissinger held a press conference at
which he reported gloomily on the difficulties that the negotiations had encountered since the October 26 press conference,
while still stating, contrary to the public record, that Hanoi had
agreed in October to separate the release of the American prisoners of war from that of other prisoners. He admitted that Saigon
had raised objections, especially to the idea of North Vietnamese
troops remaining in South Vietnam, after a cease-fire, but insisted
that they would not be decisive: "... no other party will have a

veto over our actions." He was careful to throw the primary blame for what he portrayed as the current deadlock on Hanoi, not on Saigon. Kissinger gave no hint of the next American move; the reasons may have gone beyond normal security, since there is some suspicion that he was opposed to that move.

It turned out to be a heavy bombing campaign against North Vietnam from December 18 to 29. This controversial step produced significant results, not only through its direct impact on Hanoi but also apparently because it led to further Chinese pressures on the North Vietnamese to moderate their position, rather than on the United States. Peking's reasoning apparently was that continuation of the war in Vietnam at the existing level would increase Hanoi's dependence on the Soviet Union (for military equipment in particular) and therefore Soviet influence on Hanoi, would jeopardize the Sino-American détente, and would enhance the prospects for ultimate North Vietnamese control over the whole of Indochina. Chinese pressure may have taken the form of a threat to cut off Peking's own aid to North Vietnam and to interrupt the flow of Soviet aid for Hanoi moving across China by rail.

On January 8–9, 1973, a few days after the resumption of the negotiations at Paris, Hanoi made some important concessions that the United States chose to interpret publicly as a return to what, according to the official American version, had been agreed on the previous October. According to Kissinger at another press conference held on January 24, 1973, these North Vietnamese concessions consisted of strengthening of the machinery for supervising the cease-fire, elimination of the term "administrative structure" so that the National Council of National Reconciliation and Concord looked less like a coalition government, a commitment to respect the Demilitarized Zone to the extent of not infiltrating troops across it, a clear separation of the release of American prisoners of war from that of other prisoners (the official American position was that agreement had been reached on this point the previous October but had broken down in December), and a few other less substantive concessions. President Thieu's objections, apart from the futile one to the continuing presence of North Vietnamese troops in South Vietnam, were met at least in part by some of these concessions, as well as by official American optimism than an agreement on Laos, although probably not on Cambodia, would be reached shortly; in fact, in order to ensure this the United States was prepared to put heavy pressures on the Royal Laotian Government, of a kind to be discussed later.

The South Vietnam Agreement, January 1973

On the basis of this forward step an agreement was actually signed at Paris on January 23; it was to go into effect on January 27. The problem of each side's negative attitude toward the other's junior partner was handled by having the two parties on one side sign on a single sheet, and the parties on the other side sign on a separate sheet. The agreement, in its major articles, provided that a cease-fire should go into effect and that all foreign troops on Saigon's side should withdraw within sixty days. Further foreign troops were not to be introduced on either side (the question of whether North Vietnamese troops should be regarded as foreign was left vague; indeed their presence in South Vietnam was not mentioned in the agreement). Military equipment could be brought into South Vietnam only at levels and in types sufficient to replace equipment present before the cease-fire but no longer serviceable. All prisoners of war and foreign civilian prisoners were to be released at a rate paralleling the American withdrawal, and the release of Vietnamese civilian prisoners was to be negotiated between Saigon and the National Liberation Front.

The latter two parties were to create, as soon as practicable, the National Council of National Reconciliation and Concord, which was to be composed of three equal "segments"; these were not identified but were presumably to consist of one representing the Saigon government, one representing the National Liberation Front, and one composed equally of "neutrals" nominated by one side and "neutrals" nominated by the other side. The Council was to be subject to the principle of "unanimity" (i.e., the veto) and was to organize "free and democratic general elections" to decide South Vietnam's political future. The two South Vietnamese parties were to negotiate a reduction of their armed forces. The Demilitarized Zone was to be "respected," in the sense already indicated, even though it was specified as only a provisional boundary.

An International Commission of Control and Supervision (ICCS) was to be created to police the cease-fire; its membership

was not specified, but it was generally known to be likely to consist of Canada, Indonesia, Poland, and Hungary. As with earlier
such bodies in Indochina, its official reports and recommendations would have to be adopted unanimously. The actual implementation of the cease-fire would be the responsibility of a
Four-Party Joint Military Commission, which after the American
withdrawal would become a Two-Party Joint Military Commission, representing only Saigon and the National Liberation Front,
through the elimination of the American and North Vietnamese
delegations. There was to be no foreign military activity, including
by implication movement of military personnel and material into
South Vietnam, Laos, or Cambodia, although no date was specified
on which this provision was to go into effect; thus the only way
in which Hanoi could legally send war material into South Vietnam was across the Demilitarized Zone under the supervision of
the ICCS, and, of course, at replacement levels only. The United
States was to help reconstruct North Vietnam, as well as the rest
of Indochina. The United States was to remove the mines it had
sown in North Vietnamese waters.

The published Paris agreement was allegedly accompanied by
no secret agreements, but plausible reports indicated the existence of one to the effect that North Vietnam would remove
100,000 of its troops from South Vietnam provided Saigon reduced
its forces by an equal number; if there was such an understanding,
it had to be secret, for the obvious reason that Hanoi still would
not admit publicly and formally to having any troops at all in
South Vietnam.

Kissinger visited Hanoi from February 10 to 13, mainly to
discuss the implementation of the Paris agreement, which was going none too well. He then visited Peking, partly no doubt in an
effort to encourage a cooperative Chinese attitude at the international conference that was to convene shortly at Paris to lend its
dignity to the agreement worked out in January. The release of
prisoners of war on both sides, including American prisoners of
war, was lagging behind the American military withdrawal, which
was virtually complete. Hanoi was evidently trying to get the
United States to put pressure on the Saigon government to release
its civilian prisoners. Hanoi was continuing military activities in
Laos and Cambodia and according to official American charges
was not only failing to reduce its troop strength in South Vietnam

but was actually reinforcing it. None of the Vietnamese parties was cooperating in the Four-Party Joint Military Commission or with the ICCS, which was having difficulty getting into position. There had been virtually no progress toward implementation of the political aspects of the Paris agreement.

The twelve-party conference on Vietnam (consisting of representatives of the five major powers, the four members of the ICCS, and the three Vietnamese parties, as well as United Nations Secretary General Kurt Waldheim), which met at Paris from February 26 to March 2, inevitably did more than ratify the four-party agreement already reached. In addition to doing that, it listened to strong Canadian reservations about the probable effectiveness of the ICCS and a powerful and dramatic American demand that Hanoi stop violating the cease-fire and delaying the release of the one hundred forty-odd remaining American prisoners of war. After Hanoi had promised to release them promptly, an agreement was signed that endorsed the January 27 agreement, expressed the signatories' interest in being kept informed by the parties most directly involved about progress toward implementing the January 27 agreement, and pledged the signatories to respect the independence and neutrality of Cambodia and Laos.

In several significant respects, the 1973 agreement was less favorable to a Saigon government than the 1954 agreement had been. During those two decades North Vietnam had freed itself of formal international constraints on its behavior at home (such as the importation of foreign weapons) and of one on its behavior in South Vietnam: it now had the implicit right to keep troops there. Unlike the earlier one, the 1973 agreement dealt only with South Vietnam, not with North Vietnam, let alone Laos and Cambodia (apart from the vague provisions forbidding foreign military activity on their territory). An obvious example is that whereas the 1954 agreement had provided for an ICCS in each of the three Indochina countries, including both halves of Vietnam, the 1973 agreement provided for one in South Vietnam only. Whereas the 1954 agreement had called for the regrouping of all Communist forces in Vietnam north of the Demilitarized Zone, the 1973 agreement made no reference to the presence of North Vietnamese forces in South Vietnam, much less to any obligation for them to withdraw. The official American view was, or was claimed to be, that these forces could not be supplied at a level adequate to maintain them as an effective fighting force without violating the agreement, or in other words without resupplying them through Laos and Cambodia as well as across the Demilitarized Zone. The obvious and plausible alternative possibility, that Hanoi might prefer to violate the agreement to the extent necessary to maintain the effectiveness of its forces in the South, was not discussed publicly in official American circles.

The Nixon administration claimed that the war in Vietnam was over (the President began to speak of it in the past tense), and that "peace with honor" had been brought to both Vietnam and the United States. This of course was official nonsense for public consumption. What actually happened was that the United States had ended its own direct participation in the war (apart from Vietnamization), something essentially not very difficult to achieve since it was also desired by the Communist side, had gotten its prisoners back, and had left the Saigon government intact while consigning its ultimate fate to the outcome of its interaction, political it was hoped but very likely military as well, with its Communist adversaries. Events progressively punctured a myth, widely believed by the American public and tacitly encouraged by the administration, that "Only Hanoi Knows" (to quote a frequently displayed bumper sticker) about the fate of American military personnel missing in action and not listed by Hanoi as prisoners. In reality, there is every reason to believe that Hanoi was not secretly hoarding some, let alone all, of them for some bargaining purpose, and that all or most of them had died under circumstances that would never be known.

Implementation of the Agreement

Developments during the first several months following the signing of the Paris agreements provided little basis for optimism. Canada, reluctant from the beginning to serve on the ICCS because of its previous experience in similar roles in Indochina, agreed only under strong American pressure but soon became disgusted with the violations of the cease-fire, especially Hanoi's, and with the obstructive behavior of the two Communist members of the ICCS, and withdrew at the end of July; it was replaced by Iran. In talks in Paris and Saigon beginning in late March 1973, the Saigon government and the National Liberation Front agreed

on virtually nothing and made no significant progress toward re-
solving their political differences. Neither side released its military
or civilian prisoners (apart from American prisoners of war).
Saigon continued to insist, without success, on the withdrawal of
North Vietnamese troops and on the formation of the National
Council of National Reconciliation and Concord and the holding
of elections in the near future, while its military superiority to and
political advantages over the National Liberation Front continued
to exist, whereas the National Liberation Front wanted to postpone these steps so as to have time to improve its position.

The United States, an unhappy observer unwilling to reintro-
duce its ground forces and reluctant to resume air strikes, was concerned over the ineffectiveness of the cease-fire, continued North
Vietnamese infiltration into South Vietnam, North Vietnamese
military activity in Laos and Cambodia, and the improper functioning of the ICCS and the Two-Party Joint Military Commission. Hanoi had its own grievances, including the continuation of
American reconnaissance flights over North Vietnam, American
slowness in mine-sweeping, and the delay in beginning American
economic aid to North Vietnam, a commitment that was unpopular even among doves in the United States.

From these issues came a supplementary agreement, signed by
the four parties principally involved at Paris, on June 13, 1973,
and sometimes jocularly known as Son of Cease-fire. Its main
provisions were that the cease-fire should be observed and the
supervisory machinery made to work, that the United States
should cease aerial reconnaissance flights over North Vietnam, that
the United States should resume its mine-sweeping operations and
complete them within thirty days, that the Demilitarized Zone
should be used (implicitly by North Vietnam) only for supplies
and only at replacement levels, that all prisoners should be released within thirty days, that the two south Vietnamese parties
should proceed to implement the political aspects of the January
27 agreement, that the latter's provisions regarding Laos and Cambodia should be observed, and that negotiations on American
economic aid to North Vietnam should be resumed. Clearly these
items of agreement, if taken at face value without regard to the
probability of implementation, were a mixed bag; some favored
the Communist side, others the non-Communist side. But in practical terms this agreement was subject to the same operating prin-

ciple as the earlier agreements on Indochina: observance and compliance by the non-Communist Indochinese governments and their allies, especially the United States, were relatively easy to observe and in many cases to enforce; observation and enforcement were much more difficult, and violations much easier and therefore more probable, on the Communist side. And an enormous weight of evidence indicated that Hanoi had by no means given up its determination to control South Vietnam, sooner or later and by one means or another.

Conflict and Agreement in Laos

Hanoi's interest in Laos was mainly its utility as a military supply route to South Vietnam, but this was not the only significant aspect of the Laotian question. The beginning of the Paris talks on Vietnam in 1968 stimulated an increased interest on the part of Laotian Premier Souvanna Phouma in reactivating the tripartite coalition composed of neutrals like himself, representatives of the leftist Pathet Lao, and "rightists," that had been created in 1962 but from which the Pathet Lao had soon withdrawn. This objective came somewhat closer after the United States stopped bombing North Vietnam at the end of October 1968, but increased its air attacks on the Ho Chi Minh Trail in Laos; Hanoi became interested in conciliating Souvanna Phouma in order to get him to put pressure on the United States to stop the bombing in Laos, in exchange for which Hanoi claimed to be willing to withdraw its 60–70,000 troops from eastern Laos. Souvanna Phouma was reluctant to see the end of American bombing, however, presumably because it was conducted not only against the North Vietnamese convoys moving along the Ho Chi Minh Trail but in support of Laotian government forces (including the United States Central Intelligence Agency-supported Clandestine Army composed of Meo irregulars led by General Vang Pao and a force of Thai "volunteers" that grew to 20,000 men by 1972) fighting North Vietnamese and Pathet Lao units in other parts of Laos.

The Pathet Lao for its part insisted on an American bombing halt as a precondition for talks with Souvanna Phouma. In addition, it demanded in its Five Points, published in March 1970, that all other forms of American intervention in Laos also cease, that Laos be neutralized (i.e., free of foreign interference and alignments of any kind) as called for by the 1962 agreement, that general elections be held, that a provisional coalition government be established in the meantime (not the tripartite government created in 1962, but one in which the Pathet Lao would control half the seats and from which the "rightists" would be virtually excluded), and that the zones controlled by the two sides should be reunited through consultations. Souvanna Phouma accepted the points as a basis for discussion in July 1972. His hand was very much weakened by the powerful American interest in withdrawing from Laos as well as Vietnam and by a North Vietnamese build-up in southern Laos intended to replace the "sanctuaries" in Cambodia that had been lost as a result of the crisis of the spring of 1970 (see below). In February-March 1971, in an unsuccessful effort to cope with this problem, South Vietnamese troops made an incursion into southern Laos; the United States provided air support but no ground forces such as it had sent into Cambodia a year earlier, part of the reason for the difference being a desire not to jeopardize the developing Sino-American détente as the Cambodian intervention had threatened to do.

Negotiations between Souvanna Phouma's Royal Laotian Government and the Pathet Lao began on October 17, 1972. The basic positions were that Souvanna Phouma wanted the North Vietnamese out, and the 1962 government restored, whereas the Pathet Lao wanted the United States out, American bombing stopped, and a coalition government along the lines already indicated set up; the Pathet Lao evidently hoped for a formula that would enable its North Vietnamese patrons to maintain their unadmitted presence in the highland areas. During these negotiations, the Royal Laotian Government had the diplomatic support, behind the scenes, of the United States and China; the Pathet Lao had that of North Vietnam and the Soviet Union. But in January 1973, as the United States and North Vietnam moved rapidly toward an agreement on South Vietnam, it became clear that they wanted one on Laos as well; Hanoi was reported to have agreed secretly to withdraw virtually all of its troops from Laos following an agreement between Souvana Phouma and the Pathet Lao (but not automatically following the signing of the Paris agreement on South Vietnam).

Under this pressure the pace of the negotiations in Laos was intensified, but the two sides were not under equal pressure. The United States was eager to see an agreement signed that would enable it to stop bombing in Laos before the convening of the twelve-party conference on Vietnam on February 26; in mid-February it applied the most intense diplomatic pressures to Souvanna Phouma and the "rightists" and warned them that the bombing would stop by February 25. They had little choice but to yield, in view of the indispensability of American aid and support to their survival.

The result was an agreement, signed on February 20, that was a virtual capitulation to the Pathet Lao. The Royal Laotian Government was referred to in the text as the Vientiane Government, the Pathet Lao as the Patriotic Forces. The two principal cities, Vientiane (the administrative capital) and Luang Prabang (the royal capital), were to be "neutralized," meaning that the Pathet Lao was to be allowed to station troops in them. A coalition government, composed equally of Souvanna Phouma's supporters and Pathet Lao representatives, with no provision for "rightists" except as part of Souvanna Phouma's following, was to be set up within thirty days. Within sixty days after the formation of the coalition government all foreign troops were to withdraw; the North Vietnamese were implied but not named, whereas the Americans and Thai were named. The agreement, which as a whole bore a rather close resemblance to the Pathet Lao's Five Points, included a cease-fire that was to go into effect on February 22.

The heavy fighting that had been going on in previous weeks, with the Communist side generally on the offensive, as each side tried to improve its position prior to the cease-fire, continued after February 22 in violation of the cease-fire. The United States resumed bombing for one day (February 23) in southern Laos but discontinued it so as not to complicate its position at the Paris conference. It later bombed for another day (April 16) in northern Laos. Partly for this reason, and partly because of continued American pressures on the "rightists," some of whom tried unsuccessfully to overthrow Souvanna Phouma in August, the fighting slackened fairly steadily and was virtually over by the end of the year. All but 3,000 of the Thai "volunteers" were withdrawn by August 1973.

In the meantime the emphasis of the continuing struggle came to rest on the implementation of the political provisions of the February 20 agreement. The Pathet Lao proved argumentative and obstructive, perhaps because it was short of personnel qualified to assume ministerial posts under the projected coalition government, but more fundamentally because it wanted to put off the date on which the North Vietnamese troops would be obligated to leave Laos. In addition to his problem with the Pathet Lao, Souvanna Phouma was under continued pressure from the "rightists," some of whom were in his government, and who were opposed to the political provisions of the February 20 agreement. Negotiations between Souvanna Phouma and the Pathet Lao began in March, however, under American and Soviet diplomatic pressure. In April the Pathet Lao agreed that the other side should hold the vital portfolios of Interior and Defense (as well as others) in the projected coalition government, while the Pathet Lao should be allotted (among others) the somewhat less sensitive Ministries of Foreign Affairs and Finance. This concession was less important than it might appear, given the nature of the Pathet Lao's current concerns as just indicated. An agreement on the composition of the coalition government, as well as another political matter, was reached in late July 1973 but not signed until September 14, as a result of various disagreements.

Even then implementation, as well as the beginning of the sixty-day period for the withdrawal of foreign troops, was held up by a dispute over the size, stationing, and functioning of the Pathet Lao contingents in the two capital cities. This was reached, at least on paper, on January 7, 1974, and in early April 1974 a coalition government was installed at last. During the following months the Pathet Lao's superior organization and dynamism, its newly gained presence in the two capitals, and the incompetence of the "rightists" enabled the Pathet Lao to make rapid political progress toward control of the government. Declining health on the part of Souvanna Phouma and delays in the North Vietnamese withdrawal made the situation all the more serious.

Conflict without an Agreement in Cambodia

At the end of 1973 there was no prospect of an early agreement for the third of the troubled countries of Indochina, Cambodia. In part this was because the war had come to Cambodia relatively late. Down to the mid-1960s, its able and energetic, although temperamental, chief of state, Prince Norodom Sihanouk, was remarkably successful in providing charismatic leadership for his people and in maintaining a precarious independence and neutrality for his country by conciliating China as a counterweight to his most feared neighbor, North Vietnam, and by counting on the United States to restrain his other two dangerous neighbors, South Vietnam and Thailand.

After the mid-1960's the seemingly happy situation began to come unstuck. Sihanouk's *personalismo,* the corruption in his entourage, and the weak condition of the Cambodian economy increasingly antagonized other leading political figures, intellectuals, and students. The intensification of the war in Vietnam worsened Sihanouk's relations with the United States and made him more vulnerable to North Vietnamese pressures. In 1964 he began to allow North Vietnam to establish sanctuaries, or base areas, on Cambodian territory near the South Vietnamese border in order to support Viet Cong operations in the Mekong Delta, and to maintain a so-called Sihanouk Trail connecting southern Laos and the Delta area across Cambodia. In return, he and other leading figures, including some of those who were later to overthrow him, received a substantial subsidy from Hanoi. In addition, Sihanouk permitted Chinese ships to land military and other supplies secretly along the Cambodian coast, two-thirds of them going to the Viet Cong in the Delta and one-third to the Cambodian Army.

In 1969 the North Vietnamese began to strengthen and fortify their Cambodian sanctuaries heavily, probably in order to improve their usefulness as bases for operations in the Delta aimed at exploiting the forthcoming American withdrawal. This move evoked a secret American bombing campaign against the sanctuaries. Four years later there was to be an open disagreement between Sihanouk and the United States government as to whether he had protested against the bombing in 1969; whatever the truth of this, there is no doubt that he protested publicly and vigorously against the growing North Vietnamese violations of Cambodian neutrality, which were now too flagrant to be concealed or ignored and were becoming the targets of much Cambodian public criticism.

As a logical outgrowth of this criticism by Sihanouk and others, and perhaps on his instructions, riotous demonstrations against North Vietnam and other Communist countries began in Phnom

Penh on March 12, 1970, while the Prince was out of the country. The demonstrations escalated rapidly into racially motivated attacks on and massacres of the sizable Vietnamese community in Cambodia, most of whose members were not pro-Communist. The Cambodian government, carried away by the heady atmosphere of the moment, gave the North Vietnamese a 48-hour ultimatum to abandon the sanctuaries and withdraw from Cambodia and actually expected this order to be obeyed, which of course it was not. Sihanouk's political rivals and public critics soon took charge of the demonstrations and turned them against him. The Prince for his part hoped, but vainly, to persuade the Soviet Union and China to put pressure on the North Vietnamese to withdraw from Cambodia and in this way to score a success that would restore his rapidly eroding political position at home. He was voted out of office by a unanimous vote of the National Assembly on March 18. It is worth emphasizing that neither the United States government as a whole nor the Central Intelligence Agency in particular played any significant part in his downfall. The new Cambodian government, in which Marshal Lon Nol was the leading figure, closed its ports and coastline to further shipments of arms for the Viet Cong from China. For several weeks Peking negotiated secretly with Lon Nol, its purpose being to persuade him to allow the shipments just mentioned and the North Vietnamese sanctuaries to continue in return for diplomatic recognition and a subsidy. Whatever Lon Nol's real attitude toward this proposal was, the course of events left him no effective choice but to become an American rather than a Chinese client.

Late in March, the North Vietnamese troops in the sanctuaries began to move out from them into the interior of Cambodia, probably for one or more of several purposes: to deter further Cambodian atrocities against the Vietnamese community, to support and strengthen the Cambodian revolutionary left (the so-called Khmer Rouge), to protect and strengthen the sanctuaries for future use against the Delta, to put pressure on the Lon Nol government to leave the sanctuaries alone and reopen the coastal route, and perhaps to overthrow it. Except for the first, all these actual or possible objectives were alarming to the United States government, although any major American military intervention in Cambodia could be defended before the bar of American public opinion only on the ground that it was necessary to cope with an increased threat to the Delta that might delay the American withdrawal and endanger both American lives and the success of the Vietnamization program. This accordingly was the line that President Nixon took when he announced on April 30 that American and South Vietnamese ground units, with American air support of course, were entering Cambodia in an operation confined to the sanctuary area and to a duration of two months. In addition, President Nixon appeared to believe that a failure to act in Cambodia would undermine American "credibility," especially in the eyes of the Communist powers. This view was entirely consistent with his well-known tendency to act, or react, vigorously in situations that he regarded as crises. And indeed action had to be taken promptly before the Lon Nol government collapsed and while sufficient American troops were still in South Vietnam if it was to be taken at all.

From a strictly military point of view the operation, which was terminated on schedule, was a considerable success, and it probably contributed at least indirectly to the survival of the Lon Nol government; in 1971 President Nixon was to refer to it as the "purest example" of the Nixon Doctrine in action. On the other hand, the political costs of the operation were high. There was a loud outcry on American campuses and elsewhere, and Congress passed on June 30 the Cooper-Church Amendment prohibiting the future expenditure of government funds on American military operations in Cambodia beyond those announced on April 30 (this restriction was by no means fully observed in practice, however); the Tonkin Gulf Resolution of 1964 was repealed at the same time. There was a great deal of opposition to the Cambodian operation within the executive branch, including the State and Defense Departments. The operation jeopardized the developing Sino-American détente, at least for a time; Peking cancelled a Sino-American ambassadorial conversation scheduled for May 20, and on that date Mao Tse-tung issued a personal statement denouncing the United States with ringing revolutionary rhetoric. South Vietnamese troops took revenge on the Cambodians through looting and massacring. Lon Nol, although probably rescued by the United States and certainly dependent on it, proved almost completely incompetent and refused to share authority with a much abler rival, Sirik Matak, whom the United States preferred to him. All in all, some alternative to the course actually adopted by President Nixon might have been preferable, such as negotiating at least a conditional return of Prince Sihanouk and discouraging Phnom Penh from seeking confrontation with the North Vietnamese.

In 1970–72, North Vietnamese forces expanded their holdings rapidly in northern and eastern Cambodia and presided over the emergence for the first time of the Khmer Rouge as an effective fighting force operating under the label of FUNK (an acronym for Cambodian National United Front). In the meantime, Sihanouk, snubbed by the Russians, had taken refuge as a state guest in Peking, where he was well treated with an eye to his possible political usefulness, as early as March 1970. Much as Peking saw him as its best political handle on the Cambodian situation, so he saw as his best strategy close cooperation with the FUNK, even though its leaders had been in revolt against him until very recently. To symbolize this hoped-for cooperation, not only between Sihanouk and the FUNK but on a larger scale as well, Peking sponsored a "summit conference of the Indochinese peoples," which was held on April 24–25, 1970, apparently at Canton, and at which not only Sihanouk but representatives of the FUNK, the Pathet Lao, the National Liberation Front, and North Vietnam were present. From this conference and negotiations occurring at the same time there emerged the so-called Cambodian Royal Government of National Union (GRUNK), whose nominal leadership was Sihanouk and his entourage in Peking, but whose real strength lay with the FUNK in Cambodia itself. Peking recognized the GRUNK on May 5; Moscow maintained diplomatic relations with the Lon Nol government. As the FUNK grew in strength, direct North Vietnamese influence on it and activity in its behalf tended to decline; Sihanouk admitted that he expected the FUNK's victory to lead to a Communist Cambodia over which he would not preside. In the meantime, he did his best to maintain some semblance of influence and authority. In the spring of 1973 he claimed to have just visited FUNK-controlled territory in Cambodia. Later in the year he moved his personal headquarters to Canton, probably in order to be nearer home and to appear less obviously under Peking's influence at a time when the United Nations was considering a Chinese move to substitute his government for that of Lon Nol in the United Nations; the move was defeated. His entourage mostly moved to Cambodia and merged with the FUNK.

Nevertheless, Sihanouk's international influence tended to

grow as no settlement materialized, and as the United States became increasingly eager to have one and to get Peking to use its good offices with the FUNK, through Sihanouk, to that end. In October, the Soviet Union withdrew its diplomatic mission from Phnom Penh, although without formally breaking with the Lon Nol government or recognizing Sihanouk's. Sihanouk was adamant in his refusal to negotiate with Lon Nol, or at least for a time with the United States. He insisted on termination of American support for Lon Nol, including bombing. Lon Nol for his part refused to negotiate with Sihanouk, or to consider a settlement that would partition Cambodia.

Nevertheless, under American pressure and the impact of the Paris agreement on Vietnam, the Lon Nol government agreed early in 1973 to begin negotiations with non-Communist and non-governmental groups for a coalition government with them and for a Council of National Reconciliation. Phnom Penh conceded in principle that Communists could run in a future general election. In July, it began to propose negotiations with the FUNK itself, a cease-fire, withdrawal of all foreign troops, and "national reconciliation."

By that time Phnom Penh's position was being weakened by the prospect of reduced American support in a critical field. There were a number of congressional efforts to stop American air strikes in Cambodia, and on June 29 President Nixon felt compelled to agree to a cutoff of the bombing on August 15; until that date, it continued full blast, rather than being tapered off so as to wean the Cambodian Army away from undue dependence on it. The end of the bombing created alarm in Phnom Penh and Saigon, but it seems to have made Sihanouk more interested in negotiating with the United States. It also led the United States to increase its moral support and political advice to the Lon Nol government, whose collapse would have made nonsense of President Nixon's claim that his Cambodian intervention was a shining example of the Nixon Doctrine in action. The Kissinger visit to China of mid-November 1973 produced no visible progress toward a Cambodian settlement.

Later in the year Chinese and North Vietnamese military aid for the FUNK tapered off considerably, to the point where Sihanouk complained publicly about the trend. Peking was interested in preserving its détente with the United States and was simultaneously reducing its military aid shipments to North Vietnam. Hanoi for its part was concerned over the decline in the volume of arms it was receiving and was apparently husbanding what it had for use against its most important target, South Vietnam. The declining involvement of the external powers (apart from the United States) in the war in Cambodia did not put an end to it, however. On the contrary, it continued with great ferocity, although inconclusively. At least one discouraged foreign observer remarked that he saw no reason why it could not go on forever. The alternative possibility of some sort of agreement, if not necessarily a genuine settlement, fortunately could not be ruled out either.

CHAPTER XI

Shifting American Priorities
in Asia

SINCE the mid-1960's, American public and official opinion had grown increasingly frustrated and discontented over the various costs of being heavily involved in Southeast Asia, an involvement that in the case of Vietnam had ended in what was widely, although not necessarily correctly, regarded as a defeat. For this reason, the focus of attention of American Asian policy began to shift after 1969 from Southeast Asia to Northeast Asia, and to the Soviet Union, the People's Republic of China, and Japan as against the United States' smaller Asian allies (including the Republic of China), in spite of occasional official denials that this was the case. This important political trend, which represented in effect a reversion to the priorities of the 1950s as against those of the 1960s, was paralleled by a significant military trend that was implied in President Nixon's repeated assertion that the United States would remain a Pacific power (as contrasted with an Asian power): disengagement as soon as practicable from the continent, a thinning out of the American military presence in the offshore island chain from Japan to the Philippines, and an increased reliance on more remote bases such as Guam and various islands in the Central Pacific.

Relations with Mongolia

An interesting outgrowth of the basic American political shift toward Northeast Asia and away from such Asian allies as the Republic of China was the emergence of a relationship between the United States and the Mongolian People's Republic (Outer Mongolia). In 1961 and again in 1969, a start had been made by the Kennedy and Nixon administrations respectively at recognizing Ulan Bator, only to have it vetoed on both occasions by Chiang Kai-shek, who continued to claim Mongolia as part of China. Japan, which hoped to recognize the Mongolian People's Republic but wanted to keep in step with the United States on this question, ultimately went ahead on its own and established diplomatic relations with Ulan Bator in February 1972. Chiang's attitude was apparently the only serious obstacle to the establishment of relations between the United States and the Mongolian People's Republic, and the development of the détente between the United States and the People's Republic of China was inevitably accompanied by a downgrading of American concern for Taiwan's views.

In 1973, accordingly, the United States government began talks with the Mongolian mission to the United Nations on diplomatic recognition, cultural exchange, and an expansion of trade. Since the Mongolian People's Republic is virtually a Soviet satellite, it can be assumed that Moscow has raised no serious objection to these contacts; as a matter of fact, it is probably in the Soviet interest to see Mongolia's foreign contacts expanded (as long as the expansion does not threaten the predominant Soviet influence in the country), by way of insurance against a possible growth of Chinese influence. To be sure, the Mongolian People's Republic is tied to the Soviet Union not only by a powerful and long established Soviet presence (including about eight combat divisions as of 1972) but by its own traditional fear of the Chinese, which was intensified by the elimination of all but the semblance of autonomy in Inner Mongolia during the Cultural Revolution.

Peking formally recognizes the Mongolian People's Republic as an independent "socialist" state and officially denies any claim to its territory, but there are important reasons (including a statement by Mao Tse-tung in July 1964) for believing that Peking does consider that it has some sort of claim to Outer Mongolia, if only because it does not wish to appear less nationalist in the eyes of its own people than the Nationalists on Taiwan. Consistent with its official attitude, Peking has raised no objection to the American overtures to the Mongolian People's Republic, at least in public, presumably because of its concern for the Sino-American détente and its realization of the strain that the American overtures to Ulan Bator were placing on American relations with the Republic of China. Similarly, it is unlikely that the United States government would have begun the overtures if it had believed that doing so would have jeopardized the Sino-American détente.

Military Redeployments

Shifting American political priorities in the Far East, as well as congressional pressures for economy, have been reflected in significant strategic redeployments. A central feature of this process was the reversion to Japanese civil jurisdiction of Okinawa (in the Ryukyus), which since 1945 had contained what was probably the most important base complex to be found anywhere in the Far East. Although the Japanese government was eager for political reasons to regain jurisdiction over the island and was prepared in return to allow American bases to continue to exist there, it was clear that "reversion" would initiate a degradation of the island's military utility to the United States by bringing it under the same restrictions imposed by regard for Japanese public opinion and the use of American bases in Japan itself—notably a prohibition on the storage of nuclear weapons and on the development of American forces designed to fight from these bases except in defense of Japan itself without prior consultation with the Japanese government. In spite of some opposition in the United States motivated by concern over the future of the bases and over the economic issues between the United States and Japan, a treaty providing for "reversion" and containing restrictions on the use of the bases along the lines indicated was signed in June 1971 and approved by the Senate the following November.

On the basis of an agreement reached by President Nixon and Premier Sato in January 1972, "reversion" went into effect on May 15 of that year. The Japanese Self Defense Forces assumed responsibility for Okinawa's security, and the decline of the island's utility as a combat base, which had begun when Japanese public opinion and political pressure had compelled the termination of bombing missions from Okinawa against Vietnam, continued. It seemed likely that all American bases in Okinawa would be closed down within a few years, from a combination of Japanese political pressures and congressional demands for economy. Major American bases continued to function in Japan proper, however; Yokosuka, for example, became the "home port" of the Seventh Fleet, compared to Athens for the Sixth Fleet.

Apart from Guam, which is rather remote from the Asian mainland (about 2,000 miles), the main alternative to Okinawa as a site for American air bases was Thailand. By agreement with the Thai government, which was afraid of being attacked by China or North Vietnam, or both, but which was also independent-minded enough to insist on retaining full jurisdiction over the bases, American combat aircraft began to operate over Vietnam from bases in Thailand in 1965. Early in 1967 B-52's began to be based in Thailand, which then became the major base area for American air operations in Vietnam. The American disengagement from Vietnam after 1969, and still more the Paris agreement of January 1973, raised obvious questions about the future of the Thai bases, although there was clearly a case in favor of retaining them to help deter a reversion by Hanoi to major offensive operations. As time went on, however, President Nixon's political difficulties and congressional objections to and restrictions on the rise of American military power in Indochina made the Thai bases seem less usable, and Hanoi's avoidance of major offensives made them seem less necessary. Accordingly in late 1973 some American personnel and aircraft were withdrawn from Thailand, although it was not clear how many months or years would pass before they were all gone.

An important negative decision was made in connection with the reversion of Okinawa: not to establish a major American base complex on Taiwan or store nuclear weapons there. The Republic of China would probably have been glad to see this happen, since the result would have been an increase in the sense of American commitment to it. The opposite decision was taken, apparently in 1971 and evidently to avoid strengthening the commitment and endangering the developing American détente with Peking. Furthermore, late in 1973 some of the 8,000 American military personnel on Taiwan, most of whom had been involved in logistical support for American operations in Vietnam, were withdrawn, both on account of the virtual termination of those operations and as a concession to Peking along the lines indicated in the Shanghai Communiqué of February 1972.

The basic American objective regarding disengagement from South Korea had been fixed in 1970 as withdrawal by 1975. Some 20,000 men were moved out fairly promptly, but the future of the remaining 42,000 was left rather unclear. This was partly because of congressional failure to vote the full funds necessary for the modernization of the South Korean armed forces, on which the American withdrawal was theoretically contingent, but also apparently because of the Chinese attitude. Peking was not eager to see further American military withdrawal from the region, except presumably for Taiwan, because it might lead to intrusions of Soviet influence or unilateral Japanese rearmament.

The proclamation of martial law by President Ferdinand Marcos of the Philippines put an end to most local pressures for the removal of the American military presence. The United States was accordingly able to adhere to its plan for retaining major air and naval bases in the islands, subject of course to possible budgetary restrictions.

Effects of the Nixon Doctrine

The shift of American priorities, and above all the Nixon Doctrine with its twin pillars of military disengagement and détente with China, inevitably exerted a profound effect on the United States' allies and alliances in Asia. On the whole the effect was adverse, since the United States in effect was giving a greater priority to cutting its own liability and to improving its relations with their Communist adversaries than to their security. The Republic of China felt especially strongly on this score, in view of the Nixon administration's heavy emphasis on improving its relations with Peking. The cycle of American overcommitment in the mid- and late 1960s, followed by rather rapid withdrawal in the early 1970s, tended to undermine confidence in the good sense and reliability of the United States. No one in the region believed any longer that he could count confidently on the United States for anything, at any rate beyond the end of the current fiscal year. Military disengagement tended to weaken the American ability to influence the course of events not only in military but in other matters.

Since the United States seemed less interested in the survival of its allies, it could hardly hope to exert much influence on their political development, and local elites need no longer pretend to take its views on such matters seriously. The recent antidemocratic trends in South Korea, the Philippines, and Thailand (prior to the revolution of October 1973, at any rate) appear to reflect at least in part this decline of American influence.

In the special and obviously important case of Japan, the Nixon administration worked itself up into a furor over what it took to be continuing Japanese slowness in helping to level the balance of payments between the two countries, although in fact Japan moved faster than the European Economic Community (the Common Market) in lowering tariffs on American goods and restrictions on American investment. Japanese were staggered to read, in President Nixon's "State of the World" message released in May 1973, what looked like a threat to break off the security treaty: "Without conscious effort of political will, our economic disputes could tear the fabric of our alliance." The recurrent tendency of the Nixon administration to slap the Japanese government, although perhaps understandable in the light of Japan's unpopularity with the American business community, fitted badly with repeated official American requests that Japan play a more active role in the maintenance of Asian security and stability, although without necessarily rearming much beyond the fairly modest levels envisaged in Tokyo's planning.

The 1971 Crisis in South Asia

The "Nixon shocks" to Japanese-American relations were not the only major negative monument erected by American Asian policy in 1971. Another was the American "tilt" (in Kissinger's famous phrase) toward Pakistan in the Indo-Pakistani conflict of 1971 arising out of the secession of East Pakistan (now Bangla Desh) and India's support for that step.

During this crisis, which lasted from March 1971 until approximately the end of the year, the United States made a number of ineffective efforts at mediation, suspended new commitments of economic and military aid to Pakistan in the spring of 1971 while allowing items already in the "pipeline" to continue moving, and provided some relief aid for the ten million refugees who had fled from Bangla Desh into India. Nevertheless, American policy during the crisis was clearly pro-Pakistani and was so perceived by everyone. The impetus for this policy seems to have come strongly from President Nixon himself, not from Kissinger; at a meeting of the Washington Special Action Group (WASAG, formed in 1969 to deal with crises) on December 3, 1971, minutes of which were later leaked to columnist Jack Anderson, Kissinger said that "I am getting hell every half-hour from the President that we are not being tough enough on India." As the Indo-Pakistani fighting moved to an end, the United States sent the nuclear aircraft carrier *Enterprise* into the Bay of Bengal, presumably in a show of strength, but one that in reality was more of a futile gesture.

The official explanation, given both publicly and in off-the-record briefings, for the American "tilt" in favor of Pakistan was that India had started the war by attacking West (and later East) Pakistan, and that support for Pakistan was necessary in the higher interest of Sino-American détente. Both of these arguments are dubious to say the least. The circumstances surrounding the initiation of the Indo-Pakistani hostilities are not very clear, but there is considerable evidence (including the documents leaked to Jack Anderson) that it was the Pakistani who began the fighting in the west, by attacking Indian airfields. It is true that President Mohammed Yahya Khan of Pakistan played the role of a secret intermediary between the United States and the People's Republic of China, that Kissinger took off from Pakistan on his first visit to Peking (July 9–11, 1971), and that the Chinese regarded the Pakistani as allies and "tilted" in their favor, to the limited extent possible, during the crisis. But there is no sufficient reason to believe that the Sino-American détente, which as has been shown was motivated by other considerations more important to both sides, hinged on American support for Pakistan during the 1971 crisis; it does not appear that the latter was a major subject of discussion during either the Kissinger or the Nixon visit.

The real American motives, those of the President in particular, seem to have been more complex and more devious. He and Kissinger both disliked Mrs. Gandhi, who visited the United States in November 1971, and regarded her as untrustworthy and pro-Soviet. The Soviet Union, an object of greater presidential distrust then than later, was clearly pro-Indian and indeed signed a treaty of friendship with New Delhi on August 9, 1971. The President's famous crisis mentality, and his concern for American "credibility" if Pakistan, an ally of sorts, were allowed to go under, were undoubtedly important factors. Last and perhaps most important, the President being above all a domestic politician in his reflexes (not necessarily in his actual priorities), there were matters of American politics. There was a loud outcry of congressional support for India and sympathy for the refugees; it was led by Senator Edward Kennedy, whom the President probably regarded as a potential opponent in the 1972 elections. A plausible reason for American support for Yahya was the fact that his most likely alternative or successor was Zulfikar Ali Bhutto, who was distrusted by many in Washington as leftist and unstable and who in 1950, during a controversial election campaign in which Mr. Nixon was involved, had been a campaign worker while a student at the University of California for his opponent, Helen Gahagan Douglas; later, after becoming President of Pakistan, Bhutto was to apologize for this youthful indiscretion.

After the predictable Indian victory over Pakistan, a Soviet official remarked unkindly but correctly that this had been the first occasion in history on which the United States and the People's Republic of China had been on the same side and lost together. American policy had had very little effect on the actual outcome of the crisis. The United States was discredited, at least to a degree, by its association with an ally who was not only a loser, but a vicious one. Indo-American relations, never very warm at the official level, sank to the lowest point ever reached. The United States had to accommodate itself as best it could to undeniable Indian preeminence in South Asia, for example by recognizing Bangla Desh and by trying unsuccessfully to persuade Peking not to veto its application for admission to the United Nations (in August 1972). The only consolation was a negative one: India was less important to American interests than was Japan, which was the other main victim of American official anger in 1971.

The Indian Ocean

The United States' poor relations with India were a serious problem, however, when viewed in a wider context, that of the growing American interest in the Indian Ocean. That body of water, which had been a British lake for generations and which washes the territory of none of the major powers, was the object of little strategic interest on the part of other powers until the British withdrawal from "east of Suez" began in the 1960s, a critical factor in the withdrawal being the nationalization of the Suez Canal by Egypt in 1956 and its closure as a result of the June War of 1967. The traditional Russian interest in "warm water" ports on the Indian Ocean is largely a myth, and in 1940 Stalin resisted efforts by his difficult German allies to interest him in expanding his influence in that direction rather than into the Balkans. The economic and strategic importance of the vast oil deposits around and under the Persian Gulf is so great, however, that a British announcement of impending withdrawal at the beginning of 1968 was soon followed by the appearance of a small Soviet naval presence in the Indian Ocean, one that has grown with the passage of time to a level on the order of twenty ships.

The United States understandably felt an interest in not allowing the Soviet Union to inherit the former British naval, let alone political, predominance in the region, and in being in a position to protect Japan's sea routes to the Middle East. Accordingly, ships of the Seventh Fleet began to sail westward into the Indian Ocean on occasion to establish an American presence. In addition, American nuclear submarines began to cruise the Indian Ocean, from which they could cover targets in parts of the Soviet Union and China. Apart from the submarines, the American naval presence remained smaller than the Soviet; its growth was delayed by the war in Vietnam. Both rivals were hampered by the lack of naval bases in and around the Indian Ocean. The problem was intrinsically a more difficult one for the Soviet Union, given the "short-legged" characteristics of Soviet naval vessels and the longer distances they had to travel, but American superiority in the capability of refueling at sea was somewhat counterbalanced by Soviet refueling rights in India and at various Arab and African ports. The United States is negotiating for base rights on Diego Garcia, a small British-controlled island in the central Indian Ocean.

The reopening of the Suez Canal, which at the beginning of 1974 appeared likely, would benefit the Soviet Union, both because its lines of communication from the Black Sea would be greatly shortened and because the larger ships used by the United States Navy cannot pass through the Suez Canal at its current depth. The People's Republic of China has been in no position to maintain a naval presence in the Indian Ocean but feels a keen interest in the region and attempts to maintain good relations with as many as possible of the coastal states, except for India (for the time being) and South Africa. Japan has no naval presence in the Indian Ocean and little political influence, but it has a vast economic interest because most of its oil imports originate in the Persian Gulf area. On the whole, the Indian Ocean, including the Persian Gulf, seems likely to be an area of increasing importance and interest, and one where the United States will probably have to increase its overall level of effort considerably if it is not to be seriously outstripped by the Soviet Union.

CHAPTER XII

The Trend toward
Soviet-American Détente

ASIA is by no means at the top of the list of common concerns to the United States and the Soviet Union. This has been true at any rate since the Korean War, from which the Soviet Union learned that it is not wise to challenge American interests in Asia by force as long as the United States remains a significant military power in the region and in the Western Pacific. Accordingly, Asian affairs do not figure prominently in this chapter, which concerns itself more with such matters as the basic attitudes of the two elites on general East-West relations, the strategic arms race, Europe, and the Middle East. On the other hand, the overall state of relations between the United States and the Soviet Union at any given time permeates virtually all aspects of the foreign policies of the two superpowers, including their Asian policies.

The Nixonian View of the Soviet Union

President Nixon's anti-Communist and anti-Soviet views during the years before 1968 are well known, and there are strong reasons for believing that he carried them with him, to a considerable extent at any rate, into the White House. He had no intention of being "pushed around" by the Communist powers, and still less of appearing in this light in the eyes of the American public, given the political harm suffered by the Truman administration on account of the widespread suspicion that it had been "soft" on Communism in China and Korea. President Nixon was certainly concerned over the Soviet Union's growing military might, its occasional assertiveness in Europe and the Middle East, and its aid to North Vietnam.

On the other hand, he was aware that by 1968 anti-Communism no longer had the popular appeal in the United States that it had possessed a decade or two earlier. There were several reasons for this trend, including the social trends discussed briefly in the preceding chapter and the obvious fact that the United States had not been involved in a war with one of the major Communist powers since 1953; the war in Vietnam, by its duration and inconclusiveness, had generated great weariness and frustration and a feeling of "never again." Increasing numbers of intellectuals and politicians proclaimed that the Cold War was "over." Since much, although probably not all, of President Nixon's earlier anti-Communism had been motivated by political expediency, he began to turn away from public anti-Communism as it ceased to be popular. In his 1968 campaign, he stressed his desire to improve relations with the Soviet Union, as well as to bring peace in Vietnam. Furthermore, he realized that the Soviet Union had attained approximate parity with the United States in strategic weapons and was too strong to be "pushed around."

President Nixon's idea was to proceed toward a détente with the Soviet Union on a broad front, rather than to have a "selective détente" (as he and Kissinger called it) under which Moscow could be difficult on some questions while enjoying the benefits of détente with respect to others. In other words, there was to be a "linkage" among all the major issues, so that in order to get what it wanted in such fields as trade the Soviet Union would have to be reasonable on such others as strategic arms, Vietnam, and the Middle East. As he indicated to the correspondent Howard K. Smith in an interview on July 1, 1970, he saw the Sino-Soviet dispute as a force to render Moscow more manageable from the American point of view, and improved Sino-American relations as an important means to the same end. He was in no particular hurry to move toward détente with the Soviet Union, partly because he wanted to approach China first, and partly because he was determined not to begin SALT talks under conditions that would inhibit the United States' freedom to develop an ABM system and MIRVs.

Moscow's Shift from Assertiveness to Détente

During the lifetime of the Johnson administration, the Soviet leadership tended to view the United States as being generally on the offensive and itself on the defensive, particularly with respect to Vietnam and the Third World in general. In Europe, the United States seemed to be beginning a military withdrawal on account of domestic (especially congressional) pressures, but this superficially favorable development (from the Soviet point of view) was more than counterbalanced by the prospect of greater freedom of action for West Germany, which was already embarked on a dynamic *Ostpolitik* designed among other things to weaken East Germany's ties with its East European neighbors. To counter this Moscow began in 1967 to propose a vaguely defined arrangement for "European security," whose main purposes presumably were to stabilize East Germany's position (its separateness from West Germany in particular) and substitute Soviet for American influence in the continent as a whole.

From this phase of defensive uncertainty the Soviet Union moved suddenly but briefly in 1968 into one of self-confidence and assertiveness. Its attainment of strategic parity with the United States at about that time was probably the major cause of this shift, which was more or less global in scope. One of its manifestations was that the Soviet military began for the first time to talk as though a major conventional war in Europe, one in which each side would be deterred from using nuclear weapons and Soviet conventional superiority would therefore prevail, was a realistic possibility from the purely military point of view. Soviet consciousness of parity helped to increase Moscow's interest in beginning the SALT talks, which accordingly started in November 1969. Another manifestation, as well as a source of considerable additional assertiveness, was the invasion of Czechoslovakia, which was designed to squash the liberal, reformist tendencies then operating in that unhappy country, prevent their emergence in other Communist countries (including the Soviet Union itself), and establish Soviet psychological ascendancy in Europe generally and over West Germany in particular. These aims were achieved; the West

German Social Democratic government under Willy Brandt, which came into office in 1969, eliminated the anti-East German thrust of the *Ostpolitik,* accepted the territorial losses suffered in 1945, and signed a treaty to that effect with the Soviet Union in August 1970. In the Middle East, Soviet assertiveness during this period took the form of very active support, with equipment and in other ways, for Egyptian military pressures on Israel (in the Sinai area) and for Syrian military pressures on Jordan.

During the second half of 1970, the self-confidence of the previous two years began to be replaced by a consciousness of problems and setbacks. The Soviet economy was limping, partly on account of the successful effort to achieve strategic parity; Moscow's interest in a successful outcome of the SALT negotiations and increased trade and technological contact with the Western countries and Japan accordingly grew greater. The West German Bundestag withheld ratification of the August 1970 treaty until May 1972. The United States gave strong support in 1970 to Israel and Jordan against Egypt and Syria, respectively. The Soviet relationship with Egypt was weakened by the death of President Nasser shortly afterward. The fairly rapid American disengagement from Vietnam gave the United States increased maneuverability to cope with Soviet challenges; in the autumn of 1970, the United States compelled Moscow to abandon what was apparently a plan to establish a nuclear submarine base in Cuba. Closer to home, serious unrest among Polish workers brought about a change in the top leadership in December 1970 and reminded the Kremlin that its own immunity from such disturbances could not be taken for granted indefinitely.

But most important of all was probably the appearance of signs, such as the visit of President Ceausescu of Romania to the United States in October 1970 with a message from Peking, that a détente between China and the United States was in the making. To Moscow's way of thinking, its interests could not help being adversely, and seriously, affected by any sort of "collusion" between the strongest and the bitterest of its adversaries. It was essential to do something to minimize the development of this relationship. In January 1971 secret contacts began between Brezhnev and Nixon with the aim of getting momentum into the SALT negotiations, which were then deadlocked. Probably without much hope of success, Brezhnev made a secret offer to Peking of a nonaggression pact in February 1971 but was rebuffed. At the end of March, in his report to the Twenty-Fourth Soviet Party Congress, he indicated an interest in improved relations with the United States, even though he loaded his remarks—perhaps out of conviction, perhaps for effect on Communist fundamentalists and abroad, perhaps for both reasons—with the usual denunciations of "imperialism." In spite of the importance that Moscow evidently intended to be attached to his remarks, they had no obvious immediate effect, unless one so interprets the fact that Peking proceeded to accelerate its movement toward détente with the United States, a trend that the United States was happy to reciprocate.

The converse was also true: The greater the progress toward Sino-American détente, the better the outlook for significant improvement in Soviet-American relations. It would be hard to interpret in any other way the fact that the announcement on October 5, 1971 that Kissinger would visit Peking for a second time before the end of the month—an announcement that eliminated any reasonable doubt that President Nixon would go to China as scheduled—was followed a week later by a statement that the President would also visit the Soviet Union in late May 1972. He denied of course that he was trying to exploit the differences between the two Communist powers, but the fact remained that those differences made it virtually impossible for either of the adversaries to be willingly left as odd man out while the other improved its relations with the United States. In the Soviet case, the imperative was all the stronger because a sharp turn for the worse in Soviet-American relations would jeopardize the pending ratification of the Soviet treaty with West Germany, which at that time was the keystone of Moscow's European policy.

Accordingly, Moscow gritted its teeth in comparative silence during the Peking summit and the American bombing of North Vietnam in retaliation for Hanoi's Easter offensive. It did not follow, however, that the Soviet leadership was prepared to accept the Nixon administration's views on "linkage," or in other words to cease all activities that the United States regarded as troublemaking. When Kissinger visited Moscow on April 20–24, 1972 to prepare for the summit, he met with a refusal to stop the flow of arms to Hanoi, although the Soviet leadership claimed to be unhappy about the Easter offensive and not merely about the American bombing. On the other hand, the Soviet side made a concession regarding the SALT negotiations, by agreeing at last that Submarine Launched Ballistic Missiles (SLBMs) should be counted as strategic weapons and should therefore be subject to limitation.

Nixon was afraid, however, that American public acceptance of the SALT treaty that he hoped to sign while in Moscow would be jeopardized unless the Soviet Union were more helpful on Vietnam. It was to a large extent in order to promote such helpfulness, as well as to gain general leverage that might be useful at the summit through a display of resolution, that on May 8 he ordered the mining of Haiphong harbor, a step that the Johnson administration had flinched from taking because of the Soviet shipping and supplies that passed through the port. The shock in Moscow was real, but not great enough to produce behavior likely to threaten the holding of the summit or the ratification of the treaty by the West German Bundestag (parliament). One member of the Politburo, Pyotr Shelest, who advocated cancelling or at least postponing the summit, and had had serious differences with Brezhnev on other grounds, was outvoted and purged.

The Moscow Summit and SALT I

The most conspicuous, and probably also the most important, achievement of the Moscow Summit (May 22–28, 1972) was the completion and signing of the two agreements worked out in part during the first round of the Strategic Arms Limitation Talks (SALT I). The talks and the agreements flowed from a considerable background of Soviet-American interaction since the Second World War in the field of arms control and disarmament, which it may be useful to summarize.

Probably the most important feature of the various American proposals on arms control and disarmament since the war has been their insistence that any agreement must be capable of verification as to compliance. For about two decades, verification required the ability to inspect the territory of each signatory, something that the security mania of the Soviet leadership would not permit. Moscow insisted on its sovereignty and made mostly propagandistic proposals for unverifiable measures, such as Khrushchev's advocacy in 1959 of "general and complete disarmament." The only important agreement on arms control and disarmament reached during this period was the limited nuclear test ban treaty of 1963, which was made possible by the alarm created by the Cuban missile crisis and which applied only to media where testing was fairly readily detectable (the atmosphere and underwater, not underground). In the absence of more comprehensive agreements, the Soviet Union maintained a blackmail capability against Western Europe through conventional forces and MRBMs and built up its strategic forces. The United States maintained strategic superiority (until the late 1960s) and did its best to foster Western European unity in the face of actual and possible Soviet threats, for example by taking the important step of admitting West Germany to NATO in 1955. With the rapid development of "overhead reconnaissance" (reconnaissance satellites), however, the issue of on-site inspection, which the Soviet Union still opposed, became less important. Since the late 1960s, accordingly, the United States and the Soviet Union have concluded or adhered to agreements banning the deployment of nuclear weapons in space and on the seabed, the transfer of nuclear weapons to currently nonnuclear states (the Nonproliferation Treaty), and the use of chemical weapons. Moscow continues to make disarmament proposals, for example, for a general nuclear summit conference and a cut in all defense budgets, that the United States regards as unhelpful and propagandistic.

Soviet willingness to engage in talks on possible agreements more substantial than the ones just mentioned—in the sense that they might actually limit the existing race in major offensive weapons systems—began to make itself known in 1968, for several probable reasons. Moscow would no longer have to negotiate from a position of strategic inferiority, since it had attained approximate parity in this field with the United States; it was rapidly passing the United States in the number of ICBMs, as it had done earlier in the megatonnage of its warheads and the thrust of (and hence the "throw-weight" deliverable by) its missiles, and it had an apparently not-very-effective antiballistic missile system around Moscow. On the other hand, the United States was making or about to make important technical advances; it was starting a "thin" (supposedly anti-Chinese) antiballistic missile system that could be upgraded into a "thick" (anti-Soviet) system in order to protect its land-based ICBMs, it was qualitatively ahead in SLBMs and antisubmarine warfare, and above all, it was beginning to develop

MIRVs (multiple warheads, mainly for the Minuteman III ICBM), in addition to retaining its marked advantage in bombers and overseas bases, but it was not increasing the numbers of its ICBMs (1,054) and SLBMs (656).

The possibility that SALT talks might begin in 1968 was eliminated by the atmosphere resulting from the invasion of Czechoslovakia. The situation in 1969 was complicated, among other things, by the Sino-Soviet border crisis, which not only placed some strains on Soviet-American relations but put Moscow in a bad light in the eyes of a number of Communist Parties. Accordingly, it was only after the beginning of the Sino-Soviet border talks that the SALT negotiations finally began (in November 1969). They promptly witnessed a major difference which has not yet been resolved, over the definition of a strategic weapon. The Soviet side wanted so to describe, and to bring within the scope of SALT, any weapon capable of hitting the territory of the other party; this criterion would cover many of the United States' bases overseas, but not the Soviet MRBMs targeted on Western Europe. The American side successfully resisted this argument as well as the Soviet claim for compensation in the form of a higher ceiling on Soviet ICBMs, SLBMs, and bombers; accordingly, both the American forward bases and the Soviet MRBM force were excluded from SALT I. As the result of differences over what kind of controls on MIRV would be best and military objections on both sides to restrictions on research and development, it was decided to seek no qualitative limitations on offensive weapons during SALT I, so that both sides were free to proceed with the development of MIRV and other technical innovations. The Soviet side attained its goal of including antiballistic missiles in SALT I, but abandoned (at the time of Kissinger's April 19, 1972 visit to Moscow) its insistence that SLBMs be excluded.

By the time President Nixon came to Moscow, the two sides had come very close to reaching agreement on both antiballistic missiles and offensive weapons (subject to the exclusions already mentioned). But a few remaining disagreements had to be dealt with at the highest level, notably one over the numbers (actual or estimated) that were to be accepted in each offensive category as indicating the size of the current inventories and that therefore were to serve as the basis for the permissible ceilings. The disagreements were resolved hastily in time for agreements on antiballistic missiles and offensive missiles to be signed on May 26, during the Moscow summit. The first of these, which was a formal treaty, limited each party to two antiballistic missile "deployment areas" of not more than 100 missiles each, one to protect the capital area and the other to protect its main ICBM force. The other was an interim five-year agreement covering (land-based) ICBMs and SLBMs. In principle, the maximum numbers in both categories were fixed at the level of existing missile launchers plus (in the case of the Soviet Union) missile launchers actually or allegedly under construction. These figures were 1,054 ICBMs and 656 SLBMs (on 41 submarines) for the United States, and 1,618 ICBMs and 740 SLBMs (on 56 submarines) for the Soviet Union. Within these quantitative limits, qualitative changes such as the deployment of MIRV were permitted, with two main qualifications: no additional "heavy" ICBMs such as the Soviet SS-9 could be deployed, even as substitutes for older "light" ICBMs; and no ICBMs could be substituted for SLBMs, although the reverse substitution was permitted on a one-for-one basis, up to a limit of 54 (and a grand total of 44 submarines) for the United States and 210 (and a grand total of 62 submarines) for the Soviet Union. The reason for the latter restriction was that SLBMs were regarded as more nearly invulnerable to pre-emptive attack than land-based ICBMs, and hence less destabilizing; in other words, given the comparative pointlessness of such an attack on the other side's SLBM force, there would be little incentive to launch one.

It is obvious that the agreement conceded a considerable numerical superiority in ICBMs and SLBMs to the Soviet Union, a superiority enhanced to an indeterminate degree by Soviet superiority in the "throw-weight" of its missiles and the megatonnage of its warheads. On the other hand, the Nixon administration argued, with much plausibility, that these advantages were at least offset by American technical advantages (in the MIRV program, in antiballistic missiles, in SLBMs, and in antisubmarine warfare), by the greater size of the American strategic bomber force (450 as compared to 100, approximately), and by the vastly superior American network of overseas bases; furthermore, it was argued that without the agreement the Soviet quantitative edge in ICBMs and SLBMs would have grown even greater. On the whole, these arguments appear to have enough validity so that there is no convincing basis for any other verdict than that effective parity still exists between the two sides, in the sense that the strategic forces of either could survive a first strike by the other to a sufficient degree to launch an "unacceptable" retaliatory strike.

The other public agreements that emerged from the Moscow summit were largely agreements in principle to cooperate in such fields as trade expansion, space exploration, and environmental protection. The joint communiqué contained passages welcoming the trend toward détente in Europe and expressing hope for peace in the Middle East and Indochina (in the latter case, there were differences reflecting the Soviet commitment to Hanoi). In addition, the two sides endorsed a set of "Basic Principles of Relations" stressing avoidance of war, "peaceful coexistence," further efforts toward disarmament, and continuing high level contacts, and insisting that "the development of United States-Soviet relations is not directed against third countries and their interests."

Although the Moscow summit lacked many of the flamboyant atmospherics of its predecessor in Peking, it too was obviously intended by President Nixon to make a major impact on American opinion and promote his prospects for re-election. On the Soviet side, there were strong expressions of anti-Chinese feeling in the course of the negotiations, combined with an unwillingness to make commitments adverse to Hanoi; nevertheless, it appears that the Soviet Union like China began to reduce its arms shipments to North Vietnam after mid-1972, so that some sort of tacit understanding to that effect may have been reached at the Moscow summit. In the case of the Middle East, where Soviet prestige was less heavily engaged inasmuch as none of its local partners was a Communist state, the Soviet side appears to have promised not only to prevent its military personnel then in Egypt from engaging in combat against Israel but to withdraw most of them (this was done in July 1972 under the guise of a face-saving request for withdrawal from President Anwar Sadat) and to try to discourage the Arab states from attacking Israel. The main single cause of the comparative Soviet reasonableness at the Moscow summit, apart from the overriding one of not wanting to be the odd man out facing a Sino-American détente, was probably economic: the Soviet economy, badly strained by the missile build-up and by a poor 1972 harvest, was lagging behind the West in many sectors and was in serious need of expanded trade and credits if it was to catch up.

The Second Nixon-Brezhnev Summit

During the first year after the Moscow summit, Soviet-American relations developed to the reasonable satisfaction of both parties, with certain exceptions to be noted later. On the Soviet side, there was a powerful incentive for maintaining the relationship in flourishing condition, in that Sino-American relations continued to improve. It is probably not a coincidence that the announcement in February 1973 that the United States and the People's Republic of China would exchange liaison offices (embassies in everything but name) was followed in March by indications that Brezhnev would visit the United States in June. In spite of various difficulties that delayed agreement on a date for the visit, it took place on June 18-25, 1973.

On President Nixon's side, interest in holding a second summit was at least as great as his interest in holding the Moscow summit had been; if 1972 was an election year, 1973 was the year when the Watergate controversy assumed major proportions, and the President was obviously eager for diplomatic successes, or apparent successes, that would confirm his self-image as a great statesman and help to distract the American public from the operations of his "plumbers" and other subordinates and friends. Prior to the Brezhnev visit, various United States government agencies were cajoled by the White House to think of additional agreements on Soviet-American cooperation that could be signed during the Brezhnev visit and perhaps help to create the desired effect. On the Soviet side, there was a continuing interest in not being outpaced by Peking and in expanding trade and getting credits; it is probable that Brezhnev wanted to impress as strongly as possible on official American thinking the pleasantness and advantages of détente with the Soviet Union, so as to minimize the adverse consequences for the overall Soviet-American relationship of a major Soviet initiative in the Middle East that appears to have been already in the planning stage.

This being the case, the second Nixon-Brezhnev summit inevitably consisted for the most part of atmospherics. A number of politically meaningless agreements were concluded on cooperation in such fields as trade, oceanography, and the prevention of nuclear war. More significantly, it was agreed that at the second round of SALT talks (SALT II) every effort should be made to reach a permanent agreement including qualitative as well as quantitative limits on offensive weapons in 1974.

East-West Relations: The View from Washington

It is not very difficult to identify the forces in the United States that can be described, at the cost of some oversimplification, as for and against détente with the Soviet Union.

Liberals and radicals, especially academics and other intellectuals, generally favored détente during most of the 1960s, although they were somewhat put off by the bureaucratic quality of the Soviet system. They were increasingly alienated, however, by the invasion of Czechoslovakia, and above all by the anti-Israel thrust of Soviet Middle Eastern policy and by the official repression of Soviet Jews and dissenters. By the early 1970s the liberal and radical wings of American opinion, except for actual Communists and some of the youth, were in favor of extracting a price from Moscow for détente, in the shape of concessions tending to modify the Soviet posture on the issues just mentioned.

The most powerful force behind détente with the Soviet Union in the 1970s has been not the intellectuals but the United States government. The reasons for its enthusiasm for détente are touched on elsewhere but may usefully be summarized here. They appear to be: a desire to avoid, via arms control agreements, the necessity of matching the Soviet strategic weapons build-up; a desire to moderate Soviet Middle Eastern policy, partly with an eye to pro-Israeli feeling in the United States; a desire to capitalize on the Soviet desire for trade and credits to the advantage of the American business community, of whose interests the Nixon administration is of course solicitous in the extreme; a desire to enhance the Nixon administration's image (and above all self-image) as a uniquely creative and statesmanlike innovator in the field of foreign policy, to the advantage of its domestic political standing and by way of distraction from its actual or alleged involvement in illegal activities; a desire for help, or at any rate understanding, in achieving at least the semblance of an Indochina settlement; and a desire to insure against a possible renewal of Soviet trouble-making in Europe.

All this makes a formidable list of reasons, but the administration with its characteristic lack of frankness seldom presented them in this way to the American public. Instead, détente was presented as necessitated by the urgency of avoiding a nuclear war, an argument that is self-evidently true but not highly relevant, inasmuch as both sides have been completely determined for years to avoid such a war and the measures adopted by the Nixon administration in the name of détente have gone far beyond what could reasonably be considered necessary merely for the purpose of avoiding a nuclear war. Nevertheless, the equation between détente and peace can easily be made to appear plausible, and the latter is a theme with an understandably powerful appeal to Western (and other) opinion; when President Nixon delivered his State of the Union address to Congress in January 1974, the theme that evoked the loudest applause was his references to his efforts to achieve peace. It is also a theme that Soviet propaganda has found very effective as a means of playing on Western feelings, through emphasis on the alleged devotion of the Soviet Union to peace (in plain English; getting what it wants without war). The well-known Soviet tendency to seek, or at least proclaim, détente in areas where it might be dangerous to do otherwise, while seeking every possible advantage in other areas, was minimized by the Nixon administration, in its public comments on East-West relations, with the bland statement that "selective détente" would not be tolerated. Unfortunately for this theory, the Soviet Union's highly assertive recent Middle Eastern policy (which is discussed in greater detail below) and the insult to the spirit of détente represented by the expulsion of the Soviet Union's most eminent writer, Alexander Solzhenitsyn, went unpunished by the Nixon administration.

Next to the administration, the main lobby in favor of détente is the American business community. The reasons for its enthusiasm, which are too obvious to need much elaboration, include such windfalls as the "great grain robbery" (Senator Jackson's phrase) of 1972, in which grain dealers close to the administration made a handsome profit. Under one of the agreements signed during Brezhnev's visit in the United States in 1973, ten of the leading "monopoly capitalist" firms in the United States were allowed, and in fact encouraged, to establish offices in Moscow. To them, obviously, détente has no political meaning; it means only profits.

The most important counterpressures came not so much from various private groups such as the Jewish community, for which the administration had little regard, as from an influential collection of "hawks" in Washington. Some of these were connected with the Pentagon and included former Secretary of Defense Melvin Laird, as well as his successor James Schlesinger. They tended to favor more of an effort to match the Soviet strategic build-up, quantitatively as well as qualitatively, and to have serious reservations about SALT I. The views of this group overlapped to a high degree those of the man who had become the most articulate and influential spokesman of the entire anti-détente coalition, Senator Henry M. Jackson of Washington. Senator Jackson remained profoundly suspicious of Soviet intentions and was far more attuned to the imperatives of containment than to the desirability of détente. He insisted that future SALT agreements must embody the principle of numerical equality; through his influence the American delegation to the SALT talks and the leadership of the Arms Control and Disarmament Agency were extensively purged. Jackson, among others, insisted successfully on the development of the new Trident nuclear submarine.

Unfortunately, Jackson has become unduly preoccupied with numbers, which are not the essence of the problem, at least as long as the United States retains an assured retaliatory capability against the Soviet Union. The problem rather is one of political intelligence and determination, and continuity of policy, in all of which it can be argued that the Soviet Union is superior or at any rate capable of achieving and maintaining superiority. Jackson has taken a political interest in the fate of the Soviet Jews and a humanitarian interest in the fate of Soviet dissenters. He has been instrumental, via the Jackson Amendment, in blocking most-favored-nation treatment for the Soviet Union—with the result that Soviet goods have had to pay higher import duties in the United States than goods from many other countries—as long as it restricts Jewish emigration. In 1973, obviously in an effort to meet this condition without unduly antagonizing the Arab countries, the Soviet Union relaxed its restrictions on Jewish emigration somewhat. Most-favored-nation status still eluded Moscow, however, on account of the reverberations on Capitol Hill caused by Soviet involvement in the Middle Eastern war of late 1973, which were greater than those created (publicly at least) at the White House.

The argument between the pro- and anti-détente schools continues unresolved. The former has an obvious intrinsic advantage in that the administration is still committed to détente.

East-West Relations: The View from Moscow

Soviet elite opinion on the subject of détente appears to be somewhat more complex than its American equivalent. To some extent this difference may be an illusion produced by the "closed" character of the Soviet system and the difficulty of interpreting its leaders' statements, but not entirely.

It seems very likely that there is a sizable core of agreement among Soviet leaders on matters relating to the United States. They are all influenced by, and in most cases probably share, the pervasive nationalism of the Soviet—or, more accurately, the Russian—people. At the same time, they believe in at least the central concepts and clichés of Marxism-Leninism, if only because of their proven utility in legitimating, or at least rationalizing, the authority exercised by the Soviet leadership over the people. The slogan "Soviet patriotism" obviously tries to blend these two crucial elements, nationalism and Marxism-Leninism. Both imply, or at least benefit from, the actual or alleged existence of an external adversary, and Leninist ideology in its post-1945 version has fairly consistently identified it as American "imperialism." There is accordingly a basic ideological and political hostility to the United States, and a deep-seated belief in the underlying hostility of American "ruling circles" to the Soviet Union. Specific anti-Soviet acts and policies on the part of the United States are met in Moscow with great resentment, if not necessarily with surprise; President Nixon became the object of considerable Soviet approval precisely because he took practical steps, especially in the field of technological contact and trade, that were favorable to Soviet interests. In fact, a sufficient sense of stake in President Nixon was built up in Moscow so that his political troubles aroused considerable concern there; it was only in late 1973 that the Soviet press began to mention Watergate and other such matters. By this time nearly everyone in the Soviet elite realizes that the United States is not the Wall Street dictatorship assumed in classical Marxist theory but a reasonably plural or "open" society. Partly for this reason, it is thought to be in a state of long-term decline in both its domestic affairs and its international position.

It seems reasonable to describe, at least tentatively, the dominant attitude toward the United States of the top Soviet elite, including Brezhnev himself, roughly as follows. On the one hand, this attitude is based on a desire for ultimate "victory" over the United States, without war, on a more or less global scale. It is strongly influenced by the Soviet "military-industrial complex," which finds the image of an aggressive American "imperialism" useful if not indispensable as the rationale for high military budgets. On the other hand, this dominant attitude sees détente (or "peaceful coexistence") with the United States as a desirable transitional situation, provided it is not allowed to harm Soviet interests or constrain Soviet freedom of action unduly, because it reduces the risk of a major war and facilitates economic and technological contacts through which the Soviet Union can increase its national power. American self-interest, actual or supposed, is thought to dictate cooperation in these respects, to the point where the dominant Soviet attitude seems to aim at a kind of Soviet-American global condominium, based on approximate strategic parity, as the best attainable model for the international system pending the eventual Soviet triumph. This liking for condominium, or bipolarity, is pushed to the point where it consciously conflicts with the United States' strong preference for a multipolar world order, in which China, Japan, and Western Europe would play roles of at least comparable importance to those of the two superpowers. In fact, the Soviet Union systematically tries to discourage the United States from contributing to the strengthening of these other centers of power and influence and to weaken them itself whenever this can be done without excessive risks or costs. This is one of the purposes and aspects of Soviet management of the Sino-Soviet confrontation. In the case of Japan and Western Europe, the Soviet Union has discovered an important vulnerability that it can exploit to some extent, by proxy: dependence on Middle Eastern oil. Furthermore, Soviet hostility to Israel, a virtual client state of the United States, has the ideological utility of demonstrating to Communist hardliners at home and elsewhere that détente and condominium do not require an abandonment of basic hostility to American "imperialism."

A few interesting, and at least potentially important, deviations from this dominant attitude deserve to be noted. One is the view of Mikhail Suslov, the elder statesman of the Soviet leadership, who has an unattractive reputation abroad as a militant and rigid ideologue, but whose overriding concern with the ideological soundness and political growth of the world's Communist Parties has led him to regard China as a more serious threat than the United States, to oppose the invasion of Czechoslovakia, and (in December 1973) to express opposition to his colleagues' insistence on massive military budgets. Of less political importance, but perhaps greater interest, are the views of the Soviet dissenters on the subject of détente. They are not uniform. The ideological Leninist Roy Medvedev believes that outside pressure is counterproductive for the purpose of improving the Kremlin's domestic and external behavior, that such change can come only from internal forces, and that the pursuit of détente along the lines visualized in Moscow is the best course for the West. On the other hand, the two best-known dissenters, Andrei Sakharov and Alexander Solzhenitsyn, argue that détente will only lull the West and strengthen the Soviet system unless the latter is somehow compelled to reform itself in the process. Most Soviet dissenters agree strongly with the latter view; they consider that they have done all they can, and that it is up to the West to apply all reasonable forms of pressure, even at the risk of disrupting détente in the short run, in order to make the Soviet leadership mend its ways and thereby make true détente possible in the long run.

The Middle East

Soviet policy in the Middle East, ever since it first became a significant phenomenon in the mid-1950s, has been a standing refutation of the stereotype, still occasionally encountered, that the Soviet Union is a *status quo* power. Moscow has no moral commitment to any Middle Eastern state comparable to the American commitment to Israel. No Middle Eastern country, with the possible exceptions of Turkey and Iran, is vital to Soviet security. Moscow's Middle Eastern policy has consisted almost exclusively of an unabashed search for influence. Inasmuch as Stalin's anti-Semitism and his Cold War with the United States created a pattern in the late 1940s of hostility to Israel and to the American policy of supporting it, the Soviet quest took the obvious path of cultivating the Arab states and therefore necessarily of supporting them to one degree or another against Israel. In 1967 this policy took the form of inciting Egypt to put pressure on Israel in order to deter what Moscow falsely alleged was an Israeli plan to attack Syria, in order to create a situation where Moscow could mediate, claim credit for managing a difficult situation, and compensate itself for what seemed at the time to be a series of American successes and Soviet setbacks in the Third World. An unexpectedly vigorous Israeli response, in the so-called June War, ruined this game plan and inflicted another setback on Moscow as well as a humiliating defeat on its Arab friends.

In late 1969, the Soviet leadership, looking for ways to get one up, detected what it thought was a weakening of American diplomatic support for Israel. Advanced Soviet weapons and military personnel were sent to Egypt to help the Egyptians push the Israeli back from the Suez Canal, and in the process to enhance Soviet influence on the Arab countries. This plan was checkmated by a vigorous Israeli military response and unexpectedly strong American support for Israel, in the form of arms shipments. In July 1972, therefore, most Soviet military personnel (apart from those at the Soviet naval bases on the Egyptian coast) were withdrawn from Egypt, apparently in accordance with an agreement reached with President Nixon at the Moscow summit in May; the withdrawal was skillfully and convincingly portrayed to the world, by both the Soviets and the Egyptians, as being conducted at Egyptian insistence.

The Soviet leadership then began to implement a somewhat subtler plan, one that it thought it could get by with because the United States was believed since the Moscow summit to be too deeply committed to détente to respond effectively. The essence of it was to continue large-scale military aid to the major Arab states confronting Israel, to encourage them to put repeated military pressures on Israel in order to wear it down, to withdraw Soviet military personnel whenever actual hostilities seemed about to break out, to use strong diplomatic and political pressure on Israel to deter it from capitalizing on any further military successes it might achieve, and to rely on the American commitment to détente to prevent a crunch between the two superpowers. As a parallel move, Soviet propaganda began early in 1973 to incite the Arabs to embargo oil shipments to Western countries to the extent that Arab interests might seem to indicate and to nationalize Western oil companies operating in the Arab countries.

From this Soviet strategy, plus of course Arab frustration at the fact that the verdict of 1967 had not yet been reversed, came the Middle Eastern war that began on October 6, 1973. There is no need for a discussion of it here apart from those aspects directly relevant to Soviet-American relations, except to say that the Soviet strategy inferred in the previous paragraph was carried out, faithfully and on the whole successfully. The main setback was that the Egyptian Third Army was trapped by the Israeli east of the Suez Canal. In mid-October Moscow alerted six of its seven airborne divisions, whether seriously or as a bluff. On October 24, Brezhnev sent a stern note to Nixon; although of course it has not been published it appears to have implied that Soviet troops would intervene unilaterally to free the Third Army unless the United States participated in a joint operation for that purpose, or unless at the minimum the United States put effective pressure on Israel to allow the Third Army to be resupplied (although not rearmed) from across the canal. The United States took action along the latter lines, although President Nixon also ordered a brief alert of American strategic forces on receiving the message from Brezhnev. Moscow apparently had no serious objections to President Nixon's claiming that by strenuous action he had averted the worst American-Soviet confrontation since the Cuban missile crisis. An improvement in the Nixon administration's domestic and international image was desirable, even from the Soviet point of view, after the self-inflicted political wounds that it had suffered.

In the short run, the Soviet Union had reason to feel moderately content with the outcome of the crisis. The Arabs embargoed oil shipments to Japan and the major Western countries until March 1974. The crisis created serious strains in the relationship between the United States and the West European countries, France in particular. Kissinger was predictably compelled to postpone a scheduled visit to Peking, and the Chinese were reminded that in the last analysis Moscow ranked higher on the American list of priorities than they did. The United States made no serious effort to punish Moscow for its role in the Middle Eastern crisis; at least as far as the Nixon administration was concerned, détente proceeded almost as though nothing had happened.

On the other hand, Moscow grew increasingly unhappy as the

outcome of the crisis threatened to turn into a major triumph for American diplomacy. Having tried hard, but without success, to knock Israel out of the Sinai Peninsula, President Sadat soon began to show signs of shifting to a diplomatic approach that would require American good offices, as well as a more conciliatory attitude on the part of Israel. He accepted an agreement on a cease-fire and troop disengagement arranged by Secretary Kissinger, sent an ambassador to Washington for the first time since 1967, and gave some indications that he was contemplating exchanging the Soviet Union for the United States as Egypt's patron and principal supplier of economic and even military aid. Moscow sought to avoid a serious setback of these dimensions by complicating the tasks facing American diplomacy in the Middle East; it encouraged the Arabs, unsuccessfully, to prolong their oil embargo against the West, and it incited the Syrians with greater success to maintain military pressure on Israel.

European Security

Since at least as long ago as Stalin's time, the Soviet leadership has had a powerful two-front complex, in other words a determination to avoid simultaneous crises in Europe and the Far East. A situation of this kind seemed to Moscow to be emerging in the mid-1960s with the establishment of a linkage between its European and its Chinese problems, at a time when (as indicated in Chapter VIII) it was beginning to regard Peking as a military threat. In January 1964, in a move which had anti-Soviet motives among others on both sides, France and the People's Republic of China exchanged diplomatic recognitions. More serious still, in view of Moscow's obsession at that time with West German "revanchism," was a series of secret talks between Bonn and Peking later in 1964, on a possible trade agreement and consular relations. Although frustrated by American opposition, these negotiations were very upsetting to both the East German and the Soviet leadership, especially since important voices were already being raised in West Germany in favor of contacts with the East European countries (other than East Germany), and on the part of Moscow's *bête noire,* the right-wing politician Franz Josef Strauss, in favor of efforts to exploit the Sino-Soviet dispute for West Germany's benefit.

In 1966 Soviet concern over China, already serious, was greatly heightened by the eruption of the Cultural Revolution. The need to decouple Moscow's Chinese and European problems by promoting détente in the West and to free the Soviet leadership's hands for more intense concentration on China appeared urgent. In July, the Warsaw Pact powers issued a declaration on European security that contained the essential points on which Moscow has continued to insist: general recognition of existing European fron- tiers and of the independent status of East Germany, withdrawal of foreign (i.e., American and Soviet) troops, and dissolution of both NATO and the Warsaw Pact (but not of the bilateral Soviet alliances with the individual Warsaw Pact countries, which have no counterpart on the Western side). There was little general re- sponse by the NATO powers to this overture. The response that materialized was not at all to Moscow's taste. In October 1966 the new Grand Coalition government in West Germany, which in- cluded the two major parties, the Christian Democrats and the Social Democrats, adopted its famous *Ostpolitik*. This was a pol- icy of trying to isolate East Germany, and bring about its ultimate collapse and the reunification of Germany, through the establish- ment of economic and diplomatic relations with the other East European countries, a program that Bonn vainly hoped would not arouse undue alarm in Moscow given the new Soviet commitment to détente in Europe.

The Soviet leadership chose to interpret the *Ostpolitik* as a blow at détente, at European security, at its hold over Eastern Europe, and at its efforts to decouple its China and European problems. Its propaganda began to allege the existence of a "Bonn- Peking axis" based on hostility to the Soviet Union. This propa- ganda apparently reflected both a genuine, although unfounded, fear that collusion between China and West Germany might in fact be emerging and a desire to discredit the *Ostpolitik* in East European eyes by linking Bonn publicly with Peking, which was then widely unpopular on account of the excesses of the Cultural Revolution. The invasion of Czechoslovakia was intended in part to warn the East European countries against yielding to the *Ost- politik*, to pressure them into revising their bilateral treaties of alliance with the Soviet Union (most of which lapsed in 1968) in a broader form worded so as to apply against "any state or group of states" (including China, obviously), and to demonstrate to the hypothetical "Bonn-Peking axis" the risks of trying to harm Soviet interests. Peking's alarm at the invasion of Czechoslovakia reflected in part a realization that Moscow regarded itself as faced with a problem on two fronts, and a fear therefore that Soviet military action in the West might be duplicated in the East. On the whole the invasion was beneficial to Soviet interests in Europe; Bonn promptly adopted a drastically modified version of the *Ostpolitik* stressing the improvement of relations not only with the Soviet Union but with East Germany. In August 1970 the Social Democratic government of Willy Brandt signed a treaty with the Soviet Union that in effect accepted the territorial settlement of 1945 and the separate existence of East Germany. In 1972, in order to strengthen the Brandt government's electoral position, Moscow actually gave its consent in private to the establishment of diplomatic relations between Bonn and Peking. Direct official contacts between the two Germanies got under way, and in 1973 both entered the United Nations.

Germany having been the central issue in the Cold War in Europe since 1945, these developments naturally stimulated a trend toward détente in Europe as a whole, the invasion of Czechoslovakia notwithstanding. In September 1971 an agreement was signed under which the Soviet Union promised not to interfere with Western access to West Berlin. On the Western side, the situation was complicated by growing demands in the American Congress for a reduction in the American military presence in Western Europe in view of the United States' balance of payments problem. The NATO powers decided to try to compensate for this probably inevitable reduction by bargaining it for an equivalent reduction on the Warsaw Pact side. In June 1968, accordingly, NATO proposed negotiations with the Warsaw Pact on Mutual and Balanced Force Reductions (MBFR). Moscow showed no interest in the idea at first, since it did not see why it should have to pay a price for a partial American withdrawal that it could probably get merely by waiting, and because it had a greater interest in a conference on European security along the lines outlined in the July 1966 Warsaw Pact statement. It was not until May 1971, by which time hints of Sino-American détente were making Moscow more eager to improve its own relations with the West, that the Soviet Union indicated any interest in talks on MBFR. Agreement in principle was reached at the Moscow summit, in May

1972, to hold conferences on both MBFR and European security, the latter being conditional in NATO eyes on the former.

Preparatory talks on MBFR began at Vienna in January 1973, and a full-dress conference at the end of October. The word "balanced" was soon dropped out because of a basic disagreement: the Warsaw Pact wanted equal reductions, which would preserve its own numerical superiority; the NATO powers wanted larger reductions on the Warsaw Pact side, with the aim of ultimate equality in the critical Central European sector. Another important issue was a Warsaw Pact effort to exclude Hungary, where four Soviet divisions are stationed, from the scope of the talks. One possible reason for this effort was an intent to shift to Hungary additional Soviet divisions that might have to be withdrawn from other countries; if so, the ploy was a rather sinister one inasmuch as Hungary is the strategic key to Central Europe for the Soviet Union, as Romania is the key to the Balkans. Even more difficult than the reduction of American and Soviet forces in Central Europe via withdrawal was the problem of the reduction of European forces, which would have to be achieved via demobilization.

The Conference on Security and Cooperation in Europe (CSCE) began at Helsinki in July 1973. It included nearly all European states, and not merely the members of NATO and the Warsaw Pact, as well as the United States and Canada (both members of NATO, of course). The conference's agenda was divided into four "baskets," or categories of issues, the first relating to security (nonaggression pledges, confidence-building measures, etc.), the second to various forms of cooperation (economic, technical, etc.), the third to human contacts between East and West (travel, cultural exchange, free movement of ideas across the Iron Curtain, etc.), and the fourth to machinery for implementing any agreements that might be reached. To the NATO countries, the main "basket" of interest is the third; one of the implicit, if not explicit, Soviet demands on the conference is a sanction for Moscow's domination of Eastern Europe, but NATO is willing to approve this situation only if ideas from the West can have access to the Warsaw Pact countries, where they may eventually produce constructive changes. The Warsaw Pact countries, on the other hand, and the Soviet Union in particular, are basically opposed to the free exchange of ideas, as Moscow's expulsion of Alexander Solzhenitsyn and its jamming of foreign broadcasts beaming excerpts from his *Gulag Archipelago* to the Soviet people show. The Soviet interest is in other aspects of détente, and hence in the other "baskets."

Current Issues

Both the superpowers continue to improve their strategic weapons within the rather undemanding limits of SALT I. The United States is beginning to develop a new nuclear submarine (Trident) and a new heavy bomber (the B-1). The Soviet Union tested its first MIRV in 1972 and flew one on an ICBM over the Pacific in January 1974. Activities of this kind inevitably tend to arouse fears on each side that the other is trying to achieve the capability to annihilate its adversary's strategic weapons with a first strike. On the Soviet side, this nervousness was enhanced by American Secretary of Defense Schlesinger's emphasis on retargeting American missiles away from Soviet cities to Soviet missiles.

The SALT II talks began on November 21, 1972. In line with its current emphasis on "essential equivalence" in overall strength rather than numerical equality in any one category, the American side proposed equal totals for each side for the three main categories of weapons systems (ICBMs, SLBMs, and bombers), each side to determine its own "mix" of the three. The United States also proposed equal payloads (or throw-weights) for ICBMs on both sides, obviously in order to curb development of the new "heavy" Soviet ICBMs, as preferable to controls on MIRV technology, in which the United States was considerably ahead. American forward (or overseas) bases were not to be regarded as strategic and were to be discussed within the context not of SALT but of MBFR, where they might be traded against Soviet MRBMs targeted on Western Europe. These proposals did not go down very well in Moscow, especially with relative hardliners such as Defense Minister Marshal Grechko, who evidently hoped to attain strategic superiority instead of settling for "essential equivalence."

A number of problems continued to complicate Soviet-American trade. The Soviet grain picture improved sharply in 1973, with a depressing effect on American grain sales. The Soviet interest in American investment in the development of Soviet natural resources (especially energy sources) was countered by Moscow's secrecy mania, which restricted access to sites and to other types of information needed by prospective investors. The Soviet Union wanted long-term, low-interest credits on the same basis as an underdeveloped country, whereas it seemed more logical to treat it as a developed country. Most-favored-nation treatment for Soviet exports to the United States, actually a less important question, continued to be bedeviled by congressional objections to Soviet restrictions on Jewish emigration.

A modification of Soviet Cuban policy, in a direction adverse to Castro's interests, was indicated by Moscow's interest both in achieving a détente of sorts with the United States and in getting Cuba off the Soviet taxpayer's back to a degree. The main purpose of an important visit by Brezhnev to Cuba in January 1974 was evidently to enlist Castro's sympathy for détente, to interest him in improving his own relations with the United States, and to convince the United States that the Soviet Union had no strategic stake in Cuba. He apparently had some success with Castro, but the Nixon administration felt no detectable interest in better relations with Cuba.

The third Nixon-Brezhnev summit was held from June 27 to July 3, 1974. No agreement was possible on the development and deployment of MIRVs. This impasse was part of a larger problem that had troubled the SALT talks from the beginning. The American side wanted parity in total throw-weight, a situation that would be advantageous on account of the current American lead in MIRV technology and would permit the American side superiority in the number of warheads. The Soviet side wanted parity in the number of warheads, a situation that would confer an advantage on the superior yield of the Soviet warheads and the greater thrust of the Soviet missiles. The two sides succeeded in agreeing, at the third summit, not to build the second ABM sites permitted under the 1972 treaty (around Washington and around the Soviet ICBM force), to stop testing high yield nuclear weapons underground, and to begin negotiations on the control of environmental (chemical, etc.) warfare. Nothing significant is known to have been agreed upon with respect to Europe, the Middle East, or the Far East.

CHAPTER XIII

Japan: Power and Problems

JAPAN is the only wholly non-Western country to have become a major industrial power through the process of economic and technological transformation usually known as modernization. As in the case of other industrialized countries, this transformation, which began in the nineteenth century and has accelerated since the Second World War, has increased material wealth, but at a high social and biological cost, and has conferred greater influence, but also higher risks and greater vulnerability, in international affairs. Impressive achievements are soured to some extent by continuing acute frustrations that cast serious doubt on the prediction sometimes heard that Japan will be the "superstate of the twenty-first century."

The Coming Superstate?

This prediction is based mainly on the fact that the Japanese economy is now the third largest in the world and for about a decade has been the fastest growing of all (at times in the neighborhood of 15 percent per year). But it is not plausible that this high growth will continue; the high Soviet growth rate of the late 1950s fell off in the early 1960s. The Japanese economy is almost entirely dependent on foreign sources for its fossil fuels (especially oil) and industrial raw materials, a fact that in a still unstable international environment creates a serious vulnerability.

The goal of maximum economic growth under an essentially private enterprise system has been pursued with such vigor, partly as insurance against another lapse into depression and militarism, that social justice and social investments have been badly neglected. Urban planning, public transportation, the housing fund, and the educational system are generally in a bad state. The Japanese government has been even less successful than others, in relation to the size and dynamism of the economy, in coping with those twin scourges of industrialized countries, inflation and pollution; the latter, in particular, has reached almost intolerable levels. These conditions have soured many of the less prosperous elements of the urban population on the governing Liberal Democratic Party, the bureaucracy, and the business community (sometimes known collectively as Japan, Inc.), and together with strong European intellectual and cultural influences (including Marxism) have alienated many professionals (especially academics and journalists) from the Establishment. Prosperity, in short, has not prevented, and in fact has to some extent augmented, a high level of social discontent, especially in the cities, even though the discontent has not yet assumed revolutionary proportions. Almost no one doubts that future Japanese governments will have to place less emphasis on encouraging economic growth and more on attacking the sources of this discontent through greatly increased social investment.

This shift of priorities, combined with the vulnerability to Arab pressures on the oil supply demonstrated in late 1973 and other constraints to be discussed later, make it very unlikely that Japan will try to play an international role appropriate to a "superstate." Even if it did try, it would probably not succeed. Both of the existing superstates and most of the Asian countries have fairly vivid memories of Japanese aggression, and an unduly high level of international activity on Japan's part, even if it were primarily economic rather than military, would almost certainly call countervailing pressures into being and create serious risks and costs of various kinds for Japan. Essentially for these reasons Japan is likely to remain a unique middle power, smaller economically than the Common Market countries as a whole although larger than any one of them, and inferior in both conventional and nuclear military capabilities, and probably in political influence as well, to the People's Republic of China. There is virtually no chance that Japan's economic and military strength and political influence combined will ever equal those of either the United States or the Soviet Union.

The Politics of Factionalism and Frustration

As already indicated, Japan has been governed since the end of the Second World War by a conservative coalition consisting essentially of the Liberal Democratic Party, the bureaucracy, and the business community. Of these three it is the politician, logically enough, who wields the greatest influence on politics. He usually does so, however, in a way that is aptly described by the Japanese expression low posture, since the Japanese political style favors decision by committee and rule by indirection. High posture leaders have been exceptional and usually have gotten into serious political trouble. One such was Premier Shigeru Yoshida (1946–47, 1948–54), whose great influence and long tenure were due not so much to his Churchillian personality as to the unprecedentedly fluid situation created by Japan's defeat and occupation at the hands of the United States. Another was Premier Nobusuke Kishi (1957–60), who was forced to resign by a storm of protest over his high-handed conduct of affairs, and in particular his handling of the renewal of the American-Japanese security treaty. A third was Premier Eisaku Sato (1964–72), Kishi's half brother, who tied his political fortunes mainly to external issues, notably the normalization of relations with South Korea (in 1965) and the recovery of jurisdiction over Okinawa from the United States. By the early 1970s, Sato had become widely unpopular at home as too old, too conservative, and too high posture, and he was regarded by left-wing critics, including the leadership in Peking, which refused to deal with him, as too pro-American and too pro-Chinese Nationalist; his prestige also suffered from the "Nixon shocks" of 1971.

Since Yoshida's day the ruling Liberal Democratic Party, and in particular its members in the Diet (parliament), has been largely divided into factions each of which is loyal, on the basis of personal allegiance rather than of support for particular policies, to a leading figure in the party. The factional leaders vie with each other for the party presidency, which carries with it the premiership as long as the party is strong enough in the Diet (or more accurately the lower house, the House of Representatives) to be able to control the government. There is a tendency accordingly for the premiership to rotate among the factional leaders, although a decreasing respect for age has prevented former premiers from resuming office as sometimes happened before the Second World War. Factionalism also affects the largest opposition party, the Japan Socialist Party, but its basis is less personal and more ideological than in the case of the Liberal Democrats. The Socialists are divided essentially into a left wing, whose views on domestic politics and foreign policy differ little from those of the Communists but which is more doctrinaire than the latter and lacks their tight organization, and a right wing, which is more moderate but no better organized. The Communists themselves are relatively well led and organized and have been increasing their popular and electoral appeal fairly rapidly by stressing the bread and butter issues on which the Liberal Democrats are vulnerable and by asserting their Japaneseness through a posture that is independent and in fact critical of both Moscow and Peking. The Komeito, a party originally based on the neo-Buddhist Soka Gakkai movement and attempting to combine a revivalist faith with nationalism and tight discipline, grew rapidly during the 1960s but has since found itself on a plateau. The three major opposition parties have begun to cooperate electorally against the Liberal Democrats to some extent, but the other two are wary of the Communist Party's dynamism and tight organization and afraid that it is trying to dominate them. The Liberal Democrats are much more afraid of the Communists than of the other opposition parties.

Sato regarded the reversion of Okinawa to Japanese jurisdiction, which occurred formally on May 15, 1972, as the culmination of his political career. He resigned the following month, and during the ensuing factional jockeying failed for some reason to give effective support to his preferred successor, the conservative Takeo Fukuda. The premiership went instead in July to the seemingly dynamic Kakuei Tanaka, because he favored energetic attention to Japan's domestic problems, appeared likely to be good for the Liberal Democrats in future Diet elections, favored a foreign policy more independent of the United States than Sato's had been, and was known to be acceptable to Peking. In fact, he was promptly invited to Peking by Chou En-lai, and his visit, which took place in late September 1972, did something to improve his own political position and that of his party. Nevertheless, the Communists registered gains in Diet elections held in December 1972, and the result was an unusual felt need for unity among the factional leaders of the Liberal Democratic Party. In particular, Fukuda was given a major cabinet post, that of Minister of Finance, in which capacity he killed Tanaka's ambitious and unworkable plan for the redevelopment of the country through the building of new industrial towns and made himself unpopular by advocating high taxes and the stabilization of incomes as an anti-inflation measure.

A sense of stagnation and frustration pervaded the Liberal Democratic Party and its leadership as they lost popularity on account of serious domestic problems and the opposition parties, especially the Communist Party, tended to benefit correspondingly. One of the Liberal Democrats' problems was the fact that the electoral system, a form of proportional representation in which each district elects several representatives, the seats being divided in proportion to the number of votes received by the various parties, tends to favor the opposition. In the spring of 1973, accordingly, Tanaka tried to push a reform plan calling for a single member district system through the Diet but failed. This was merely the most serious of a number of setbacks sustained by Tanaka and the Liberal Democratic Party in 1973.

The *immobilisme* and factionalism of the Liberal Democratic leadership, the gradual decline of its popularity, and the considerably faster decline of Tanaka's have led to the recent emergence of a number of new groups of younger party members eager for a change. The most interesting and important of these is the Seiran-kai. Like the prewar Japanese nationalists, it is conservative and demands a higher level of public morality and responsiveness (although within a more or less authoritarian framework) to social needs. It objects to Tanaka's diplomatic break with Taiwan and his recognition of Peking, which in fact were widely unpopular within the Liberal Democratic Party and were supported mainly by the business community, fascinated by the lure of the supposedly vast market on the mainland.

In an election for the House of Councillors (the upper house of the Diet) held in July 1974, the Liberal Democrats' bloc of seats was eroded to a bare majority. On the other hand, the main losers were members of factions other than that of Premier Tanaka, who accordingly appears to have strengthened his position within the party somewhat. One result was the resignation of several important cabinet members, notably Finance Minister Fukuda, probably in preparation for the lower house elections and a contest for the premiership in 1975.

The Economics of a Vulnerable Giant

The Japanese economy has been one of the wonders of the postwar world. Probably the main causes of its extraordinary growth have been: the supply of skills inherited from the prewar period, social stability, a high rate of savings, a high educational level, high labor discipline and productivity (especially in relation to wages), able management, high levels of investment, the large-scale borrowing under license and adaptation of foreign technology and a resulting low budget for research and development, government support for economic growth and export expansion, low defense and welfare budgets, the postponement of much social investment in the interest of rapid economic growth, a shortage (until 1973) of artificial obstacles to access to foreign level resources and industrial raw materials, the undervaluation of the yen (until 1973) and resulting low prices for Japanese exports, generally good economic and political relations with the United States until 1971 (including large amounts of American offshore procurement of supplies in Japan in connection with the Korean and Vietnam Wars), and a great demand in much of the world for Japanese capital and goods.

Like other good things, this impressive list of assets has not been immune to erosion. Japanese labor costs have risen and are now high by Asian standards. The work ethic has declined considerably, especially among the younger age groups. The neglect of the environment and of social needs by the ruling establishment has become a major political issue. There have been powerful American pressures on the Japanese government since 1971 to revalue the yen (upward) and take measures to wipe out the large Japanese payments surplus with the United States. The oil crisis of late 1973 dramatized Japan's risky dependence for 80 percent of its petroleum imports (which total about 200 million tons per year) on the volatile countries of the Middle East. As a result of two revaluations of the yen (1971, 1973) and a substantial liberalization of tariffs and of controls on foreign investment in Japan in 1973, all under American pressure, Japan not only ceased to run a payments surplus in 1973 but incurred a $9 billion deficit. The outlook is for further trouble, since Japan like other petroleum importers will have to pay higher prices for its oil, not only from the Middle East but from other areas as well (Indonesia, for example). There is a faint hope, but no more, that substantial amounts of oil will be available at reasonable prices from the Soviet Union or the People's Republic of China, or both.

After the outbreak of war in the Middle East on October 6, 1973, the Arab countries demanded that Japan cut off trade with Israel, break diplomatic relations with it, and sell arms to them. The Japanese government was very reluctant to comply, partly because it feared that compliance would seriously harm its relations with the United States. The latter argument was weakened by a lack of interest on the part of the United States government in Japan's predicament, however, and the need to protect Japan as far as possible from cuts in oil shipments from the Arab countries seemed urgent. Accordingly, late in November, Tokyo publicly urged that Israel withdraw to its pre-1967 frontiers, a step that fell far short of meeting the Arabs' demands and yet constituted a striking departure from the postwar Japanese practice of avoiding like the plague controversial issues in international politics. The Arabs soon shifted their demands on Japan to a more significant and realizable one that Japan help them with its technology in return for assurances that its imports of Arab oil would not be seriously affected. A number of large contracts for industrial projects in the oil-producing Middle Eastern countries accordingly began to be negotiated and signed by Japanese interests at the beginning of 1974. As a result of this prompt capitulation, or virtual capitulation, Japan's actual oil imports were not seriously affected, although prices of course went up and a panic psychology prevailed for a time. Japan's normal imports were disrupted for a few weeks, then resumed at higher prices.

It is possible that Japan will agree to sell arms to Middle Eastern countries. Another possibility is that Japan may try to interest the latter in using some of their huge foreign exchange reserves to finance a long-discussed canal across the Kra Isthmus (in southern Thailand). This would enable Japanese tankers to avoid the Straits of Malacca, which are claimed by Indonesia and Malaysia as their territorial waters and in any case are too shallow for supertankers, and the Lombok Strait (between Bali and Lombok), which is deep but out of the way. On the other hand, the Kra Canal would be difficult to construct unless nuclear explosives were used, with possibly devastating effects on the environment, and would also be unable to accommodate supertankers. A depressing concluding note on Japan's economic and social future: in 1923 there was a catastrophic earthquake in the Tokyo-Yokohama area. The facts of geology make it very likely that there will be another, whose effects may be buffered somewhat by modern construction techniques but may still be disastrous.

The Search for a Foreign and Security Policy

The shock of defeat and occupation reduced Japanese foreign policy to virtual nonexistence, and even now no real consensus have developed as to what Japan's role in the world should be.

The alliance with the United States, and the presence of American bases in Japan and Okinawa, have been unpopular with the left, which would greatly prefer neutrality and friendlier relations with the Communist powers, but the ruling establishment regards the American connection as essential for the purpose of deterring possible Soviet attack and as helpful in maintaining its own political and economic position at home. Down to the mid-1960s, the establishment considered it unnecessary and even undesirable to go much beyond following the American lead on major international questions such as China policy. At that time Premier Sato chose to normalize relations with South Korea and begin pressing for the reversion of Okinawa, but these were not steps likely to put a serious strain on the tie with the United States.

Unaccustomed as it was to major initiatives in foreign affairs, the Japanese establishment made only a hesitant response to the Nixon administration's pressures on it, beginning in 1969, to increase its level of armaments somewhat and play a more active role in Asian security to help compensate for American disengagement from the region under the Nixon Doctrine. To be sure, the Fourth Five-Year Defense Build-up Plan, announced in the spring of 1970, proclaimed a "self-reliant" defense posture and projected a modest increase in the defense budget to slightly over one percent of the gross national product (still a very low figure in percentage terms, but a respectable one in absolute terms in view of the size of the Japanese economy). Meanwhile, in the Nixon-Sato communiqué (November 1969), the Japanese government had agreed to allow the United States to use its bases in Japan and Okinawa for the defense of South Korea and Taiwan (the actual wording achieved this effect by asserting a Japanese interest in the security of those areas), in exchange for an American pledge to return civil jurisdiction over Okinawa to Japan.

The "Nixon shocks" of 1971 greatly increased Japanese uncertainties about the reliability of the United States as an economic partner and ally, although the establishment for the most part remained eager to preserve the relationship. The Japanese government became less willing to follow the American lead where Japan's security was not directly involved, especially in China policy. Sato began to make overtures to Peking but was rebuffed. As we have seen, it was his successor Tanaka who managed to establish diplomatic relations with the People's Republic of China.

Tanaka's Foreign Minister Ohira and some of his subordinates advocated, at least for a time, a policy of "equidistance" for Japan with respect to the three major powers (the United States, the Soviet Union, and the People's Republic of China), an idea that would involve the abrogation of the security treaty with the United States in favor of treaties of friendship with all three, as well as closer ties with Western Europe independently of the United States. Recently, however, this idea seems to have lost ground, partly because of continuing difficulties in Japan's relations with the Soviet Union and China. The American tie remains the centerpiece of Japanese foreign policy, even though a seemingly less reliable one than many Japanese would like.

Japan's Self-Defense Forces, although small, are well armed for conventional warfare in the home islands, while lacking nuclear weapons and any significant offensive capability against foreign countries. Japan makes some of its military equipment under license from American manufacturers, but it also produces some very good items entirely of its own design, a fighter bomber and a heavy tank, for example. For political reasons, there is no conscription, and the Self-Defense Forces are manned entirely by volunteers. Apart from maintaining internal security in the unlikely although possible event of insurgency (presumably leftist, although conceivably rightist), their function is essentially to hold out for a few days in the event of a major Soviet attack (which is considered unlikely) and act as a tripwire for the anticipated American response, military or otherwise. If there were no American response, they would probably surrender. Unlike Israel or Switzerland, Japan has no plans for involving the population in defense of the homeland; the reasons are partly political but relate primarily to the heavily urban character of contemporary Japanese society. There appear to be no plans for naval action to protect Japan's shipping routes, which are vulnerable to Soviet submarines, except perhaps for some antisubmarine operations in case of actual war.

It is obviously possible that Japanese democracy might collapse in favor of some authoritarian alternative, for example in the event that a leftist electoral victory were met with a coup from the side of the establishment, but this does not appear likely in the near future. It is also obviously possible that Japan might decide to rearm massively and even "go nuclear," either under the present political system or some other. But here again, the likelihood is not very great. Japanese public opinion is growing more nationalistic but is not turning to militarism, partly because of memories of the past experiment in militarism and partly because of a realization that such a step would set up serious domestic political strains and create serious external risks from the direction of major powers whose military might Japan could not hope to match, as well as exacerbating Japan's political relations with many other countries. This would apply particularly to a decision to acquire nuclear weapons. Japan's "nuclear allergy," inherited from 1945, is still operative, although curiously enough public opinion polls show a high percentage of the respondents expecting the eventual acquisition of nuclear weapons while not actually favoring it. Japan is "keeping its options open" on this score by not ratifying the Nonproliferation Treaty, which it signed in 1970, allegedly because of fear that a discriminatory (as compared with the Western European countries) system of inspection of Japan's peaceful nuclear program would be imposed. There is of course no doubt that Japan has the economic and technical capacity to "go nuclear" in short order if it ever took the decision to do so, but it would probably have to base its nuclear weapons at sea on account of its high population density.

Japan and the United States

The Year of Europe in American foreign policy, 1973, saw an American effort to bring about trilateral economic cooperation among the United States, Japan, and Western Europe, to a large extent in order to improve the American balance of payments situation. There was a good deal of talk in the United States, among academics as well as others, about a Japanese-American-West European triangle, paralleling in the economic sphere the Sino-Soviet-American triangle in the political and military spheres. But both the Japanese and the West Europeans have been rather suspicious of American intentions and of each other; on the whole, they prefer to deal with each other independently of the United States. Furthermore, there is very little substance to the idea of a Japanese-American-West European triangle. What is actually involved is three bilateral relationships, not particularly dependent on one another, whereas the Sino-Soviet-American relationship is a true triangle in which a major change in the relations of any pair of the three directly affects the other two relationships.

Since the period of the "shocks," Japanese-American relations have begun to be set on a somewhat more even keel. A possible additional "shock" was prevented, for example, when the United States raised the level of its soybean exports to Japan. On the other hand, the giant American oil companies, from which Japan buys much of its oil, have been unwilling to ship the large quantities desired by the Japanese at the frozen price that the Japanese government is willing to pay; the price has had to rise.

The "shocks" have been understandably traumatic for the Japanese and especially for the establishment in view of its sense of commitment to the American connection. Some Japanese appear to fear that the official American obsession with détente with the Soviet Union may have rendered the American security guarantee worthless. Perhaps in an effort to breathe more life into the Japanese-American security relationship, some Japanese claim to believe in the continued effectiveness of the Sino-Soviet alliance, as a counter to which the Japanese-American security agreement was originally concluded.

The oil crisis of late 1973 drove many Japanese, confronted with their country's virtual helplessness in the face of the Arab bloc, to think of Japan as a virtual satellite of the United States to a greater extent than had been true for some years. Some hoped, to no avail as yet, that the United States would make itself responsible for Japan's access to foreign sources of energy, as it had for Japan's external security.

Japan and the Soviet Union

The Japanese and the Russians are highly culture-bound peoples cordially disliked by most of their neighbors, including one another. It would be hard to name any pair of peoples less well suited by temperament and culture to get along with each other. On the Soviet side there are memories of the Russo-Japanese War (1904–05), the Japanese military intervention in the Soviet Far East and Eastern Siberia (1918–22), and occasional aggressive acts by the Imperial Japanese Army in the 1930s. On the Japanese side, there are memories of the Soviet attack in August 1945. The Soviet Union regularly ranks in Japanese public opinion polls as the most disliked of foreign countries. It has been regarded by Japanese since 1945 as the only serious external threat to their country's security.

The Soviet Union refused to sign the San Francisco peace treaty in 1951 and has not yet negotiated one of its own with Japan, although diplomatic relations were established in 1956. Having seized some territory from Japan in 1945 (southern Sakhalin and the Kurile Islands) and held Japanese prisoners of war without a proper accounting, the Soviet Union has been fairly consistent since then in treating Japan with a heavyhandedness that is unusual even for Moscow. Soviet military aircraft overfly Japanese islands, and Japanese fishing vessels alleged to have intruded into the rich fishing grounds in Soviet Far Eastern waters are often seized. It is little wonder that the Japan Communist Party has found it advisable to cultivate an image of independence from Moscow, as well as from Peking.

On the other hand, Japan has benefited somewhat from the Sino-Soviet dispute, and in particular the growing Soviet perception of China as a threat, as well as from Soviet concern that American military disengagement from the Far East might create tempting opportunities for Peking. In 1966 Moscow began to encourage the participation of Japanese credits and technology in the development of the resources of Siberia and the Soviet Far East, especially oil and gas. The biggest project envisaged has been to build a pipeline from Irkutsk to Nakhodka on the Pacific to carry oil from the Tiumen fields in western Siberia. So far this project is almost entirely in the talking stage, mainly because of Japanese unhappiness over Chinese objections to the project (on the ground that some of the oil would be used by Soviet forces facing China) and over Soviet reluctance to provide enough technical data or give firm assurances about quantities and prices of oil to be made available to Japan, in addition to a Japanese preference for seeing American interests also involved in the project.

An even more serious issue arises from the fact that Japanese opinion is virtually unanimous in demanding the return of the "northern territories," which consist of what Moscow regards as the four southernmost islands of the Kurile chain. Even though this issue is a less emotional one for the Japanese than the demand for the reversion of Okinawa was, the Japanese government has gone on record as being unwilling to sign a peace treaty with the Soviet Union unless the four islands are returned. Occasional tentative conciliatory statements on this question notwithstanding, Moscow has adopted a basically uncompromising stand. It is afraid that even a small breach in the territorial settlement of 1945, of which it is the major beneficiary, might open up much larger breaches to the benefit of China and possibly even some of the East European countries.

The Soviet Union has been considerably irritated by what it interprets as Premier Tanaka's pro-Chinese attitude. When he visited Moscow in October 1973—partly for domestic political effect, as had been the case when he visited Peking a year earlier— he got no visible concessions on the "northern territories" or the Tiumen pipeline project. The latter appears to be in suspense.

Moscow's proposal for a "collective security" system in Asia, which it has been promoting since 1969 and in particular since 1971 (as a counter to the Sino-American détente), includes a call for the abrogation of the Japanese-American security treaty. This idea, as well as the obvious anti-Chinese overtones of the proposal and its vagueness from several points of view, has led Tokyo to refuse to take part in any such arrangement unless Peking also participates. Of that there is very little likelihood.

Japan and China

Japan and China are involved in a unique love-hate relationship. Most of the love is on the Japanese side; most of the hatred is on the Chinese side. The Japanese feel a profound admiration for and indebtedness to Chinese culture, a burden of guilt for past aggression, no real fear even though China has nuclear weapons, and a patronizing sense of superiority in the departments of economic growth and technological sophistication. The Chinese remember and resent Japanese aggression, are aware in private that it was not they who beat the Japanese, lack the comforting certainty that they could beat them in the future that the Soviets feel with respect to the Germans, fear that Japan might rearm and relapse into aggression, dislike Japan's conservative and essentially pro-American orientation, and are uneasily awed by Japan's phenomenal economic resurgence.

Japan's relations with the People's Republic of China, which originally regarded it as an American satellite, were predominantly hostile until Peking's virtual economic break with the Soviet Union in 1960 led it sharply to increase its trade with Japan. Peking tried to use this trade in a variety of ways to put pressure on the Japanese government to cut its diplomatic ties with Taiwan, and ideally its security ties with the United States. Seeing that it would be the object of great resentment on the part of Japanese firms if Chinese annoyance at Tokyo's policies were allowed to disrupt trade, the Japanese government allowed the (private) Japanese trade negotiators to sign any statements Peking wanted, no matter how critical. Trade was not in fact disrupted, but the Chinese side increased its psychological ascendancy in this strange relationship. This ascendancy was enhanced by the pro-Peking attitude of the major Japanese newspapers, which reflected not only the leftist tendencies of some of the editors but also the fact—revealed later by some of their correspondents who had served in Peking—that in 1964 and 1968 they made secret agreements with the Chinese to keep their coverage favorable, as the price for being allowed to retain bureaus in Peking.

A violent anti-Japanese propaganda campaign got under way in the spring of 1970 and raged until the autumn of 1971, when it began to taper off. Japan was accused not merely of intending to rearm but of actually rearming and engaging in expansionist activity. To some extent the emotion expressed was probably genuine and reflected concern over the Japanese Fourth Five-Year Defense Build-up Plan, as well as a warning to Japan not to take over responsibility for Asian security as the United States disengaged. But the campaign was also partly for effect, to acquire leverage over the Japanese political situation and to rationalize in

China the initiation of détente with the United States, to which
Lin Piao and some others were evidently opposed; Chou En-lai's
argument, expressed in rather esoteric terms, was essentially that
Japan being China's main enemy, it was good strategy to split it
from China's secondary enemy, the United States, at a time when
Japanese-American relations were tense in any case, by improving
relations with the United States. It can hardly be a coincidence
that the anti-Japanese campaign began to subside almost immediately after Lin's fall in September 1971.

An important part of the anti-Japanese campaign was a dispute over some small islands known to the Chinese as the Tiao
Yü T'ai and to the Japanese as the Senkaku. They lie on the edge
of the continental shelf about one hundred miles northeast of
Taiwan, in an area where there are believed to be large oil deposits. Furthermore, control of them would give Japan a foothold
on the continental shelf as a whole, which may be very rich in oil.
Peking became enraged in December 1970 because South Korea,
the Republic of China (Taiwan), and Japan had been granting
concessions to American firms to prospect for oil on various areas
of the continental shelf. Peking asserted its own claim to the resources of the entire continental shelf, a claim for which there is
some basis in international law. In the interests of the emerging
détente with Peking, the State Department directed the American
firms to cease and desist. Peking thereupon unleashed a propaganda offensive asserting its own claim to the islands and attacking Japan, the Chinese Nationalists, and the relationship between
them. The campaign was used skillfully to foster support for Peking as the guardian of China's national interests among Chinese
and Taiwanese students overseas, especially in the United States
and Canada. By the spring of 1972, however, Peking's general anti-
Japanese offensive was fading away in any case, and in mid-May
the reversion of Okinawa to Japanese jurisdiction brought the
Self-Defense Forces into the vicinity of the Tiao Yü T'ai (or
Senkaku). Peking accordingly dropped the issue as suddenly as it
had taken it up.

In mid-1971, Chou En-lai announced "three principles" that
must be accepted by Japan if Sino-Japanese relations were to be
normalized. They were to the effect that the government of the
People's Republic of China was the sole legitimate government of
China, that Taiwan was an integral part of China, and that the

peace treaty between Japan and the Republic of China was illegal and must be abrogated. Although it was not clear whether acceptance of these was regarded as a prerequisite for the beginning of negotiations on normalization, the effect was to enhance Chinese leverage on Japanese politics and foreign policy; in this and other ways, Peking acquired a virtual veto over the selection of the next Japanese premier in succession to Sato.

The Japanese establishment, and still more the opposition, was rendered increasingly receptive to Peking's rough wooing by the "Nixon shocks" of 1971, to which injury insult was added when the United States insisted that Japan cosponsor a resolution proposing that the United Nations General Assembly admit the People's Republic of China while retaining the Republic of China (unless expelled by a two-thirds vote). When Peking was admitted and Taipei expelled instead, on October 25, Tokyo took this development as a sign that the time had come to alter its China policy. Since Sato was *persona non grata* in Peking, it was left to his successor to make the change. Tanaka, as we have seen, was in a mood to do so, and Peking was in a mood to reciprocate because Chou En-lai did not want to wait any longer to bring Japan into the essentially anti-Soviet network of relationships that he was in the process of creating.

Tanaka's visit to China, which occurred at the end of September 1972, resulted in a joint communiqué that had virtually been agreed on in advance as a result of pressure on Tanaka to be conciliatory from the Japanese left and the business community. In the communiqué, the Japanese side expressed its "understanding" of Chou's "three principles," recognized Peking as the sole legal government of China, stated that it "understands and respects" (only just short of "accepts") Peking's claim that Taiwan is part of the People's Republic of China (not simply China, as stated in the Chou-Nixon or Shanghai Communiqué), and declared that it "deeply reproaches" itself for the aggression of the past. Tokyo had accepted the first of Chou's "three principles" in full and the second in part, and Ohira in a separate statement said that Tokyo regarded the Japanese treaty with the Republic of China as no longer valid. The Chinese side renounced its demand for reparations, which had never been serious in any case. The two sides announced that the "abnormal state of affairs" (i. e., undeclared war) between them was terminated, agreed to establish diplomatic relations, pledged mutual friendship, denied that this friendship would be directed against any third party and that either side aimed at hegemony in the Asia-Pacific region, and agreed to hold negotiations on such matters as a peace treaty and trade expansion.

This seemingly spectacular turn in Sino-Japanese relations evoked great expectations on the part of some Japanese and some foreign observers. Writing early in 1973, the able American journalist Selig Harrison concluded that the Japanese establishment, out of concern to avoid a destructive rivalry with China in Asia, was making major concessions to Peking. Those were said to be recognition that Peking would eventually control Taiwan, termination of Japanese financial support for the Taiwanese independence movement, a tendency to clear with Peking in advance any major proposed new investments in Taiwan in the hope of salvaging the Japanese economic position there after Peking assumed control, plans for extensive cooperation with Peking in the economic development of the China mainland and in exploitation of the resources of the continental shelf, toleration of a moderate amount of Chinese revolutionary activity in Asia apart from Japan, cooperation with overseas Chinese firms in Southeast Asia, and the leaving to Peking of the Asian market for light industrial goods. Peking for its part hoped, by dealing with Japan more or less along these lines, to increase its leverage on Taiwan, exploit the tensions in Japanese-American relations, keep Japan away from the Soviet Union, and discourage Japanese rearmament. It appears that there are substantial elements of exaggeration in this analysis, which was written while the honeymoon atmosphere created by the Tanaka visit to Peking still lingered.

Peking having achieved much of the effect that it desired, namely the creation of a major incentive for Japan to prefer a Chinese to a Soviet orientation, simply by the fact of the visit, the honeymoon tended to evaporate in early 1973. To be sure, Tokyo's relations with Taipei were reduced to the level of a semiofficial trading office, Japanese firms hesitated to invest in Taiwan, and Japan's trade with the China mainland continued to expand. Tokyo made it clear that it would not consent to the use of American bases in Japan (including Okinawa) for the defense of Taiwan. Some fairly small sales of Chinese oil to Japan occurred. A 55-man Chinese "friendship" delegation visited Japan in the spring of 1973, mainly in order to familiarize its members with the Japanese scene and make contact with all major sectors of Japanese opinion (except the Communist Party). On the other hand, there was no noticeable progress toward a peace treaty, and some aspects of the commercial negotiations proved difficult. Peking tried to use them as a lever for gaining full Japanese recognition of Taiwan as a part of the People's Republic of China. Peking demanded that the profitable flights by Japan Air Lines and China Air Lines (the Nationalist air line) between Japan and Taiwan be terminated as the price of Japan Air Line's being allowed to make much less profitable flights to the mainland, partly in order to avoid the embarrassing possibility that aircraft from both the Communist and Nationalist Chinese airlines might find themselves using the same facilities in Japan.

After the middle of 1973, however, the atmosphere improved somewhat. Peking was probably disturbed over the apparent improvement in Soviet-American relations symbolized by Brezhnev's trip to the United States, by the disenchantment in Japan over the dissipation of the honeymoon atmosphere in Sino-Japanese relations, and by Premier Tanaka's approaching visit to the Soviet Union. Chou En-lai took care to make it clear, although not for the first time, that he had no serious objection to the Japanese-American security treaty (presumably because it minimized the chances of massive rearmament or a turn toward the Soviet Union by Japan) or a modest level of Japanese rearmament; neither of these things, as a matter of fact, had been criticized by the Chinese side in the Chou-Tanaka communiqué. Chinese attacks on the Siberian pipeline project stopped. In January 1974 a formal intergovernmental trade agreement was signed, and in April one was signed on air line rights essentially on Chinese terms.

The logic of the situation seems to suggest that the Sino-Japanese relationship is not likely to take the form either of open enmity, from which both would have too much to lose, or close cooperation, to which there are too many obstacles, but is likely rather to oscillate near the middle of the scale. It could be pushed toward enmity by another bout of Japanese militarism, but that seems unlikely. It could move toward closer cooperation if large oil reserves are actually found on the continental shelf and if Peking and Tokyo decide to exploit them jointly for the common benefit, that of the oil-hungry Japanese economy in particular.

Japan and Asia

The Japanese have generally felt a sense of contemptuous superiority to other Asians, apart from the Chinese. This feeling does not seem to have been much affected by the fact that Asia, again apart from China, is less important to them than it once was. This is true partly because Japan was defeated in its bid to establish what it called a Coprosperity Sphere in Asia, nominally for the benefit of others but actually for its own, but even more because it is now an industrial giant investing and trading worldwide, not primarily in Asia. Furthermore, whereas it was obviously the strongest power in Asia between the two World Wars, it is now outclassed politically and militarily by three others.

But even though non-Chinese Asia is no longer of prime importance to Japan, the converse does not hold; Japan is still very important to the rest of Asia as the largest single foreign investor and trading partner for the region as a whole. Although Japan's lack of military "reach" and of an active foreign policy toward the region has limited its political influence to a level considerably lower than that of the other three major powers, its enormous economic role has intensified the lingering resentments, especially in the Philippines, over the brutality of Japanese conquest and occupation in 1942. Japanese businessmen, who manage somehow to be both aloof and abrasive in their contacts with Asians, are sometimes called "yellow Yankees." They look for fast profits regardless of almost everything else. Their extractive operations (iron in the Philippines, oil in Indonesia, etc.) are conducted in a way reminiscent of strip mining; the terrain is left looking like the mountains of the moon. Japanese economic activity, whether formally classified as reparations payments (for the Second World War), aid, credits, or investment, is essentially and obviously export promotion and has little developmental effect. Japan runs large favorable balances with the Asian countries. Japan has been reluctant to become deeply committed to multilateral agencies such as the United Nations Economic Commission for Asia and the Far East or the World Bank's International Development Agency and has emphasized the Asian Development Bank, which is essentially Japanese-controlled. To an even greater extent than their American counterparts, Japanese official and commercial activities in Asia

tend to bolster the political *status quo* as a means toward stability
and profits. Thus, Japanese contacts, which include occasional corrupt ones, are useful to the Asian establishments, including even
the Communist ones but especially the right-wing ones, which,
like authoritarian regimes elsewhere, often promote economic development as a means of distracting public attention from the
shortage of political freedom. These connections are widely disliked by students, intellectuals, opposition politicians, local businessmen, and some of the ordinary people. The United States,
which used to encourage Japan to increase its economic activity in
Asia, does not do so any more.

For obvious geographic and historical reasons, Korea occupies
a special place in Japan's Asian concerns, even though the Japanese look down on the Koreans even more than on most other
Asians. Although the old feeling that Korea is a "dagger point at
the heart of Japan" has somewhat subsided, the Japanese elite
apart from the extreme left prefers to see the peninsula divided
and the southern half under a more or less friendly government and
under American protection, as the best situation from the standpoint of Japanese security. The satisfaction stemming from the
large and profitable Japanese stake in South Korea is somewhat
impaired by embarrassment caused by the highly authoritarian
character of the South Korean government. This was particularly
acute when the South Korean Central Intelligence Agency kid-
napped opposition leader Kim Dae Jung in Japan in 1973 and
brought him secretly back to Korea. Japan has a slowly growing
economic relationship with North Korea, but no diplomatic relations.

The Japanese establishment tended to approve of the American intervention in Vietnam after 1965, at least initially, both
because it seemed likely to promote stability and hold back Communism in Asia as a whole and because it resulted in huge Japanese profits from "offshore procurement." The opposition,
especially intellectuals and the left-wing parties, were of course
strongly opposed to it. The establishment resents the fact that the
United States has excluded Japan from the Vietnam settlement—
the Paris conference and the ICCS, specifically—at the same time
that it was inviting Japanese contributions to the reconstruction
of both halves of Vietnam.

In January 1974, Premier Tanaka took what turned out to be a memorable trip to Manila, Bangkok, Singapore, and Jakarta. For reasons already indicated, he was well received by the governments and establishments but denounced by some other elements. Students staged demonstrations in Manila and Bangkok (where they had organized a brief boycott of Japanese goods in late 1972), and a serious riot in Jakarta. In the latter case, however, the students were obviously venting their general frustrations on a variety of targets, including their own government and overseas Chinese merchants. Wholly owned Japanese firms were the objects of a great deal of hostility during the Tanaka visit, but this was much less true of enterprises owned jointly by Japanese and local firms. Tanaka and many of his thoughtful countrymen were shaken by these expressions of resentment. There was a general feeling that Japan and Japanese businessmen must try to adopt a lower posture in Southeast Asia and conduct their activities in ways less offensive to local feeling, but of course not withdraw from the region. What would actually be done was not clear.

CHAPTER XIV

India's Ascendancy over Pakistan

THE CRITICAL factor in the international politics of South Asia has been the power balance and general relationship between India and Pakistan. With its two widely separated halves held precariously together by a common Islamic heritage and a shared fear and hatred of India, and with the support of military aid from and an alliance (even though not valid against Indian attack) with the United States, Pakistan was able for a time to hold up its end of the adversary relationship with its larger neighbor. But this was possible only as long as the Pakistani political system offered enough to the people of East Pakistan to keep them within the same fold as the culturally very different West, where the political and military power lay. When that ceased to be true, in 1970–71, Pakistan broke in half, and the power balance in the subcontinent tilted sharply in favor of India, which enjoyed comparative political stability and superior national power.

The Rise of Indira Gandhi

It was a striking testimonial to the vigor of the parliamentary system in India and to that of the Congress that the death of Nehru in May 1964 was not followed by chaos or a military takeover. A majority of the senior Congress leaders combined to exclude the conservative and authoritarian Morarji Desai from the succession and to pick instead as the next Prime Minister Lal Bahadur Shastri, a capable and conciliatory man lacking Nehru's intellectual qualities and cosmopolitan background.

Under post-Nehru conditions, and given Shastri's personality, it was almost inevitable that the force of tradition and regional feeling ("fissiparous tendencies," as they are often called by Indians) should assert themselves. But the concessions made to them by the Shastri government were essentially statesmanlike compromises that had the purpose, and the effect, of easing tensions and preventing "fissiparous tendencies" from getting out of hand. There were three serious crises in 1965: a food shortage, tension resulting from the provision in the 1950 constitution requiring that Hindi (spoken only in the north) become the national language that year, and a war with Pakistan. The food shortage was gotten over through large imports of American grain for the poorer states, while the more prosperous ones were allowed to keep most of what they produced. The language crisis was eased by permitting the continued use of English for official purposes in the non-Hindi-speaking provinces. The war with Pakistan grew out of a Pakistani effort to force India to agree to a plebiscite in Kashmir (the greater part of which was controlled de facto by India although most of the population is Moslem) and resulted in an Indian victory which, although not decisive, was sufficient to enhance Shastri's prestige considerably. He died in January 1966, at the Soviet Central Asian city of Tashkent, after negotiating an end to the war under Soviet mediation.

The Congress leadership again maneuvered successfully to exclude Desai from the succession and chose instead as the next Prime Minister Nehru's daughter, Mrs. Indira Gandhi,* mainly because her name and prestige would be helpful in what promised to be a difficult general election in 1967. Like her father, she belonged to the left wing of the Congress and stood far enough to the left to be reasonably acceptable to Moscow and to the pro-Soviet mainstream of the Indian Communist movement, from which a pro-Chinese group calling itself the Communist Party of India (Marxist) (CPI[M]) had split off in 1964 as a consequence of the Sino-Soviet dispute.

* Not related to Mahatma Gandhi.

Rather widespread public discontent, with the Congress among other things, ate into the Congress vote in 1967, although it won 56 percent of the seats in the lower house (the Lok Sabha) of the Parliament whereas no other party won more than one-sixth as many. The Congress's postelection position in several of the states was considerably shakier. In West Bengal, a leftist coalition led by the CPI(M) came to power only to be faced with an armed revolt of some of its own extremist members, usually known as Naxalites (from Naxalbari, their initial area of operations), who took part in forming a new militant movement calling itself the Communist Party of India (Marxist-Leninist). The Naxalites took to random violence in the Calcutta area until they were largely crushed by severe police pressures in the early 1970s.

The 1967 election produced considerable demoralization in the Congress leadership, some of whose senior members were defeated in their home constituencies. One result was a temporary mood of party unity; Desai was brought into the cabinet, as Deputy Prime Minister and Finance Minister. More important was the fact that Mrs. Gandhi's position was beginning to be strengthened by an influx of younger voters tending to prefer left-wing Congress candidates to their right-wing counterparts. More and more the Congress leadership polarized into its left and right wings, and a series of issues in 1968–69 produced a split between them. One of these was the question of cooperation between the Congress-controlled central government and the non-Congress governments in some of the states; Mrs. Gandhi favored cooperation, the right wing opposed it. Another was Mrs. Gandhi's favorable tendencies toward the Soviet Union, India's main arms supplier, and in particular her public support for the invasion of Czechoslovakia. The leadership of the Congress machine had tried with little success to dominate the Prime Minister during the tenure of Mrs. Gandhi's father; it now hoped for better results in her case. As its alternative candidate for Prime Minister the machine, sometimes referred to as the Syndicate, selected the previously rejected Morarji Desai, probably because the weakness of his power base would tend to make him receptive to the Syndicate's guidance.

Mrs. Gandhi met the challenge head on, and successfully, in 1969, the centennial of Mahatma Gandhi's birth and a year whose associations therefore tended to strengthen her hand as the living embodiment of the Gandhi-Nehru tradition. Both more autocratic and less powerful than her father, she forced a break with her adversaries, rather than managing them while keeping them within the Congress as her father had done. In July she picked a fight with Desai by compelling his resignation as Finance Minister over the issue of nationalizing the banks, which he opposed. She then secured the adoption of legislation nationalizing the fourteen largest banks; her position was the popular, although not necessarily valid, one that the banks would now make credit more readily available to ordinary people. At the same time she challenged Desai's backers, the Syndicate, by maneuvering the election by the state legislatures of her candidate for the presidency of the Republic over the Syndicate's candidate; this was an important victory inasmuch as it is the President's prerogative to proclaim emergency ("President's") rule in states where normal parliamentary government is held to have broken down, and as we have seen there were differences between Mrs. Gandhi and the Syndicate on this question. In the latter part of 1969 the Syndicate and its supporters seceded and began to function as a separate party, usually known as the Old Congress, within the Parliament and in the country at large. Mrs. Gandhi's following, usually referred to as the New Congress, was clearly the stronger of the two. Much of her popularity arose from her endorsement of an appealing, if probably unrealizable, program of social reforms designed to "stamp out poverty."

The Fall of Ayub Khan

In 1962, President Ayub permitted political parties to function again in Pakistan. He intended to strengthen his authority by being elected to the presidency in 1965 by the 80,000 Basic Democrats, who in turn had been popularly elected in accordance with his nonparliamentary system of Basic Democracy. The latter was more democratic in name than in fact and rested essentially on the support of the armed forces and the bureaucracy.

Disturbed by the narrowness of his victory in the presidential election of early 1965, Ayub began to rely more than ever on the support of the essentially conservative bureaucracy and the armed forces. Angered by the Kennedy administration's liking for India, he had already begun to depend on China rather than the United States as his main external support against India, a tendency which was also favored by his brilliant, leftist, hawkish Foreign

Minister, Zulfikar Ali Bhutto. Encouraged and possibly incited by Peking, Ayub decided in mid-1965 to use force in an effort to make progress on the deadlocked Kashmir question, and in particular to bring about a plebiscite in which most of the region's Moslem majority could be expected to vote for union with Pakistan, in preference to accepting a continuation of the existing *de facto* partition of Kashmir between India and Pakistan.

In August 1965, Pakistani troops invaded the Indian-held part of Kashmir, and in September the fighting spread southward to the much more sensitive border region between the two countries properly speaking. The United States suspended aid to both sides in protest, and American influence in the subcontinent sank to one of its numerous low points. Being larger, although not necessarily better, the Indian armed forces began to gain the upper hand over their Pakistani adversaries, both in Kashmir and farther south, and it appeared that they might come into control of the tributaries of the Indus River, whose water is vital to the survival of West Pakistan. In mid-September, accordingly, Ayub first requested American and then accepted Soviet mediation. This step was opposed by Bhutto, who received some loud but ineffective propaganda support from Peking in the shape of (empty) threats designed to arouse in New Delhi fears of another Chinese border attack like the one of 1962. The main effect of this Chinese performance was to bring increased American and (above all) Soviet diplomatic pressure on both sides for a settlement, precisely in order to remove any basis for Chinese intervention. Meeting under Soviet auspices at Tashkent in January 1966, India and Pakistan agreed in effect to a return to the *status quo ante*. Pakistan had gained neither a plebiscite in Kashmir nor anything else; far from strengthening his political position, Ayub had impaired it.

China appeared more than ever as Pakistan's main foreign friend. Peking was credited, plausibly but not necessarily correctly, with having deterred any Indian move against East Pakistan during the 1965 war. Chinese military aid flowed to Pakistan in substantial amounts. By contrast, Pakistan began in 1969 to squeeze the United States out of bases near the Northwest Frontier from which certain activities in Soviet and Chinese Central Asia, notably signal communications and missile tests, had been electronically monitored for the previous decade.

Ayub's political decline continued, for reasons that included some basic social forces. Pakistan's remarkable economic growth under his political leadership had been achieved within the framework of a capitalist economic system. This meant that a few firms and families had grown disproportionately rich, that they could and did corrupt civil servants and politicians, and that the poor benefited relatively little and grew increasingly discontented. A long illness that Ayub suffered in 1968 helped to increase the level of opposition political activity, the most important manifestation of which was the emergence of Bhutto (whom Ayub had sacked as Foreign Minister in 1966) at the head of a new (1967) party, the Pakistan People's Party. In the autumn of 1968, Bhutto began to give effective political leadership to an anti-Ayub movement centering on student demonstrations, strikes, and other forms of disorder in the cities of West Pakistan, the main purpose being to prevent Ayub from being re-elected President in 1970.

Under mounting pressure of this kind, Ayub explored the possibility of proclaiming martial law, but the armed forces refused to implement it while he remained President. He then agreed (in February 1969) to a restoration of parliamentary government and announced that he would not be a candidate for the presidency in 1970, but the violence continued (mainly in West Pakistan), and political leaders in East Pakistan were loudly demanding autonomy. Ayub accordingly resigned on March 25, and the violence promptly subsided.

Ayub was succeeded by the senior figure among the military leadership, General Mohammed Yahya Khan. Even though the violence was virtually over, the new regime promptly proclaimed martial law. Although it was administered less rigorously than had been the case after the 1958 coup, it was regarded by many among the politicians and the public as unnecessary and excessive and accordingly got the new era off to a rather unpromising start on what was to turn out to be a disastrous career.

The Emergence of Bangla Desh

Perhaps even more than the quarrel with India, the tension between East and West was Pakistan's most serious single political problem. There was not only a geographic but a racial and cultural distance between the two halves; indeed, virtually their only common bond was an Islamic heritage and a distrust of India and

Hinduism. The population of the East (about 70 million) was more than half of Pakistan's total population, and the East through its exports of primary products such as jute generated most of the country's foreign exchange earnings. Yet the center of political and military power lay emphatically in the West, which was the home of some of what the British had called the "martial races" of the subcontinent and of nearly all the leaders of the original movement for Pakistan. The foreign exchange earned by the East was controlled essentially by the Western-dominated central government and used to a large extent to strengthen the armed forces, and in this way also the ascendancy of the West. The impressive economic development of the Ayub period, which had been fueled to a large extent by American aid, had occurred in and benefited the West far more than the East. It is not hard to see why the majority community of the East, the Bengali, wanted constitutional changes that would give the East political equality with, and autonomy with respect to, the West. Such in essence was the program of the East's principal political party, the Awami League, and its charismatic leader, Sheikh Mujibur Rahman (often known simply as Mujib).

In late 1969, President Yahya Khan promised general elections for one year later. The outcome was to be the first National Assembly in the history of Pakistan to be elected on the basis of one person, one vote, so that a majority of the seats would be filled by Easterners. But shortly before the date on which the election was to be held a huge storm and tidal wave struck the low-lying coast of East Pakistan, causing many thousands of deaths and severe property damage. The elections were postponed for two months. An international relief effort was mounted, but it was directed largely by the Pakistani central government, which proceeded to display both monumental inefficiency and a considerable indifference to the suffering of the victims. The result was further alienation of the East.

When the elections were held, in December 1970, the Awami League won 167 seats, representing all but two of the total allotted to the East. The League had been expected to win, but no one had predicted a landslide of these proportions. In the West, Bhutto's Pakistan People's Party won a majority of the seats, although a much less commanding one (81 out of 138). On the basis of these results, Mujib's position was that he should become Prime

Minister of Pakistan (and not simply Chief Minister of East Pakistan), that the capital should be moved to Dacca (in the East), and that the East's demands for equality and autonomy should be granted. Bhutto objected strongly to this and announced that his party would boycott the National Assembly; he evidently preferred a breakup of the country, in which case he would stand a good chance of coming to power in the West, to a condition of unity under which he would have to play second fiddle to Mujib. Caught between these two intransigent positions, Yahya moved closer, as time went on, to his fellow Westerner Bhutto, and as political methods failed he turned increasingly to the approach that he as a soldier understood best.

Yahya announced at the beginning of March 1971 that the convening of the National Assembly would be postponed. This step was interpreted in the East as a surrender to Bhutto and an effort to nullify the elections. Demonstrations and rioting spread rapidly in the East, and Mujib was forced by his own extreme followers into an uncompromising position. Yahya simultaneously tried, without success, to negotiate with him and Bhutto began a build-up of military strength in the East.

On March 25, the second anniversary of the proclamation of martial law, the Pakistani forces began systematic attacks on the largely unarmed population of the East, whom they regarded as little different from Indians. The emphasis was on the Hindu minority, and on educated people. Several hundred thousand people were killed during the ensuing weeks; some estimates run as high as three million. The troops also engaged in an orgy of raping and looting. They were helped by some members of the minority Bihari community, the Bihari being non-Bengali Moslems in East Pakistan. A huge stream of refugees, ultimately totaling about ten million and obviously including many Moslems as well as Hindus, began to pour into India, or more specifically into West Bengal. Mujib was promptly seized by the military and taken to the West, where he was kept under detention and was scheduled to be tried for treason. On April 17, some of his followers proclaimed the independent state of Bangla Desh as the successor to East Pakistan; they also began to organize a guerrilla resistance movement known as the Mukti Bahini. But actual independence was much more of a hope than a fact.

The 1971 War

The fact that Bangla Desh actually became independent was
due largely to Indian intervention. New Delhi was appalled by
the massacres in East Bengal and even more by the influx of refugees, who increased the already impressive political instability of
West Bengal and placed an intolerable burden on the economy
not only of that state but of India as a whole, in spite of the emergence of a substantial international relief effort on behalf of the
refugees. From India's point of view, it was imperative that the
refugees go home, but there was obviously no chance that they
would go home as long as the Pakistani Army was on the rampage
in East Bengal. This consideration alone would probably have
been enough to lead India to eliminate the Pakistani Army from
East Bengal, but there were others as well. Mrs. Gandhi's party had
just won a huge victory in the general election of March 1971,
which had been called a year ahead of the next election in the
states so as to separate national issues from local ones and give
Mrs. Gandhi a clear national mandate. Her party won 350 out of
518 seats in the Lok Sabha. She was therefore in a strong position
to take decisive action as the crisis over East Bengal unfolded, and
doing so would tend to strengthen her political position even
further and distract public attention from the difficulty she would
inevitably have in fulfilling her pledge to stamp out poverty. By
supporting the emergence of an independent state in East Bengal,
India would obviously contribute to the dismemberment of Pakistan, the weakening of its armed forces, and the attainment of clear-
cut Indian ascendancy over Pakistan. New Delhi had no serious
interest in assuming full responsibility for East Bengal's problems
by absorbing it. New Delhi accordingly insisted from the beginning of the crisis that Yahya must negotiate in good faith with
Mujib, even though it did not recognize Bangla Desh for the time
being.

One probable reason for this caution was Moscow's similarly
cautious attitude, which was influential because New Delhi relied
on the Soviet Union to deter Chinese intervention in the event of
an Indo-Pakistani war. But Moscow committed itself increasingly
to the Indian side, mainly because it felt a need for the support
of India as a counterweight to what seemed to be an emerging
Sino-American détente. Accordingly, after two years of incon-

clusive negotiations Moscow and New Delhi finally signed a treaty of friendship (not a formal alliance) on August 9, 1971; its most important part is Articles 8 and 9, which say by clear implication that if China should try to intervene in an Indo-Pakistani war, the Soviet Union would do whatever was necessary to cope with the problem. For extra insurance, India kept six divisions along the Sino-Indian border and waited until snow began to fall on Himalayan passes before intervening directly in East Bengal.

By about the middle of 1971, the Indian Army was providing arms and training for the Mukti Bahini, whose units moved back and forth across the border between East and West Bengal and made life increasingly difficult for the Pakistani forces. The latter tended to redeploy near the border and concede much of the interior to the Mukti Bahini. In October, both India and Pakistan massed troops near their common border in the West. Of the two adversaries, India was obviously the stronger, and in the refugees it felt that it had an issue that both required and justified intervention. It probably hoped that by intervening it would free Bangla Desh without bringing on a general Indo-Pakistani war, but it was also prepared for the latter eventuality. On November 20, Indian troops made limited penetrations into East Bengal and began to engage the Pakistani forces they encountered. Determined not to lose East Bengal without fighting what it termed the "final war" with India, Pakistan launched a surprise air attack against Indian airfields in the West on December 3. The Indian Army immediately began a full-scale invasion of East Bengal, while remaining essentially on the defensive in the West. On December 16 the Pakistani forces in the East had to surrender, and the fighting in the West ended at the same time.

During the entire crisis and particularly during the actual fighting, Chinese political and propaganda support for Pakistan was loud and strong. Any sympathy in Peking for the Mukti Bahini as a "national liberation movement" was much more than outweighed by the sense of commitment to Pakistan and hostility to India built up over the previous decade or more. Peking may have believed that acquiescence in the loss of East Bengal to Pakistan would weaken its own claim to Taiwan and encourage Soviet pressures on Chinese border territories. Soviet support for India and the White House's sympathy for Pakistan (which was not shared by many in the United States government) also contributed to Peking's attitude. But Chinese support for Pakistan was almost purely verbal, down to the end of the war, and two of its strongest propaganda broadcasts were timed to coincide with the Pakistani surrender in Dacca, when there was no chance that they might have to be acted on. Peking was prevented from doing more than make propaganda by snow in the Himalayan passes, by the presence of six Indian divisions along the Sino-Indian frontier, and above all by the possibility of Soviet retaliation.

The Aftermath of the Indian Victory

Normally the country most affected by a war is the loser. The first political effect of losing the 1971 war to India was another change of government in Pakistan. A scapegoat had to be found, and the military leadership fixed on the obvious candidate, its own senior member, Yahya Khan. Being politically discredited by its excesses in East Bengal, and its defeat, the Army permitted Bhutto to become President at the end of 1971. He remained obviously vulnerable to potential removal by the Army, but the prevailing political climate made this unlikely as long as he did not permit a further break-up of the country following the loss of the East.

Bhutto was very much on his mettle to hold what was left of Pakistan together and begin healing the wounds suffered in 1971. An able and energetic man, he responded in a most remarkable fashion. By frequent dramatic public appearances, he rallied popular support for his leadership and program. With a judicious combination of force and political concessions, he successfully combatted secessionist tendencies and incipient insurgencies in the western state of Baluchistan (where they were supported by Iraq) and in the Northwest Frontier Province (where they were supported to some extent after July 1973 by Afghanistan).

In April 1973 Bhutto restored the parliamentary system after a lapse of about fifteen years. He became Prime Minister, with a largely figurehead President as chief of state. Less on account of any dictatorial tendencies on Bhutto's part than because of continuing instability, there was nevertheless a tendency toward government by decree, fairly rigorous censorship, and other such departures from the practice of a liberal democracy.

Although a rich man, Bhutto was a socialist of sorts and

favored greater equality of incomes and a curb on the influence of the twenty-two wealthy families who had emerged at the top of the economic heap during the previous two decades. He nationalized heavy (but not light) industry, promoted social legislation, and fought corruption. His problems were formidable; they included the strains of the war, the loss of the East's export earnings and a resulting acute shortage of foreign exchange, a major flood (in August 1973), and the agricultural difficulties normal in a poor agrarian country.

Bhutto effected some major changes in Pakistan's foreign policy. He appeared genuinely to accept the verdict of 1971 and adopted a relatively conciliatory line toward India and Bangla Desh, except for a probably ritualistic revival of propaganda on the Kashmir question. It is likely, although not certain, that the Army leadership joined him in accepting the verdict of 1971. By way of insurance, Bhutto was careful not to antagonize the Army and public opinion by moving too rapidly toward reconciliation with India. He withdrew from SEATO and increasingly emphasized ties with the Middle Eastern countries, notably Iran; there was a possibility that Pakistan might emerge with Chinese aid and support as a major producer and supplier of arms to the Middle East. He continued to cultivate friendship with China, which rewarded him with a continued and substantial flow of economic and military aid. He was less successful with the United States, which regarded itself as a political friend of Pakistan but declined to resume large-scale arms shipments. The Soviet Union, unwilling to leave the field entirely to China, engaged in a limited aid-and-trade relationship with Pakistan.

As with many wars, it was not certain that the victor of 1971 was much better off than the loser. The Indian economic and social system was badly strained by the refugees, the war, continued and virtually uncontrolled population growth, serious commodity shortages (including grain), the persistence of caste barriers, insufficient social change (including land reform), educated unemployment and widespread underemployment, and a greatly increased bill for oil imports as a result of the Middle Eastern crisis of 1973. These conditions inevitably found a reflection in the political sphere. There were rather numerous strikes, riots, and other manifestations of discontent, including student demonstrations. In spite of severe police repression, the Naxalite movement lingered on. Mrs. Gandhi's recognition of English as a national language (in 1967) notwithstanding, agitation over language problems persisted in the southern states.

Although Mrs. Gandhi and her party retained the Congress's traditional dominant role in the central government, and in most of the state governments through a series of state elections in 1972 and afterward, there was inevitably some erosion. Part of it was due to Mrs. Gandhi's secretiveness and lack of forcefulness, her indecisiveness on domestic policy questions, and her tendency to rely on cronies rather than on individuals of real political stature for advice. The bureaucracy through which she had to work was cumbersome, inefficient, and often corrupt. The Congress leaderships in the states showed increasing unwillingness to be manipulated or controlled from New Delhi. The narrowness of the Congress's victory in some important state elections in 1974 made Mrs. Gandhi more dependent than before on the support of the pro-Soviet wing of the Indian Communist movement, the Communist Party of India.

Clearly Mrs. Gandhi regarded the Soviet Union as India's main foreign friend. A major indication of this fact was a visit by Brezhnev in November 1973. The Soviet side agreed to continue its substantial economic aid to India, although on the understanding that Indian economic planning would be modeled to a greater extent along the centralized lines favored by Moscow. Soviet military aid and general Soviet-Indian cooperation in foreign policy were also to continue, although the Indian side declined to give public endorsement to the Soviet concept of "collective security" and (apparently) to grant naval bases or special port facilities as Moscow evidently desired.

Although under considerable Soviet influence, India was by no means a Soviet satellite and was determined not to become one. It was partly for this reason—in the hope of maintaining a counterweight to Soviet influence, in other words—that New Delhi began to show an interest in improving its relations with the United States, which had reached a record low in 1971. Another, even more important, reason was a felt need for American economic aid, which was quietly resumed in 1974, and above all for American grain. On the other hand, tensions in Indo-American relations remained. Mrs. Gandhi criticized the American bombing campaigns in Vietnam in 1972, and the United States excluded India from any role in the Vietnam settlement, including participation in the ICCS. Indian official and public opinion was hostile to American naval activity in the Indian Ocean, and in particular to the American plan to construct major naval facilities on the island of Diego Garcia.

Again as a counterweight to the possibility of excessive Soviet influence, New Delhi showed an interest in improving relations with Moscow's main adversary, Peking, even though Sino-Indian relations since the late 1950s had usually been only slightly less bad than Indo-Pakistani relations. But there was little overt response from Peking, which was still angry over what had happened in 1971, lacked Bhutto's reasons for conciliating India, and regarded Mrs. Gandhi as unduly receptive to Soviet influence. On the other hand, there were some elusive indications that Peking might be prepared to moderate its stand if Mrs. Gandhi should become willing to weaken her ties to Moscow. In any case, the only significant source of Chinese influence in the subcontinent was being reduced to the extent that Indo-Pakistani relations improved.

When it began its independent career, Bangla Desh was described, unkindly but not inaccurately, as an "international basket case." It had been devastated and decimated by war. Thousands of its women who had been raped by Pakistani soldiers, and in many cases made pregnant, were having great difficulty in being accepted by their families. There was continuing civil violence, especially among the Biharis, some of whom had collaborated with the Pakistani. There was considerable political instability, and the new government by no means enjoyed universal support. There were serious shortages, and the economy was burdened by the gradual return of the refugees. On the other hand, there was no massive blood bath and no massive famine. The latter blessing was due to a large extent to a sizable international relief and aid program, in which the Soviet Union, India, and the United States figured prominently.

At the beginning of 1972 Bhutto released Mujib unconditionally, and he returned triumphally to become Prime Minister of the new state. In elections held in March 1973, his Awami League won a huge electoral victory; the opposition parties were almost wiped out. The Awami League's political position was somewhat eroded with the passage of time, however, by internal factional

bickering, Mujib's inadequacies as a policymaker and adminis-
trator, and economic problems. Bangla Desh gathered in a growing
number of diplomatic recognitions, including those of the Soviet
Union and the United States. Its application for admission to the
United Nations, however, was vetoed by China in August 1972,
at the request of Pakistan and contrary to the wishes of the United
States. Pakistani recognition of Bangla Desh in February 1974,
however, was followed by indications that Peking might do the
same.

The legacy of the 1971 war to the international relations of the
subcontinent was a complex and bitter one. Indian troops soon
withdrew from Bangla Desh, but they remained in occupation of
limited areas of West Pakistan. India was holding 93,000 Pakistani
military prisoners, including some Bihari irregulars. Hundreds of
thousands of Bihari in Bangla Desh and of Bengali in Pakistan
wanted to go to Pakistan and Bangla Desh respectively; the Bihari
in particular were having a very difficult time where they were.
Difficult though these problems were, and great though the bitterness was, the domestic situations of the three countries were too
serious to permit the luxury of further international conflict, and
progress toward a relaxation of tension on the subcontinent was
on the whole surprisingly rapid. In July 1972, India and Pakistan
agreed to establish a state of peace and friendship between them,
to return to the military *status quo ante* (except with respect to
Bangla Desh), and to begin negotiations on exchange of prisoners,
repatriation of civilians, and a Kashmir settlement. Although
Indian troops withdrew from West Pakistan by the end of the
year, implementation of the political aspects of this accord was
delayed and complicated by Mujib's position, to which India felt
compelled to pay some attention. He was demanding both Pakistani recognition and war crimes trials for a sizable number of the
Pakistani prisoners. Bhutto was willing to consider the first of
these demands, but only if the second were dropped; if he had
accepted the second, he might have been overthrown by his own
military leadership. In this and some other respects Bhutto essentially prevailed, partly because of his own dynamism and partly
because of the reluctance of Mrs. Gandhi and Mujib to risk his
downfall and the further balkanization of Pakistan. In August
1973, another Indo-Pakistani agreement was reached that provided for the repatriation of all Pakistani prisoners of war and

some of the two civilian groups already mentioned, the dropping of all but a small number of war crimes trials, Pakistani recognition of Bangla Desh, and the end of Pakistani opposition to Bangla Desh's admission to the United Nations. Pakistan recognized Bangla Desh in February 1974, on the occasion of a conference of Moslem nations at Lahore. The repatriation process was under way by that time. In April 1974, Pakistan apologized to Bangla Desh for the behavior of its Army, Bangla Desh dropped the idea of war crimes trials completely, and India and Pakistan agreed to move ahead with the development of the ties visualized in the accord of July 1972.

A further major shift in the international politics of South Asia could occur if India were to become a nuclear power. India has long had the technical capability of doing so but has been restrained by a combination of domestic and external considerations, including cost. The 1971 war tended to tip the balance of the argument in the other direction, however, by intensifying India's self-image as the major power of South Asia and yet one still subject to "nuclear blackmail" as long as it lacked its own nuclear weapons. Such was the Indian public reaction to the entry of the American nuclear aircraft carrier *Enterprise* into the Bay of Bengal in December 1971 (see Chapter XI); soon afterward Indian officials were saying privately that it was only a matter of time before India became a nuclear power. The first Indian nuclear detonation, an underground one alleged to be for peaceful purposes and conducted in May 1974, obviously brought that day closer. In spite of the considerable improvement in Indo-Pakistani relations that had occurred by that time, the effect on Pakistan of this advance in the Indian nuclear program seemed likely to be serious. To the extent that it was, it also appeared likely that Pakistan would be driven further into the arms of Peking, and that Sino-Indian reconciliation would be put off if not prevented altogether. All this would be a high price to pay for an Indian nuclear capability that would be of little use against China (or any other adversary beside Pakistan), since Chinese missiles and bombers could threaten major Indian cities from bases in Tibet far more easily than Indian missiles and bombers could threaten major Chinese cities.

After a generation of intermittent struggle, a clear Indian ascendancy over Pakistan had been established and had gained recognition from everyone except perhaps a few Pakistani die-hards. India's fairly close relationship with the Soviet Union further enhanced its international position and rendered very unlikely the possibility of another humiliation of India at the hands of China like the one of 1962. More than ever before, India's main problems were internal rather than external. This important new situation seems to have had at least an indirect causal effect on two political shifts that occurred along the northern rim of the subcontinent in 1973. In April, political demonstrations by the Nepalese majority against the ruling minority of Lepchas in the Himalayan principality of Sikkim led to Indian intervention in favor of the former and an increase in India's already considerable political influence; Sikkim is highly strategic because it lies astride the main route through the Himalayas between Tibet and eastern India. In July, the King of Afghanistan was overthrown by a leftist military coup, with the result that Soviet influence increased somewhat and Afghanistan began again, after a lapse of ten years, to work toward the detachment of the Pushtu areas of Pakistan and their establishment as an Afghan-dominated state to be known as Pushtunistan.

CHAPTER XV

Southeast Asia:
Diversity and Change

SOUTHEAST Asia's record of instability since the Second World War and the massive American military involvement in Indochina have tended to repel public opinion in the United States and much of the rest of the world and threaten to make the region become the object of comparative international neglect. This is an unfortunate trend, since Southeast Asia remains an important and interesting region, the only one in the world that contains valuable natural resources, includes some ten recently independent states in varying conditions of vigor, and is still a theater of interaction among four major external powers. In a case like this, public neglect is not the proper corrective to official overinvolvement. Whatever else happens to Southeast Asia, it will not evaporate.

Burma: Socialism via Military Dictatorship

Early in 1960 the civilian U Nu resumed office as Prime Minister of Burma following an interval of military rule (1958–60). His fervent piety and talk about a Buddhist state tended to alienate the predominantly non-Buddhist border minorities, while his geniality led him to promise them increased autonomy. Fearing that this trend might give rise to secessionist movements and to

Thai control over the Shan States (in the northeast), and convinced that parliamentary government had failed in Burma, the military under General Ne Win seized power for the second time in March 1962.

Governing through a self-appointed Revolutionary Council composed of military leaders and leftist intellectuals, Ne Win set out to achieve a socialist political and social system for Burma via a military dictatorship, and to gain the kind of immunity from interference by foreign powers (above all China and the United States) that was conspicuously lacking in Indochina, by means of an isolationist foreign policy. He began to build a one-party state by forming in 1962 the Burma Socialist Programme Party (BSPP), which consisted of only a handful of members at first but began to acquire something of a mass base about 1970. Shortly before that, elective councils had been formed in both the urban and the rural areas, as a means of political mobilization of the population; they were wholly controlled by the BSPP and performed few useful functions except to serve as a channel of communication between the leaders and the led.

Ne Win tried to cope with the several ethnic and leftist insurgencies by inviting their leaders to a conference in 1963. In the case of the Burma Communist Party (BCP, the orthodox or White Flag Communists), he had been encouraged to do this by Liu Shao-ch'i, who visited Burma in the spring of 1963 in his capacity as Chairman of the People's Republic of China. Although some of the other negotiations achieved limited results, those with the BCP broke down. The BCP went back into insurgency but was soon driven out of Lower Burma by the Army. It then withdrew to the vicinity of the Chinese border and became increasingly dependent on support from Peking, which at first proved to be very limited in nature (apart from propaganda).

Ne Win tried to cope with the problem of disaffection and continuing, although not very serious, insurgency among the ethnic minorities by a policy of very limited concessions combined with an essentially assimilationist policy backed by much repression. Much of the Indian community, which contained valuable entrepreneurial skills, was compulsorily repatriated. The Chinese community was left largely alone at first, because of the peculiarly important place that China occupies in Burma's view of the world.

To a large extent Ne Win's isolationist foreign policy, which reduced Burma's role in regional and international organizations almost to zero, was motivated by fear of the giant Chinese neighbor and a desire not to give it the slightest pretext to intervene in Burma—apart conceivably from supporting the BCP. This objective was largely achieved, not only through Ne Win's efforts but on account of Peking's preoccupation with other matters (such as Vietnam) and the countervailing diplomatic roles in Burma of the Soviet Union and the United States. Peking conceded a rather favorable (to Burma) settlement of the Sino-Burmese boundary dispute in 1960–61, for roughly these reasons and greatly to Rangoon's relief. Peking's growing propaganda support for the BCP after 1963 placed no great strain on official Sino-Burmese relations as long as it was accompanied by no overt action. Nevertheless, Ne Win was disliked by the radical Maoists in China because of his association with Liu Shao-ch'i (who was purged in 1966–67) and his campaign against the BCP. It was probably as a result of this attitude that Rangoon witnessed a more violent explosion of militancy during the Cultural Revolution on the part of Chinese radicals, especially students, than did any other area outside China with the possible exception of Hong Kong. The resulting demonstrations (in June 1967) were first banned by Ne Win and then became the object of retaliation by troops, police, and mobs. A huge diplomatic and propaganda crisis in Sino-Burmese relations ensued, and Peking terminated its economic aid program in Burma.

In 1969, as part of his program for institutionalizing the BSPP's rule, Ne Win solicited the constitutional advice of the civilian leaders whom he had ousted in 1962, including U Nu. The majority of them favored a return to parliamentary government. When Ne Win rejected this idea, U Nu went abroad and for about four years led an insurgent movement based just across the Thai border; although backed to a limited extent by the Thai government, by some Hong Kong Chinese business interests angered by Ne Win's nationalization program, and by some others hopeful of offshore oil leases if U Nu returned to power, this movement achieved few results apart from exercising some influence in the adjacent Karen State (in southeastern Burma).

In the early 1970s, Ne Win proceeded with his political program. He declared himself a civilian in 1972 and the following year had the BSPP draw up a draft constitution purporting to legitimate its own rule. A referendum and election held at the beginning of 1974, also under the BSPP's leadership, ratified the constitution and put it into effect. In reality, the regime's political repressiveness, although not unusually severe, had alienated many of the students and intellectuals, and its economic policies had antagonized the peasants. On the other hand, at least in rural areas the Burmans (the majority community, as distinct from the ethnic minorities) had a tradition of acquiescence in existing authority as long as it was not impossibly severe or inefficient.

In the industrial sector, or what little there was of it, Ne Win's policy of nationalization (i.e., expulsion of foreign capital) and socialization (i.e., elimination of private enterprise) did not work too badly. But in the rural areas limited incentives, including low state-fixed prices for agricultural products, and official propaganda (not backed by much action, to be sure) in favor of collectivization contributed to a virtual stagnation of rice output and therefore of the export of Burma's main foreign exchange earner. Indeed, the economy as a whole was stagnant, and absolute production levels declined in some sectors. Since this situation could not reasonably be attributed to Burmese culture and society, which showed considerable creativity and vigor, it had to be due largely to the stultifying effects of Ne Win's brand of authoritarianism and socialism.

Next to the economic situation, Ne Win's most serious problem was probably the Communist insurgency and its relationship with Peking. In 1967 the BCP became the only non-Chinese Communist Party to take Peking's advice to launch its own Cultural Revolution; the major reason for this decision was probably a desire to make Peking take the BCP seriously for the first time. The main practical effect was that by the end of 1968, the party's top leaders had killed each other off. Peking, presumably under the pressure of its own radical elements, then decided to rebuild the party as an effective guerrilla movement. Under leaders with strong pro-Chinese sympathies and with Chinese equipment (including pack and anti-aircraft artillery), a new model BCP manned largely by local (non-Burman) tribesmen soon emerged in the small but strategically situated Wa State, just on the Burmese side of the border with China. For six weeks in November-December 1971, this force besieged Kuenlong, the main town of the Wa State, but ultimately without success. After that the insurgents expanded southeastward into the Eastern Shan States, in the direction of northern Thailand. Meanwhile, as though to support the new model BCP and prevent it from becoming depressed by the resumption of full-fledged ambassadorial relations between China and Burma in 1970–71 after a hiatus of about four years, Peking started a "liberation radio" in Yunnan in April 1971 that beamed anti-Ne Win revolutionary propaganda at Burma. Apart from the Chinese radicals' dislike of Ne Win and their sense of commitment to the BCP, plausible explanations for this pattern of Chinese behavior included a desire to warn Rangoon against an abandonment of its isolationism and above all against affiliating in any way with the Indo-Soviet entente, and a desire for a base area that could be helpful in subverting northern Thailand; the latter consideration grew in probable importance as Peking withdrew most of its military personnel from northwest Laos in 1973–74, following the agreement on ending the civil war in that country, and as Chinese involvement in Burmese insurgency appeared to increase.

Less serious, but still a problem, was the presence in northeast Burma of Chinese soldiers and adventurers referred to by the Burmese as KMTs (for Kuomintang), or KMT Irregulars. Some of them apparently remained in contact with Taiwan, which presumably thought that it got some value from them, but for the most part they simply engaged in smuggling opium out and guns in and generally lining their own pockets. The United States was concerned over their activities in connection with its campaign against the international drug traffic, but Rangoon showed little interest in cooperating in an opium suppression campaign until it became clear in the early 1970s that some children of high Burmese officials had become addicted to heroin. At that point the Burma Army began to intensify its activities against the KMTs and in 1973 drove the "opium king" of Burma, an overseas Chinese named Lo Hsing-han, into Thailand, where he was promptly captured and returned to Burma to stand trial. Obviously opium suppression in Burma, where more opium was produced than in any other Southeast Asian country, was making at least some progress.

By about 1973, Ne Win's twin policies of socialism and isolationism were under sufficient strain so that some minor modifications were beginning to be made. Ne Win traveled increasingly abroad, partly on account of illness but also in order to establish closer ties with foreign countries. Burma showed a gradually increasing interest in an informal invitation that had been extended to it to join the Association of Southeast Asian Nations (ASEAN; see below), as well as in United Nations aid and Japanese credits. All this reflected a perception of Burma's economic difficulties and the increasingly fluid international situation in Asia resulting from American disengagement from Indochina and the Sino-American détente, and probably also concern over Chinese policy toward Burma.

Thailand: Away from Dictatorship

The powerful and effective Marshal Sarit Thannarat, who governed Thailand for five years (1958–63), was succeeded by a duumvirate consisting of two more marshals, Thanom Kittikachorn and Praphat Charusathien, the latter being in effective control of the police. Theirs was a corrupt, inefficient, and increasingly unpopular regime, but the devotion of most Thai to Buddhism and the monarchy kept active opposition at a minimum as long as the King, the widely revered Bhumibol Aduldet, refrained from speaking out against the duumvirate. It was not a very repressive regime by the standards of modern garrison or police states, but the level of active political freedom was rather low, and the process of economic development, fueled by American aid and Japanese investment, tended to produce increased social inequalities.

In the early 1960s, as the crisis in Indochina escalated, the Thai government grew increasingly concerned over the presumed threat by China and North Vietnam to Laos and the adjacent regions of north and northeast Thailand. Indeed, an insurgency, more of a political than a military variety and supplied and directed to a considerable extent by China, North Vietnam, and the Pathet Lao, began among the population of the Northeast, who are Thai but are closely related to the Lao. By the late 1960s a guerrilla insurgency, supplied by China but not really Communist in nature, began among the non-Thai Meo mountaineers of Northern Thailand. Since the late 1950s, the ethnically Chinese Malayan Communist Party had been maintaining its major base areas in extreme Southern Thailand, where although its main thrust was against Malaya it posed something of a threat to Bangkok's control over the rather disaffected Moslem minority in the South. In addition to these domestic problems, the Thai government's relations with all its neighbors were uneasy at best; with Japanese support, it had taken territory from all of them during the Second World War only to be compelled to return it afterward and was still suspected of wanting to regain it.

Bangkok reacted to this difficult situation by a combination of modest and none-too-successful counterinsurgency programs (except in the South, where progress was achieved in the early 1970s) and closer alignment than before with the United States. In 1965 Bangkok began to allow American aircraft to be based in Thailand and to bomb the Ho Chi Minh Trail in Laos and Communist installations and forces in both halves of Vietnam; in early 1967 this American presence was expanded to include B-52s. In addition a small contingent of Thai troops went to fight in South Vietnam, followed by a larger one that went to Laos (see Chapter X). All this naturally hardened Peking's and Hanoi's attitude toward Bangkok more than ever.

Accordingly, the Thai government was seriously concerned when its supposedly powerful and reliable American patron began to indicate in March 1968 an apparent intention to reduce its military involvement in Vietnam and the rest of Southeast Asia; the Nixon Doctrine of 1969 was of course a still more positive affirmation of this intention. Bangkok's response was an effort to render itself less dependent on the United States, to improve its relations with the non-Communist Southeast Asian countries and with the ASEAN nations (Malaysia, Singapore, Indonesia, and the Philippines, in addition to Thailand) in particular, and to establish private contacts with Peking aimed at a lessening of Sino-Thai hostility. Some progress was made in all of these directions, but with characteristic Thai caution; Foreign Minister Thanat Khoman, who wanted to move farther and faster along these lines than his military colleagues cared to go, was ousted in 1971. Peking showed an interest in trade, cultural relations, and diplomatic recognition—provided Bangkok broke with Taipei—but was unwilling (presumably for domestic political reasons for the most part) to reduce its support for insurgency in Thailand.

In 1968–69, the ruling duumvirate implemented a constitution (the latest of several that Thailand had had since 1932) and permitted a parliamentary election and a limited emergence of party politics. One reason for this interest in institutionalization was that both Thanom and Praphat were approaching the legal retirement age for Army officers, that the King expected them to retire on schedule, that Thanom at least intended to comply, and that they were not likely to be able to retain their political power for long after their retirement from the Army. Several factors combined, however, to render this turn toward parliamentary government a short-lived one. Praphat intrigued actively to succeed Thanom after the latter's retirement and to postpone his own retirement somehow. The military elite as a whole and the bureaucracy rapidly became irritated at the inevitable bickering among the politicians and the efforts by the latter not only to criticize the government but to influence its behavior. Given the already-discussed and difficult international situation facing Thailand, the military elite wanted greater freedom of action than it was likely to have under a semiparliamentary system. Accordingly, in November 1971 the government executed a "coup in office" that put an end to the constitution and the parliament. Apart from opposition politicians and students, the population took the coup fairly calmly, but it sowed the seeds of serious future trouble for Thanom and Praphat.

For a number of reasons, Thailand was struck by serious economic difficulties, including inflation and labor unrest, in 1972. Partly as a distraction, the government encouraged students to stage demonstrations against Japanese economic influence in Thailand. But once aroused the students soon began to direct their activities against a more meaningful target, the government. There was a series of student demonstrations in 1973 over a variety of issues, of which the most important was Praphat's ambition to succeed Thanom. In October the demonstrations swelled to massive proportions over the government's arrest of a group of student leaders. Thanom apparently differed with Praphat and with his own son, the powerful and unpopular Colonel Narong, who was Praphat's son-in-law, over how to handle the crisis, which was marked by the killing of a few hundred demonstrators by police and troops—the first such tragedy in Thailand's history. Significant elements of the Army refused to support Thanom and Praphat. Most important of all, the King sided openly with the students and insisted successfully that Thanom, Praphat, and Narong resign and leave the country. The King then appointed a conservative civilian, Sanya Thammasak, as Premier and in effect forbade the Army to overthrow him.

The public euphoria that greeted this sudden and potentially important change of government tended to evaporate as the leaders of the student organizations, although not especially leftist, were excluded from real political influence by a coalition of military men and bureaucrats almost as conservative, although not so dictatorial, as the preceding one. Growing political turbulence led to a cabinet reorganization in May 1974. Thailand still had a long way to go before it could claim to be a genuine parliamentary democracy. But it had apparently begun to move in that direction, at a time when most of the non-Communist Asian states were moving in the opposite one, and it might conceivably serve as a valuable example for the others.

The Sanya government made only marginal changes in the foreign policy of the old one. It appeared slightly more favorable to the withdrawal of the American military presence, which actually began in 1973. It was somewhat more conciliatory toward Peking, which responded with some vague and not necessarily binding pledges about reducing its support for insurgency in Thailand. Peking was interested not only in conciliating the new Thai government but in encouraging the United States not to withdraw too rapidly, since its military presence in Thailand tended to serve as a check on possible increased Soviet influence and to deter Hanoi from re-escalating the war in Indochina.

As a relatively homogeneous and self-confident country located in the center of continental Southeast Asia and lacking the unsettling legacy of a colonial tradition, Thailand is one of the two intrinsically most important countries of the region, the other being Indonesia. Its future political development is likely to exert a considerable influence not only on the welfare of its own people but on its neighbors and on the international politics of Southeast Asia. This fact, which has been obscured by the general preoccupation with Vietnam, has emerged more clearly into view as the military situation in Vietnam and Laos has quieted down, for the time being at any rate.

Vietnam "at Peace"

It is obvious to even the most casual newspaper reader that the January 1973 agreement brought peace to Vietnam only in theory.

In reality, the struggle went on, although to date at a level of violence significantly lower than before the signing of the agreement. As nearly always in the past, the Communist side was basically on the offensive. As usual in the past, the cause and eventual outcome of the struggle seemed likely to depend on the degree of viability of the non-Communist regime and the policies of the major foreign powers.

The question of the viability of the Saigon government is a complex one, and the answer is uncertain. President Thieu appears determined to keep Communists and possibly pro-Communist neutrals from entering it in the manner envisaged eventually in the January 1973 agreement. Instead he has been trying to prolong his own grip on the presidency by various maneuvers. In 1973 he formed a government party, the so-called Democracy Party, and although he has allowed a slightly greater degree of personal and political freedom to his non-Communist opponents than used to be the case, he has effectively prevented them from coalescing into a third force. Although his government is neither the most repressive nor the most inefficient in Southeast Asia, it ranks fairly high on both counts. Authoritarianism of this kind is perhaps understandable in a regime fighting for its life but is not necessarily the best system under which to do so. From the standpoint of ideology and organization, the two main sources of dynamism and effectiveness in politics, the Saigon government is clearly inferior to its Northern adversary and the latter's Southern allies. In the rural areas, landlords have been reacquiring land once distributed to peasants under the land reform program, and local government is closely controlled from Saigon. The economy has been hit by commodity shortages and a galloping inflation, in spite of the virtual disappearance of spending by American military personnel. The partial Americanization of the regime has probably made it less able in some ways than it would otherwise be to cope with its problems, notably its contest with the North.

In the North, in spite of war weariness and extensive bomb damage the Hanoi leadership shows no signs of slackening in its determination to dominate the South, at first through the NLF and then directly, and Laos and Cambodia through local proxies. To be sure, Hanoi is heeding Soviet and Chinese advice, and the call of common sense, to the extent of devoting considerable energy and funds to economic reconstruction. Clearly it would be reluctant to sacrifice this to American bombing through overeagerness in the South. On the other hand, Hanoi regards its economic program as a basis for, not an alternative to, further efforts to "liberate" the South. To the latter end it is trying hard to build up the so-called Third Vietnam, the substantial territory along the western edge of South Vietnam controlled by the NLF and its Provisional Revolutionary Government of South Vietnam (PRG), as a rival to and eventual replacement for the Saigon government. Hanoi has tried, with some success, to insist that countries wishing to establish diplomatic relations with itself must also recognize the PRG, and in this way the PRG has gained a few diplomatic recognitions from non-Communist as well as Communist countries. A choice of sorts is involved; a government can maintain relations simultaneously with Hanoi and Saigon, but not with Saigon and the PRG. North Vietnam has effectively annexed the northern portion of the territory nominally controlled by the PRG. The North Vietnamese Army has been rapidly extending and expanding the road network linking the DRV with the Third Vietnam, as an alternative or supplement to the Ho Chi Minh Trail. Artillery, armor, and other military equipment have been accumulated in the Third Vietnam via these roads at levels higher than those that existed at the time of the Easter offensive. Since the Soviet Union and China have apparently reduced their deliveries of military equipment to North Vietnam since January 1973, this must mean that nearly all the DRV's stocks of such equipment are in South Vietnam. By the same token, nearly the whole of the North Vietnamese Army is outside its home territory, in South Vietnam, Laos, and Cambodia—a phenomenon unique in the world. North Vietnamese troops being withdrawn from Laos are apparently being moved into South Vietnam.

All this means, of course, that Hanoi is in a strong position to launch a major offensive in South Vietnam at any time it chooses. It has been restrained, however, by a number of considerations. One obviously is Saigon's military powers of resistance, which are fairly formidable even in the absence of further American air support, as a result of the Vietnamization program. Another is the attitude and policy on military aid of Peking and Moscow, which are essentially unfavorable at present to another offensive. Most important of all, probably, is uncertainty regarding the American response to a North Vietnamese offensive; Hanoi evidently has no desire to see any more B-52s and probably is not sure the United States would refrain from using them if challenged. In addition, there is the fact that the Viet Cong infrastructure is rather weak in the largely government-controlled areas (i. e., outside the Third Vietnam). For these reasons, more or less, North Vietnamese Defense Minister Vo Nguyen Giap, who apparently favors another major offensive, has not been able to make his views prevail. Instead, the strategy to date has essentially been one of keeping limited military pressure on the South Vietnamese Army in the hope of eroding its morale and producing defections, and of trying to rebuild the Viet Cong infrastructure, especially in the Mekong Delta. This strategy has achieved some success, but obviously not decisive success. Its implementation has involved Hanoi in substantial violations of the restrictions on infiltration of personnel and equipment imposed by the January 1973 agreement. There is evidence that the Viet Cong leadership would like to see an even higher level of such violations than the North Vietnamese have so far been willing to commit.

Given this situation, the political contacts looking toward elections and a coalition government provided for in the January 1973 agreement have gotten nowhere. There have been no secret negotiations between Saigon and the NLF, such as would be needed to produce a workable compromise, but only exchanges of propaganda broadsides. In May 1974 the Two-Party Joint Military Commission and the political talks between the two sides at Paris virtually broke down. Neither side has felt enough confidence in itself and trust in the other side to go through with the arrangements envisaged in January 1973 on some mutually acceptable basis. The main achievement was the exchange by March 1974 of all political prisoners that the two sides had admitted to holding; Saigon released approximately 31,000 (as against the 200,000 it was alleged by Hanoi, probably with much exaggeration, to be holding), and the NLF 6,000. Saigon complicated the process by trying to turn over to the NLF some of its leading non-Communist political prisoners on the ground that they had pro-Communist sympathies, but most of them refused to be released under these conditions.

American aid and support obviously remain critical to the survival of the Saigon government. The United States is reasonably enthusiastic along these lines, because it based its military with-

drawal from Indochina on the public premise that Vietnamization could be made to work. But since 1970 the administration
has been subjected to gradually increasing pressures from Congress, in the form of bills, amendments, and failures to vote the
full appropriations for Indochina requested by the administration,
to lower its profile still further. The administration's reply has
been that, although the January 1973 agreement may have terminated previous American commitments to the survival of the
Saigon government, the agreement itself has created a new commitment of this kind. This ingenious proposition has not been
convincing to congressional critics.

The situation in South Vietnam is complex and obscure enough
so that a fairly wide variety of outcomes is possible. The most
probable outcome, however, appears to be one in which American
aid and support for Saigon are reduced gradually, and perhaps
rapidly after 1977, and Hanoi's significant superiority in ideology,
organization, and geopolitics begins to tell, eventually to the point
of victory. If so, the outcome may not be pretty to watch; the long
struggle has generated enormous bitterness, and there is abundant
evidence in North Vietnamese and NLF documents of a plan for
systematic "repression" of political enemies after victory, perhaps
on the scale of a blood bath.

Malaysia: Prosperous but Tense

Malaysia's basic problem is the cultural antipathy between its
two major ethnic communities, the Malays and the Chinese. The
Malays, who constitute a plurality of the total population, are
Moslems and for the most part farmers and fishermen. The Chinese, who are almost as numerous, are far ahead in commerce and
industry and are therefore resented by the Malays. During the
colonial period the British favored the Malays in a variety of ways
as the original inhabitants and the underdogs. Before the attainment of independence in 1957 by Malaya (known as West Malaysia
since the formation of Malaysia in 1963), the leaders of the two
communities agreed that the political system would be essentially
Malay-dominated, but that the Chinese and other minorities
should enjoy reasonable freedom of economic activity and access
to citizenship. This compromise was not too difficult to reach, because the country as a whole basked in the glow of comparative

prosperity based on abundant rubber and tin, and political tempers were not yet running high. The compromise was reflected in the makeup of the dominant political party, the Alliance Party (or Alliance); its major component was the United Malay National Organization (UMNO), and the other principal component was the Malayan Chinese Association (MCA). Under the firm but benevolent rule of the Alliance and its leader, Prime Minister Tengku Abdul Rahman, and given general prosperity (by Asian standards), Malaya had few serious problems during its first few years of independent existence. The insurgency maintained by the Malayan Communist Party had already been reduced to almost negligible proportions by the British.

But this happy situation rested on two foundations that were not necessarily stable: prosperity and a continued willingness on the part of the Chinese community to accept what amounted to second-class citizenship. Prosperity was threatened by the competition of synthetic rubber produced in industrialized countries and had to be maintained through an indigenous industrialization program that produced strains of its own. Chinese political passivity (apart from the activities of the Chinese-controlled Malayan Communist Party) began to be eroded in the 1960s. The first influence in that direction came from neighboring, and overwhelmingly Chinese, Singapore. An apparent sharp leftward trend in Singaporean politics in 1961 led Prime Minister Rahman to accept the British idea that a federation, to be known as Malaysia, should be formed out of Malaya, Singapore, and the British territories in Borneo; within this wider framework, it was hoped that Singapore could be prevented from going Communist, by external intervention if necessary. But in reality Singapore was in little danger of going Communist; the position of its vigorous Prime Minister Lee Kuan Yew was never seriously threatened. The main practical results of the formation of Malaysia in 1963 were two: the outraged Indonesians proclaimed a state of "Confrontation" with Malaysia and Britain that lasted until 1966, and Lee Kuan Yew and his dynamic People's Action Party (PAP) began to extend their organization onto the Malayan mainland. This intrusion constituted a serious challenge to the flabby MCA, to the Alliance as a whole, and to the notion of second-class citizenship for Malayan Chinese. Singapore was accordingly expelled from Malaysia in 1965 and became an independent state. This action was an insult not only to Singapore itself but to the politically conscious elements of the Malayan Chinese, especially the youth.

Following this episode, some new Chinese political parties emerged that were both more radical and much more anti-Malay than the MCA. On the Malay side, this development was paralleled by the formation of new parties some of which were more radical, and some of which were more conservative (i. e., Islamic), than UMNO. In general elections held in May 1969, some of these parties scored impressive electoral triumphs at the expense of the Alliance; the MCA in particular suffered losses to the new Chinese parties. Postelection celebrations turned rapidly into widespread communal riots, which were suppressed by the overwhelmingly Malay Army and police. The government promptly declared a state of emergency, suspended the parliamentary system, and governed by decree until early 1971, when the parliamentary system was restored. During that interlude Prime Minister Rahman retired and was succeeded by the slightly more Malay-minded Tun Abdul Razak. In effect, the Malay-dominated establishment had showed its teeth, and the lesson was widely understood. The new parties lost much of their support to the Alliance, and the MCA in particular staged something of a comeback. On the other hand, the basic issue persisted.

As a counterpart and stimulus to this trend toward domestic restabilization, Razak launched a program of creative diplomacy. In mid-1971 he proposed that Southeast Asia (meaning really the states belonging to ASEAN) be "neutralized" under the guarantee of the major powers, which he listed as China, the Soviet Union, and the United States (note the order, and the omission of Japan). He also favored an improvement of relations, and the establishment of diplomatic relations, with Peking, because it was illogical not to have such relations with a power that Malaysia was inviting to help guarantee its security, because he hoped for increased trade with China, and because he hoped to persuade Peking to stop supporting the Malayan Communist Party. This policy reflected a realization that Britain and the United States were withdrawing militarily from Southeast Asia, that the Soviet Union was showing an increasing interest in the region, and that many Malaysian Chinese were in favor of relations with Peking. Relations between Kuala Lumpur and Peking have warmed up somewhat, and diplomatic recognitions were exchanged in mid-1974. Peking has pro-

duced a split within the leadership of the Malayan Communist
Party by urging it to give up insurgency and stress political action.

Singapore: One-Party Democracy

Singapore is a small country with interesting problems and policies. Its population is about three-fourths Chinese, but its neighbors (Malaysia and Indonesia) are predominantly Malay and tend
to regard Singapore as a potential Trojan horse for future expansion of Peking's influence in Southeast Asia. In order to help calm
this suspicion, or more accurately in order to avoid intensifying it
by appearing as Chinese as it really is, and also with the aim of
avoiding communal tensions like those that erupted in Malaysia in
1969, Singapore officially stresses what it calls the "Singaporean
identity" of the country and its population. Being small, largely
urban, and highly vulnerable to external events and pressures
(such as expulsion from Malaysia, and the British military withdrawal from Singapore in 1971), Singapore cannot afford to move
so far to the left that it scares away foreign trade and investment
or alarms its neighbors.

Singapore's politics and general situation reflect these conditions and the personality of Prime Minister Lee Kuan Yew, who is
highly dynamic and leftist but anti-Communist. He expelled the
Communist elements from his People's Action Party (PAP) by
1960, and when they went into active opposition he put their
leaders in jail, where they have been ever since. What political opposition remains is divided and ineffective, and the PAP normally
gets about 70 percent of the popular vote in elections. It earns this
impressive level of support not only by having the only effective
political organization in the country but by running a highly effi-
cient welfare state that provides the population with good social
services. The PAP government has been imaginative and successful in attracting foreign capital and improving the level of skills
of its own people, so that Singapore is emerging as a regional
headquarters for foreign firms operating in Southeast Asia and as
the repository of many modern skills and processes needed by the
rest of the region.

Whether trusted or not, Singapore has therefore made itself
more or less indispensable. It has tried with some success to cultivate better relations with its closest neighbors, Malaysia and Indo-

nesia. Prime Minister Lee has encouraged the United States not to reduce its military presence (especially in Thailand), which he regards as important to the stability of the region. He pursues a warily friendly policy toward the People's Republic of China; he is determined not to go too far or too fast in that direction because of the possible impact on both Singapore's Chinese majority and its neighbors.

The Philippines: Martial Law

As a combined result of its Malay, Spanish, and American heritage, the Philippines passed through a quarter century of independence (1946–71) with glaring social inequalities, a high level of concentration of economic and political power in the hands of a few dozen families, and considerable potential for unrest. The political system, modeled outwardly on that of the United States, was democratic in form, but not in essence. The existence of a huge number of firearms in private hands, another point of resemblance to the United States, was conducive to a high level of violence, although it also acted as a deterrent to any possible trend toward a centralized dictatorship.

Ferdinand Marcos, who was elected President in 1965, was a brilliant lawyer and an ambitious politician. He also claimed, perhaps sincerely, to be anxious to find a solution for the country's serious economic and social problems. This goal and his own ambitious temperament led him into increasingly autocratic behavior. He was determined to be the first Philippine President to be reelected, and he achieved this result in 1969 through an election campaign that was corrupt even by the standards of the Philippines. Among other things, it left the public works budget badly depleted. His second inauguration was greeted by some fairly serious student demonstrations, which were forcibly suppressed.

Soon afterward a Constitutional Convention met and began to debate ways in which the obviously unsatisfactory political and social systems could be improved. The Convention showed itself unreceptive to some of Marcos's ideas, including his tentative suggestion that his beautiful and imperious wife might be a candidate to succeed him. There can be little doubt that Marcos's personal ambition and sense of mission contributed heavily to disgusting him with this sort of bickering and to pushing him toward drastic action.

In September 1972, following a period of serious floods and an alleged attempt on the life of the Secretary of Defense, and insisting that there was an urgent need to cope with Communist insurgency, Marcos proclaimed a state of martial law and moved to cement his political relationship with the military leadership in a variety of ways. He jailed a number of political opponents, imposed heavy censorship on the previously exuberant press, and terminated the existing constitution and the Constitutional Convention. In 1973, with the support of a rigged referendum, he began to introduce a new, more or less parliamentary (as contrasted with presidential) constitution under which he would serve as both President and Prime Minister. As time went on, he relied less and less on the none-too-credible argument that the country had been seriously threatened with insurrection in 1972 and emphasized instead the need for a strong government to implement vital social reforms. In this connection he inaugurated a land reform program that had at least the possibility of becoming the first effective one in the country's history. Administrative efficiency was considerably improved. Increased political and economic stability attracted the approval and capital of foreign (especially American) investors, to the point where the regime's critics sometimes suggested—not necessarily correctly—that Marcos's coup had had active foreign backing from the beginning.

Even if exaggerated in official statements, there was a leftist insurgency of sorts. In protest against the degeneration of the earlier Huk movement into banditry, a Maoist party was formed in 1968 and proceeded to generate a guerrilla arm calling itself the New People's Army. It flourished best in the traditionally discontented area of central Luzon but also began to send offshoots into some of the islands farther south. Although troublesome, it was not a serious threat to the government's survival, and there was no convincing evidence that it received much more than propaganda support from Peking.

There was a more serious insurgency in the large southern island of Mindanao. The predominantly Moslem population had resented for some years an influx of Christian settlers, whom they regarded, apparently correctly, as enjoying governmental support. In addition, the Moslems objected to the operations of large logging companies in their area. This situation worsened after the proclamation of martial law, because the new regime made a serious effort to collect a large number of private firearms. These were particularly numerous in the Moslem area, where they were regarded as necessary protection against oppression from the outside. The result was a sizable revolt, against which the Philippine armed forces employed aircraft and artillery. In spite of frequent and alternating official claims that the Moslem insurgency had been crushed or had been ended through a negotiated settlement, the fighting went on. The revolt could not really be suppressed, because the government was unable to isolate it from the south. From that direction arms flowed to the insurgents by sea from Sabah (in North Borneo), whose Chief Minister was a militant Moslem; there were credible reports that this flow of arms was financed with Libyan funds.

Apart from continuing to enjoy the benefits of American aid, military as well as economic, the Marcos government in its foreign policy devoted considerable attention to trying to establish some sort of relationship with Peking. There were two main considerations behind this: a desire for trade, and a hope of insuring against serious Chinese support for the New People's Army. More generally, the Philippines tried to eradicate its widely held image as some sort of American satellite and to gain acceptance as an authentically Asian nation.

Indonesia: Is Development Enough?

A period of rapid leftward movement in Indonesian politics and foreign policy came to an abrupt end in late 1965 after President Sukarno and the Communist Party (PKI) attempted a disastrously unsuccessful coup against the comparatively conservative Army leadership. There ensued a huge massacre of actual and alleged leftists, the fall of Sukarno, the reduction of the PKI to the status of an ineffective underground organization, a massive setback for Peking's previously considerable influence in Indoneisa, and a negotiated settlement of the "Confrontation" with Malaysia.

A further consequence was that Indonesia came to be, and has remained, essentially under the political leadership of the Army and the security forces, with General Suharto as President of the Republic. To a large extent the military exercise their political influence through what is actually a government party (although theoretically a nation-wide movement) usually known by its acronym, Golkar. The military thoroughly dislike the other political parties, which they regard as divisive, and the Islamic elements of Indonesian political culture, which they consider reactionary. The military themselves have a progressive, even revolutionary, ideology derived from the post-1945 struggle against the Dutch, but their practice tends to be more conservative than their ideology. Having overthrown Sukarno's leftist "Guided Democracy," they have replaced it not with the obvious alternative of parliamentary democracy but with an authoritarian military regime devoted to economic development and rationalizing the absence of democracy on that ground. Partly sincerely and partly opportunistically, the military also cultivate the image of a security threat from Peking and the Indonesian Chinese community, which does not in fact exist to any significant extent (since 1965) but is a useful myth for the regime's purposes.

Although potentially very wealthy on account of its abundant natural resources, Indonesia faces serious economic and social problems. Population growth and the mushrooming of urban slums are proceeding rapidly and almost unchecked. There is a strong inflationary trend that is sometimes compounded by governmental economic mismanagement, as was notably the case at the time of a rice shortage in 1973. Official corruption and unemployment are widespread. The educational system is inadequate in size and inadequate in quality to a near-disastrous degree. Development, the regime's watchword, is realistically possible only through letting in foreign (mainly Japanese) capital or unleashing the economic energies of the local Chinese, or both. In reality both these things have been done to a degree, and there has certainly been some development, but as usual in non-Communist countries the process has widened the range of social and economic inequality. Furthermore, Japanese investment, which has gone mainly into extraction, has been carried on with a get-rich-quick mentality and as a strip-mining operation. The Chinese are an even more serious problem; by no means all of them are Indonesian citizens, and they are all disliked, distrusted, and oppressed in various ways by the military-security establishment and by many ordinary Indonesians, for a number of reasons some of which have validity but most of which do not.

The current Indonesian political system concedes its citizens some passive freedoms but not many active ones (such as the freedom to organize and propagandize). West Irian, acquired from the Netherlands in 1962–63, was integrated into the country as a whole in 1969 in a way that left almost no room for any opposition to express itself. The elections in 1971 to the People's Consultative Assembly (not a true parliament) were managed by the Army and Golkar so effectively, through a combination of coercion and persuasion, that Golkar got 63 percent of the popular vote. In 1973, under governmental pressure, the Moslem parties merged themselves into one, and the non-Moslem opposition parties did the same. The establishment portrays itself as the main barrier to a resurgence of the PKI, which is a possible although not probable development, and uses this as one argument for the maintenance of fairly rigorous security controls. It was against all this—lack of democracy and social justice, economic problems, etc.—that large-scale student demonstrations amounting to riots occurred in January 1974, on the occasion of a visit by Premier Tanaka of Japan. The demonstrations were directed at first against exploitation by Japanese and local Chinese capital but soon turned into an anti-establishment movement; troops and police suppressed the demonstrations with considerable force.

What economic development has occurred since 1965 has resulted to a large extent not only from foreign investment but from funds loaned by what is known informally as the Aid to Indonesia Club, one-third of whose capital is contributed by the United States government, one-third by the Japanese government, and one-third by other governments (especially the West German). Although very helpful, this aid has added significantly to the large foreign debt inherited from the pre-1945 period. A major bright spot on the economic horizon is the government oil monopoly, known as Pertamina, which sells licenses for petroleum extraction (mainly in Sumatra) to foreign enterprises and distributes refined fuels within Indonesia; it is well run, and its profits finance most of the military budget over and above housekeeping expenses.

Indonesia has always visualized itself as the major indigenous power, actual or potential, of Southeast Asia. In Sukarno's time it tried to play up to this role rather actively, and after 1960 in close cooperation with Peking. Like Sukarno's other policies, this one was substantially reversed after 1965 in favor of a low profile and a cautious approach, although Indonesia sees itself as intrinsically the leading member of ASEAN. The situation is complicated by the absence of any real external threat against which Indonesia can claim to provide leadership and protection, although Jakarta tries to cast Peking and the local Chinese in this role. Relations with Indonesia's neighbors have improved considerably since the end of "Confrontation." Post-1965 relations with the United States have been reasonably good; President Nixon visited Jakarta in 1969, and it was at American initiative that Indonesia was invited in 1973 to serve on the ICCS for South Vietnam. Relations with the Netherlands, which were very bad under Sukarno, have also improved, and Dutch capital and skills are now welcomed. As part of its general campaign of normalizing its foreign relations and competing with Soviet influence, Peking would like to establish diplomatic relations with Jakarta (they were broken off in 1967), as well as with the other ASEAN states. But for reasons already suggested Jakarta has been fairly cool to the idea, and Indonesia is likely to be the last of the ASEAN states to act on it.

The Emergence of Regionalism

The countries of Southeast Asia are so geographically divided, politically dissimilar, and economically competitive (i. e., similar) that the emergence of regional sentiment, regional organization, and regional cooperation has been a slow and tentative process. In the course of it, some regional organizations have fallen by the way-side. SEATO (the Southeast Asia Treaty Organization), which was formed by the United States in 1954, essentially to protect Thailand, has slowly disintegrated through the inactivity or withdrawal of France, Britain, Pakistan, and Australia. ASPAC (the Asian and Pacific Council), an Asia-wide anti-Communist organization whose moving spirits have been the Republic of Korea (South Korea) and the Republic of China (Taiwan) virtually collapsed in 1973 because some of its members wanted to expel Taiwan as an aid to improving relations with Peking.

Practically speaking, there remains only one functioning regional organization in Southeast Asia. Beginning with some very limited and tentative cooperation among Indonesia, the Philippines, and Thailand in the early 1960s, ASEAN (the Association of Southeast Asian Nations) was formally established in 1967, after the end of the "Confrontation," through the inclusion of Malaysia and Singapore in addition to the three states already mentioned. Given the inherent obstacles, cooperation among the five members has grown slowly, but it has grown. ASEAN has survived, and there is at least a reasonable chance that it will prove viable and will continue to survive; whether it will ever become truly important is another matter. To date it has only a weak central organization, and no joint military headquarters or staff. Its main activities and achievements have been in the economic field; it has negotiated with some success with the industrial countries (especially the Common Market) for better prices for its primary products, and at the time of the oil crisis of late 1973 it persuaded Japan to limit its exports of synthetic rubber (which is produced from petroleum). It has tried to promote coordination among its members in collecting economic data and framing their economic plans. It coordinates the planning of (anti-Communist) counterinsurgency operations, especially in regions bisected by national boundaries (in particular Thailand-Malaysia and Indonesia-Malaysia). All this is not much, but it is something, and it is one reason for not accepting uncritically the notion that Southeast Asia is a "power vacuum" in which the major external powers can act as they please.

Interaction among the Major Powers

Enough is said in other chapters about the roles of the major powers in Southeast Asia so that this discussion can be brief.

Japan's political influence and military power were of course eliminated from the region in 1945, have not returned since, and show no signs of returning in the near future, in spite of the rapid growth of Japanese trade and investment in the region in recent years.

Weakened by war although not defeated, Britain began to withdraw from the region, politically and militarily, in 1947. The process was accelerated after the end of the "Confrontation" in 1966 and was virtually completed (except for Hong Kong, which of course is not usually considered a part of Southeast Asia) in 1971.

After a decade or so of increasing political and military involvement in the affairs of the region (especially Indochina), the United States began in 1969 what looked likely to become a complete military disengagement (except perhaps for its bases in the Philippines). This has inevitably been reflected in a decline of American political influence, although by no means to zero. The United States still aspires to play a significant role in Southeast Asia, if only as a counterweight to the other major powers.

Australia has decided not to try to fill the partial vacuum created by British withdrawal and American disengagement. Nor does it have the resources to do so even if it wished. Australia's military involvement in Malaysia and Vietnam, which was significant at one time, has been terminated, and there remains only a modest Australian military presence in Singapore. The Labor government of Prime Minister Gough Whitlam, which came to power at the end of 1972, opposes overseas activity of this kind and is interested in improving its relations with Peking. Early in 1974, it granted at least formal independence to Papua New Guinea, which occupies the eastern half of that island and which until then had been controlled by Australia.

Soviet diplomatic, commercial, and naval activity in the Indian Ocean and Southeast Asia have increased somewhat since about 1969, when Brezhnev announced his vague proposal for a "collective security" system in Asia as a means of enhancing Moscow's influence and coping with Peking's. But the process has not been a dramatic one, and there are serious geographic, cultural, and political obstacles in the way of significant progress in the future. China and the United States, on the whole, probably have capabilities for exercising influence in Southeast Asia that are superior to those of the Soviet Union; there are some local exceptions to this generalization, notably the case of North Vietnam.

For obvious geographic and cultural reasons, it would appear that if any power were in a position to "dominate" Southeast Asia it would be China. And in fact Peking probably entertains ambitions for ultimate pre-eminent influence in the region. But influence, even of the pre-eminent kind, is not the same thing as domination; the latter condition is almost certainly unattainable, and on the whole Peking behaves as if it is aware that this is so. Its power, prestige, dynamism, and diplomatic skill are in its favor, but it lacks military "reach," is regarded with considerable suspicion by local elites (especially military elites), and is counterbalanced to a significant extent by the other major powers. At present it is preoccupied much less with any thought of "dominating" Southeast Asia than with coping and competing with the other major powers. This requires a policy of conciliating the regional governments, except for those in Saigon and Phnom Penh. That in turn requires a reduction of efforts by Peking to support local Communist insurgencies and manipulate local Chinese communities to roughly the minimum level acceptable to Peking's radical Maoists; Burma appears to be an exception to this generalization. On the whole, Peking benefits from a widespread belief that China will always be a significant factor in the international politics of Asia, including Southeast Asia. Accordingly, there is a general, although not universal, tendency on the part of the regional governments to accommodate to Peking as the United States disengages.

Under the impact of American disengagement and the Sino-Soviet confrontation, Sino-American relations in Southeast Asia have become much less contentious than they once were. Peking wants at least passive American support against the Soviet Union, and it wants the United States not to reduce its military presence in Southeast Asia (and the rest of Asia with the possible exception of Taiwan) any further, at least in the near future, because such disengagement might create a "vacuum" that would be "filled" by the Soviet Union.

Soviet-American relations in Southeast Asia have developed along somewhat similar lines. The Soviet Union is anxious not to antagonize the United States to an extent that would be counterproductive in connection with the Sino-Soviet confrontation. Moscow does not want an American military withdrawal from Asia to occur under conditions that would benefit Peking. On the other hand, Southeast Asia is much less important to the Soviet-American relationship than it is to the Sino-American relationship, and Moscow can therefore afford to be somewhat more difficult with the United States over Southeast Asia (especially Indochina) than Peking can without seriously endangering the overall détente. This fact, as well as the Soviet Union's superior ability as compared with China's to supply heavy industrial and military equipment, goes far toward accounting for Moscow's somewhat greater influence on Hanoi (as against Peking's).

Ideological, political, and diplomatic rivalry between Peking and Moscow is at a high level in Southeast Asia, as elsewhere. Above all, China is determined to frustrate the Soviet design for some sort of "collective security" arrangement. In this Peking has been successful so far, largely because the regional states are reluctant to antagonize it by adhering openly to the Soviet proposal. Peking remains anxious on this score, however. Its action in driving South Vietnamese troops forcibly off the disputed Paracel Islands (in the South China Sea) in January 1974 was probably not motivated solely by territorial claims and the possibility that there is offshore oil near the islands. Soviet naval vessels had been in the vicinity of the Paracels shortly before the clash; if Saigon should make its claim to the islands good and then succumb to North Vietnam, Hanoi might decide to make the islands available to the Soviet Union as a base for the Soviet fleet, under the rubric of "collective security."

In 1971 Indonesia, Malaysia, and Singapore declared the narrow Straits of Malacca to be their territorial waters. Although they are not yet in a position to deny passage to foreign naval or commercial vessels, this claim could be a problem for Japan, which gets most of its oil from the Middle East via the Straits of Malacca. There have been some vague proposals, including one by Prime Minister Lee Kuan Yew, that Japan strengthen its navy and patrol the straits, but this is very unlikely to happen unless the situation becomes much more serious than it is at present. The United States and the Soviet Union both continue, for naval and commercial reasons, to regard the straits as an international waterway; China, which so far has no naval presence and few commercial interests in the region, has endorsed the Indonesian-Malaysian-Singaporean position for the sake of improving its image in the region.

There does not appear to be much of a future in Southeast Asia for Soviet-style "collective security," Malaysian-style "neutrality," or Chinese "domination." Except for the three non-Communist Indochinese governments, none of the regional governments is in serious danger of being overthrown from within (by a Communist revolution, at any rate), or coerced from without to an unmanageable degree. For this situation to change significantly, some dramatic development not now in prospect—and it is hard to imagine one—would have to occur. The probable outlook is for uneven but real progress by the regional states (again with the possible exception of the non-Communist Indochinese states) toward political stability and some degree of economic development, under cover of a mutual standoff or multipolar balance among the major powers.

CHAPTER XVI

Conclusion:
A Multipolar Balance?

FOR ABOUT half a century after the Napoleonic Wars, the international politics of Europe were governed by the principle of multipolarity, or to put it a little differently rested on a multipolar (or multilateral) balance of power. The alliance designed to contain Napoleonic France soon disintegrated as France appeared to accept its defeat and to pose no further threat to the security of Europe. For a time after that, no two major powers were at war, and no two were closely allied; relative international stability paralleled this situation and probably derived from it to a considerable extent. The first serious threat to stability and multipolarity arose when one major power, Prussia (later the German Empire), in effect challenged the system by attacking and crushing another, France (in 1870–71). The French determination to get revenge then became the main, although not the only, force that led to the displacement of multipolarity by two rival coalitions centering respectively on France and Germany (although the most aggressive members of these coalitions were Russia and Austria). This situation was highly unstable; a quarrel between any two members of the rival coalitions had a tendency to bring on a general confrontation, and the outcome was the First World War, from which Europe has never fully recovered. Germany, the leading member of the defeated coalition, refused to accept the verdict of 1918 and under Hitler's leadership transformed itself into a militarized colossus both stronger and more aggressive than any of the other European powers; the latter, even though faced with a common danger, were unable to coordinate their policies and defenses effectively. The outcome was the Second World War.

The moral of all this seems to be that given the nonexistence of any supranational authority with effective powers of enforcement, multipolarity, like any other international arrangement, can remain viable as long as, and only as long as, it remains acceptable at least to those powers whose nonacceptance would be sufficient to disrupt it.

It is plausible that the European experience, and the lessons derivable from it, have some relevance to the contemporary Far East, even though in that case the powers involved have a good deal less in common with each other in the ideological and political spheres than the European powers did, at any rate prior to the First World War. On the other hand, it is possible that this difference is cancelled out by a greater interest today in the avoidance of a major war in view of the presumed consequences of a large-scale resort to nuclear weapons.

China since the Cultural Revolution

For about a century prior to 1949, China was the sick man of East Asia. Its weakness was the most important single cause of and incitement to whatever expansion on the part of other powers occurred during that period, the most important cases being tsarist Russia in 1900 and imperial Japan in 1894–95, 1904–05, and 1931–45. The situation since 1949 has been sufficiently complex so that it is impossible to say categorically whether a strong and united China is more likely to be conducive to international stability in Asia than a weak China was, but the probable answer is yes. Certainly, true multipolarity in the Far East is impossible unless China, whatever its political orientation, plays an active and constructive international role. The chances of its doing so are bound to be influenced by a number of basic factors, the most obvious, and probably the most important, of which is its domestic political development.

The Red Guard movement, and in reality the Cultural Revolution as a whole, was terminated in late 1968 by military suppression, on Mao Tse-tung's personal although reluctant order. This left the Army even more effectively in control of the provinces than it had been since it was ordered by Mao to intervene in the Cultural Revolution (in January 1967). This new political prominence of the Army made the civilian Communist Party leaders uncomfortable, however, and as soon as it had performed the indispensable giant-killer's role that it alone could perform, by suppressing the Red Guards, plans were made for cutting back first its prestige and then its power.

This was a difficult task for a number of reasons, including the fact that the senior member of the military leadership, Defense Minister Lin Piao, had been proclaimed Mao's principal deputy and heir. Other factors tending to make him a formidable figure were his militantly Maoist ideological tendencies and his powerful ambition. Against him there was, in addition to the natural tendency for the suppression of the Red Guards to be followed by a reduction of the political role of the armed forces, the fact that his ambition and (paradoxically) his political incompetence precipitated a powerful coalition in opposition to him of which Premier Chou En-lai was the moving spirit, and to which Mao himself gave his support at some point. Lin's ambition and radicalism were compounded by his primitive adherence to the dual adversary strategy, which was then going out of vogue (in fact although not in theory) in favor of the "tilt" toward the United States; he took the Soviet threat lightly and opposed the "tilt" in the other direction. Seeing his influence decline, he tried to insist that a National People's Congress be convened in the autumn of 1971 to formalize his position as Mao's heir in the state system, as the Ninth Party Congress (April 1969) had already done for his status in the party hierarchy. When this ploy failed, he apparently attempted some sort of coup against Chou En-lai, his principal adversary, but failed and was killed on September 11 or 12, 1971. Even in death he was a fairly formidable political figure, and accordingly a huge "disinformation" campaign, including the charge that he had been killed in an airplane crash in the Mongolian People's Republic while trying to escape to the Soviet Union, was mounted against his memory by the victors. His supporters were purged or demoted.

The turn to the right represented by the suppression of the Red Guards, the effective termination of the Cultural Revolution, the purge of Lin Piao, and the rehabilitation of many party leaders disgraced during the Cultural Revolution (Vice Premier Teng Hsiao-p'ing, in particular) has angered many of the militant Maoists, including former Red Guards, and made them more determined than ever to preserve the influence of Mao Tse-tung's "thought" and the legacy of the Great Leap Forward and the Cultural Revolution. They apparently fear that they may find themselves in trouble after his death (he was born in 1893), and they evidently reason that they had better do everything they can to enhance their influence and protect themselves while he is still alive.

The main actual political trend, however, is something quite different. While maintaining a fairly low personal political profile for purposes of self-protection, Chou En-lai, with the substantial although not necessarily complete support of Mao and a coalition of moderate civil and military colleagues, has been presiding over a program aimed essentially at stabilizing the political system—through the rebuilding in somewhat different form of the political institutions thrown into turmoil during the Cultural Revolution, and the avoidance of further such "mass campaigns"—and developing the economy over the long haul rather than by "leaps." It appears to be Chou who has engineered the rehabilitations already mentioned. To enhance acceptance of his leadership and program by the elite and the population, he has skillfully cultivated the sense of a Soviet threat, but not to the point of inducing panic or despair; he has insisted, for example, that the main thrust of Soviet "expansion" is toward the West, not against China. He has been trying since at least as long ago as the summer of 1973 to convene a new National People's Congress to help legitimate his policies, but as of September 1974 he had been unable to do so.

At first, and particularly until the fall of Lin Piao, Chou faced a serious problem on the right, in the shape of the power influence of the commanders of the Military Regions on the provincial politics of the country. He has been able to win some over to his side, and in fact he has long had close personal ties with certain sections of the military leadership. Others, more difficult in one way or another, have been gradually separated from their sources of influence and encouraged to give up their political roles in order to concentrate on their military functions. The biggest single step in this direction since the fall of Lin Piao was taken in December

1973, when Peking was able to move the most powerful of the Military Region commanders to new commands, where they have been denied the political positions and influence that they had enjoyed before. The time may have appeared favorable because the Soviet Union was still considerably preoccupied with the crisis in the Middle East, and in any case December is not the ideal month in which to launch a military campaign in Inner Asia.

Since then Chou's most serious known political problems have originated on the left, from the direction of the radical Maoists. They launched a campaign of propaganda and political agitation against his policies in August 1973. They probably took their cue from the fact that Mao had given his public endorsement to the Red Guard movement just seven years before, and that he had said at about that time that China ought to undergo a "great upheaval" every seven or eight years. Chou has let them have their say to a considerable extent, because he does not want to gain a reputation for suppressing criticism, because it would be difficult to silence them in any case, and because they have some claim on Mao's support. He has launched propaganda campaigns and slogans of his own, some of which have a militant sound but the more important of which—these have been especially prominent since the beginning of 1974—stress the importance of order, discipline, and moderation.

Chou's main domestic problem may no longer be the regional military or even the radical Maoists, but rather his own age (he was born in 1898), health, and declining energies. He has maintained a ferocious working schedule and carried enormous responsibilities for many years, and in the spring of 1974 there was convincing evidence that his health had begun to fail and that he had had to curtail his schedule. This situation, combined with the continuing propaganda emanating from the radicals, has deceived some foreign observers into thinking that he had lost Mao's support or for some other reason was politically finished. This is almost certainly not the case. As already indicated, he has not been running a one-man show but has been leading a coalition, some prominent members of which to be sure are only a little younger than he if at all. Some of them have begun to represent him at public functions, and perhaps in other ways as well; this is particularly true of Teng Hsiao-p'ing, whose spectacular re-emergence culminated in his re-election to the party Politburo by January 1974 and his attendance at the special United Nations session on raw materials problems in April of that year. The real test of the viability and stability of Chou's team (or "collective leadership") and policies will probably begin after his incapacitation or death or Mao's, whichever comes sooner.

Something has already been said (mainly in Chapter VIII) about China's post-Cultural Revolution foreign policy, which in effect is Chou En-lai's; this discussion will therefore be brief.

In foreign relations and diplomacy, the keynote is normalization, with the purpose of eliminating the damage done by the Cultural Revolution and enhancing China's international contacts and prestige. Ambassadors have been sent back to nearly all countries where Peking maintained them before the Cultural Revolution, about forty new diplomatic recognitions have been acquired (usually at Taiwan's expense), and entry into the United Nations has been achieved.

To a large extent for domestic political reasons—on account of the continuing influence of the radical Maoists, in other words—Chinese foreign propaganda still stresses opposition to both "superpowers" and friendship for the "small and medium states" of the world, and Peking still gives some actual support to leftist revolutionary movements in carefully selected areas (northern Burma, for example). But all this is much less important in reality than the "tilt" toward the United States, which is intended as a counterweight to the Soviet Union, an approach to progress on the Taiwan question, and a means of expanding trade; the effort to deter the Soviet Union through conventional and nuclear military modernization and to compete vigorously with it in virtually every region and situation; and the attempt to achieve and maintain a relationship with Japan just friendly enough so that Tokyo does not rearm massively or move too close to the Soviet Union. This is an active policy, but it hardly deserves the continual Soviet charges of "militarism" and "expansionism."

The Outlook for China

More than most countries, China in the past has surprised those who have tried to predict its future. It will probably do so again, in this case as well as others. But the attempt is still worth making, as an aid to intelligent discussion.

The dominant force in contemporary Chinese politics is not ideology (i. e., Communism, and the "thought" of Mao Tse-tung in particular) but nationalism. Virtually all politically conscious Chinese are convinced, and have been convinced for many years, that national disunity breeds weakness, which invites foreign intervention, something that they do not want in the slightest. To them it follows, obviously, that China must be strong, and therefore that it must be united. Communism and the "thought" of Mao Tse-tung have achieved their rather impressive level of acceptance and success in Chinese political life largely because they, more than any available alternative, seemed to provide the best ideological and organizational basis for strength and unity; they have, in short, achieved a high level of legitimacy. It is almost certainly significant that none of the powerful leaders of China's border regions, when threatened and sometimes overthrown by Red Guards and other militants during the Cultural Revolution, is known to have contemplated invoking Soviet support, even though it would probably have been feasible to do so.

On the other hand, Chinese nationalism is not to be equated with Communism in its present or any future form. There is also a substantial component of what, for the sake of brevity, can be called tradition. Whenever its programs were not working well for any reason, Communism in China has had to make significant concessions to tradition, more at the local than at the national level. Although there is not likely to be a reversion to a purely traditional (i. e., pre-Communist) political system, either through evolution or through revolution, it does appear probable that further concession to tradition will have to be made, and will be made. An important reason for believing this is that the "thought" of Mao Tse-tung is likely to begin to lose its vigor after the death of the thinker, even though at present it has many young adherents, as the regime has to grapple more and more earnestly with the increasing pressure of population on the economy, especially the food supply. Problems like this will not be solved through further "great upheavals" of the Maoist variety; accordingly, there will probably not be any more of them, or if there are the result may be disaster. The only likely occasion of another "upheaval" would arise if Chou En-lai were to die before Mao, and if the radicals were then able to overthrow or bypass Chou's moderate team and persuade the Chairman to order an "upheaval."

Another, very different, form of disaster would be defeat in a major war, presumably at the hands of the Soviet Union. But there is at least a good chance that China will avoid a disaster of either variety. If so, and especially if Chou survives Mao, there also appears to be a good chance of avoiding a bruising succession struggle in favor of a reasonably orderly transition to a younger "collective leadership" to replace the one currently ruling. This may include some Maoist radicals, but more as window dressing than anything else. Its genuinely important constituents are likely to be the leading representatives of the principal functional constituencies or power systems: the party apparatus, the state system (especially the government administration and the security forces), and the armed forces. Because of China's antimilitary political tradition, and the Chinese Communist preference for subordinating the Army to the Party, there is unlikely to be a full-fledged military takeover except perhaps in the face of some imminent disaster. It is entirely possible that the pressure of population growth and rising consumer demand on a limited national product will lead the regime to tighten its security controls over the people. The re-emergence of bureaucratic institutions that has been going on since the end of the Cultural Revolution is likely to continue, in spite of protests from the radicals.

In the economic sphere, there is likely to be slow and difficult progress, rather than a spectacular breakthrough or a spectacular failure, in the three critical fields of agricultural development, population control, and industrialization. Progress could probably be accelerated if the regime were to improve the educational system through reducing its currently excessive ideological and political content. The ideological preference for "self-reliance" will probably continue to hold down, although of course not to prevent, China's participation in the international economy, and in particular its willingness to seek or accept long-term development credits or joint ventures with foreign capital.

In the military sphere, China will probably continue to improve its conventional capabilities, which are already impressive from a defensive standpoint, and will probably be able to launch damaging blows against Soviet Asia if the occasion should arise. The same goes for China's nuclear weapons force, which is already able to inflict serious damage on targets well within the Soviet Union and is probably already partially invulnerable (through hardening, dispersal, and warning measures) to a possible Soviet first strike. Within several years China will presumably develop an ICBM; development in this field to date appears to have been held back not only by technical difficulties and the emphasis on shorter-range missiles adequate for hitting Soviet targets but by a desire not to alarm the United States. By now, however, development of a Chinese ICBM would probably not be enough by itself to disrupt the Sino-American détente. Given the technical problems, the cost, and the possibly disturbing effect on its foreign relations, China is likely to be rather slow in developing a significant conventional strategic "reach" (an ocean-going navy, amphibious and airborne forces, etc.).

Nationalism is likely to be the dominant force in China's foreign policy as well as in its domestic politics. This means that China will continue to be conscious of its national dignity and sensitive to real or imagined slights. It does not necessarily mean that China will be aggressive or expansionist, even when its national and military power is considerably greater than it is at present. Then, as now and in the past, there will be significant constraints in the form of military risks, practical difficulties (terrain, etc.), economic costs, and political consequences. Although domestic politics will continue to affect foreign policy, as is true in every country, specifically Maoist pressures on foreign policy (such as demands for support of "people's wars" abroad) are likely to diminish, for reasons already indicated. China is likely to expand its already significant participation in the formal aspects of international relations (the United Nations, international conferences and agreements, etc.). This assumed trend toward greater pragmatism and flexibility will probably facilitate, and may also be intensified by, a search for a formula under which two currently indigestible morsels, Taiwan and Hong Kong, can be assimilated into the Chinese body politic. One of Chou En-lai's internal arguments in favor of the détente with the United States is that it will promote the "liberation" of Taiwan; since "liberation" has not come perceptibly closer since 1971, he has felt compelled to resort (through statements by his supporters) to the argument that it is not desirable to press the United States for more rapid disengagement from its commitments to Taiwan because a sudden American withdrawal might panic the Republic of China and drive it into Moscow's arms. In the long run, it seems likely that the mainland and Taiwan will work out some formula under which they can reunite, formally at least.

To a considerable extent, the future of China's foreign policy, and to some extent even the future of its domestic politics, depend on the future of its relationship with the United States and the Soviet Union. These subjects are important enough to deserve separate examination.

The Future of Sino-American Relations

The common interests that led to the Sino-American détente have already been discussed (mainly in Chapter IX). Stated as simply as possible, they amount to a shared desire to resolve, or at least cool, existing Sino-American conflicts of interest in Asia in order to be better able to cope with the more serious problems presented by the Soviet Union. Obviously this is an unstable basis for a constructive Sino-American relationship in the long run.

A search for other bases for such a relationship uncovers something, but not so much as might be desirable. On the American side, there is a rather synthetic euphoria about China and Sino-American relations in some official and public circles anxious for better relations and closer contacts with China for one reason or another. Secretary Kissinger has said that the Sino-American détente is independent of changes of administration in the United States and in that sense "irreversible"; in reality, it should be obvious to any one that even if he happens to have made a correct prediction in this respect he has no power to bind future administrations. Out of concern for Chinese sensitivities, and perhaps at Peking's specific request, the United States government has discouraged public, and especially official, discussion of Chinese politics and foreign policy unless it is certain to be conducted in flattering terms. Contacts between American officials and private China specialists have also been discouraged, although not entirely prohibited; this policy is sometimes referred to as the China Blight. The American side has allowed Peking to manipulate private contacts for its own political and propaganda purposes; the Chinese side entirely controls the flow of travelers, etc., in both directions, partly for domestic political reasons. In this way American policy helps to perpetuate, by consciously refraining from challenging it through a serious effort at normal contact, the immature and unself-critical view of themselves and the world held by most Chinese.

On the Chinese side, there is virtually no euphoria about the United States, even though a generation of intense anti-American propaganda has had less effect on public thinking than might have been supposed. The mainstream of current Chinese foreign policy making, as led and symbolized by Chou En-lai, regards the United States as useful, and in fact indispensable, but hardly as an object of affection. The radical Maoists evidently still object to the United States on the ground that it is "imperialist" and a super-power, and, in spite of the fact that the Chairman himself has seemed to put his seal of approval on the Sino-American détente by receiving President Nixon and Secretary Kissinger, they have still been sniping at the détente and at Chou's alleged failure to extract more advantage from it. The height of the radicals' propa-ganda campaign against Chou, in the early months of 1974, saw something of a chill in Sino-American diplomatic and cultural contacts, including an absence from their posts for several weeks of the heads of the two liaison offices, David Bruce and Huang Chen. Chou En-lai's illness obviously raises the possibility of trou-ble for his policies, including his commitment to détente with the United States.

On the other hand, this is merely a possibility, not a certainty, and not necessarily even a probability. Reasons have already been given for doubting that Maoist radicalism is the wave of the future in either Chinese politics or Chinese foreign policy.

Now that the Soviet Union rather than the United States has become China's main adversary in Asia, there is not likely to be serious Sino-American friction, for some time at any rate, over such former trouble spots as Japan, Korea, Indochina, South Asia, or even Taiwan. If any such friction does arise, it is likely to be managed through political and diplomatic, rather than military, means, at least as long as each side continues to be preoccupied with its Soviet problem.

Even though Chinese Communism is a much less serious prob-lem in American public thinking than it once was, President Nixon still appeared to be sufficiently in need of right-wing support in his struggle against impeachment so that he was unwilling to transfer diplomatic recognition from Taipei to Peking as many other governments have done. The same consideration probably

explains the fact that the Republic of China has recently been allowed to open two new consulates in the United States, and that
the American ambassadorship in Taipei has been kept continu-
ously filled whereas some other important diplomatic and State
Department positions have been left vacant. President Nixon in
effect made it clear, on the other hand, that he regarded the People's Republic of China as much more important to American
interests than the Republic of China. Secretary Kissinger has never
visited Taiwan, whereas he has visited the mainland six times
(1971–73). It is possible that a future American administration
might transfer diplomatic recognition by raising the liaison office
in Peking to the level of an embassy and reducing the embassy in
Taipei to the level of a liaison office. The success of such a ploy
would depend on acceptance by both Chinas, and there is no sign
at present that acceptance would be forthcoming. On the other
hand, the United States is already unique in being able, obviously
on account of its importance to both Chinas, to have a liaison office
in Peking while maintaining an embassy in Taipei, and conditions
might arise in the future in which a reversal of status would be
feasible.

Sino-American trade has already expanded enormously (although not to the level of American trade with Taiwan), from
nothing before 1971 to almost $1 billion (both ways) in 1973 and
an anticipated figure of well over $1 billion for 1974. The trade is
heavily (about ten to one) in the United States' favor, since American exports (mainly food, fibre, and some high technology items)
are in much more demand in China than Chinese exports are in
the United States. It is likely that there will be further trade expansion, the main constraint being China's limited foreign exchange reserves, a large part of which are derived from exporting
food and water to Hong Kong. Negotiations are under way to set-
tle Chinese claims for assets blocked by the United States and
American claims for property confiscated by China; if these claims
are settled, the result should be a further stimulus to trade expansion. Still another stimulus would be the granting of most-favored-
nation status to China by the United States, which has not yet
been done (as of fall 1974). Peking is already accepting short-term
trading credits, which it prefers to call deferred payment arrangements, from American and other sources; developmental credits

and other forms of aid are not now in prospect but are an obvious possibility—although perhaps nothing more—in the future. Joint enterprises and other forms of foreign (including American) investment in China appear to be a very unlikely possibility, given Chinese sensitivities to any semblance of foreign exploitation.

The most important aspect of Sino-American relations, although it is an aspect that is the subject of very little public official discussion on either side, relates to the Sino-Soviet confrontation. No one expects the United States to give China any kind of formal military guarantee against possible Soviet attack. Peking has not asked for one, because it is too proud, because it expects that the answer would be negative, and probably because it considers that even if a guarantee were given it would not necessarily be reliable (any more than the Soviet guarantee seemed reliable to Peking by the late 1950s) and might even trigger a Soviet attack. The most that can reasonably be expected under present conditions is that the Sino-American relationship should be, or at least should appear in Moscow to be, sufficiently close so that there is a significant element of uncertainty as to what the American response would be in the event of a Soviet attack on China. This uncertainty appears actually to have been created in Moscow, at least until recently. On the other hand, the Soviet leadership has recovered to a considerable extent from the initial shock created by the dramatic developments of 1971–72 in Sino-American relations, which have tended to become somewhat routinized since 1972 and to develop the strains inevitable in a working international relationship. It is likely, therefore, that Moscow takes the Sino-American relationship a little less seriously as a constraint on any possible Soviet decision to attack China. Partly for this reason, the Soviet attitude toward China appears to be more dangerous than at any time since 1970 or 1971.

Since 1969 the United States government has said very little, in public at any rate, to discourage a Soviet attack on China. On the contrary, American official hands have been largely kept off this issue, again so far as the public record shows. There was no reference to the Sino-Soviet confrontation in the Shanghai Communiqué, and Kissinger has never taken a Soviet specialist with him to China (presumably because to do so might anger and alarm Moscow). This comparative silence is obviously maintained in the interest of the notion of American "equidistance" as between Moscow and Peking, the Soviet-American détente, and of course the avoidance of a military clash with the Soviet Union.

If in fact Sino-Soviet tension has recently increased, the question can reasonably be asked whether the United States should do more. A major Sino-Soviet war would probably result in a defeat for China and a serious disruption of the international stability and multilateral balance in the Far East that it is one of the main aims of United States foreign policy to foster. At the minimum, it would seem advisable for the United States government to say publicly, and therefore authoritatively, that it is no longer committed to the idea of the "irreversibility" of the Soviet-American détente and that a Soviet attack on China would lead to immediate American re-examination of the entire relationship. It could be left to Moscow to wonder what the outcome of that re-examination might be. It would also be worth while for the United States government to consider seriously what it would do if the following scenario, or "hypothetical horrible," materialized, wholly or in large part: at a time of political crisis in the United States, Mao Tse-tung dies and a political crisis ensues in China, the Soviet Union attacks China, North Vietnam attacks South Vietnam, and the Arabs attack Israel. It is not an inconceivable situation.

Sino-Soviet tension short of war, such as exists at present, is a very different matter from an actual war, from the standpoint of American interests among other things. As already indicated, this level of tension has resulted in significant advantages for the United States, which probably could have been exploited more effectively than has been the case. Any marked change in the current Sino-Soviet relationship in either direction, whether toward conflict or toward accommodation, would tend to be bad for American interests, at least under present conditions. What are the main factors bearing on the likelihood that such a change will occur?

Sino-Soviet Relations: Conflict or Accommodation?

The early months of 1974 witnessed what appeared to be a potentially serious worsening of Sino-Soviet relations. To a considerable extent it seemed to flow, like the simultaneous difficulties in Sino-American relations, from the upsurge of protest by Chinese radicals against Chou En-lai's domestic and foreign policies. The radicals' devotion to the dual adversary strategy, or in other words the assumed obligation to struggle simultaneously against, or at least express defiance of, both American "imperialism" and Soviet "revisionism" (or "social-imperialism"), evidently lingered on. It was not clear to what extent certain gestures along these lines were forced on Chou En-lai over his objections, private or explicit, or were taken by him in order to appease his critics and avoid the necessity for still more vigorous gestures; there were probably elements of both things in the situation. To the extent that he took action against the Soviet Union on his own initiative, he may have intended to show the United States that the anti-American gestures did not portend a Sino-Soviet reconciliation. If so, the message was none too clearly conveyed or understood.

On the whole, it seems probable that Chou En-lai was in reasonably effective charge and was managing this apparent reversion to the dual adversary strategy in a way compatible with his established policy of claiming, not very convincingly, to maintain an even-handed opposition to the two "superpowers" while in reality "tilting" toward the United States. The sharp and successful Chinese military action against South Vietnamese forces in the Paracel Islands (in the South China Sea) on January 20 was obviously directed at a client of the United States. The simultaneous expulsion of three Soviet diplomats and two of their wives from China for undiplomatic activity (to be precise, stealing public mailboxes and examining their contents) completed the picture of an almost balletic exercise in the application of the dual adversary strategy. On the other hand, as already indicated, the conflict in the Paracels also had strong anti-Soviet overtones on account of the presence in the area shortly beforehand of Soviet naval vessels and the existence of a North (as well as South) Vietnamese claim to the islands. Here, evidently, was Chou En-lai's "tilt" in operation, at least in a negative sense.

A probably more serious episode occurred about two months later, while both David Bruce and Huang Chen were absent from their respective posts in Peking and Washington. On March 14, a Soviet helicopter strayed across the Central Asian sector of the Sino-Soviet border into Sinkiang and either had to land on account of mechanical difficulties or landed and was unable to take off again. On the following day Moscow privately requested the return of the three-man crew; the helicopter itself was of less interest since it was presumably not operational and since the Chinese already had many of the same type. The incident and the request presented Peking with a difficult problem. Simply to comply would expose Chou-En-lai to domestic charges of being "soft" on "social-imperialism"; not to comply would risk further tension with the already dangerously aroused military leadership of China's most formidable adversary. The problem was complicated by the existence of a reasonable possibility that the crew had been reconnoitering, from the air or even on the ground, Chinese missile sites on which work had been suspended for the winter; the area in question is about two thousand miles from Moscow, roughly the range of an IRBM. In this difficult situation Peking kept silent for the time being, and on March 20 the Soviet side made a public statement of its version of the incident, which was to the effect that the helicopter had been on a medical evacuation mission and had not intended to violate the border. Peking then published (on March 23) a strongly worded refutation of the Soviet version and presented its own, which was to the effect that the helicopter had been engaged in espionage and that there had been other recent Soviet overflights in the same area. It is worth noting that Peking timed this statement, which was obviously likely to go down very badly in Moscow, for the day after David Bruce's return to Peking, a development that strengthened Peking's hand and sense of security by showing that its relationship with the United States was still viable; it was also the day before the start of a visit to Moscow by Secretary Kissinger, and therefore a time that seemed appropriate to the Chinese for reminding the United States and the world that the Soviet Union was not to be trusted. On May 3, the Soviet side made another statement on the helicopter incident and warned in rather strong language of "inevitable consequences" if the crew were not returned. In reality this statement may have been less threatening than it appeared; for one thing, it was issued close to the time of the May Day celebrations in Moscow and therefore at a time when the Soviet military leadership may have needed some sort of compensation for the fact that it had not been allowed to stage a military parade on that occasion since 1968. (The 1969 parade had been cancelled almost at the last minute, probably because the party leadership thought that its military colleagues were already seeking too much publicity through exploiting the clashes with the Chinese on the Ussuri River in March.) In any case, however, Peking was still in a predicament. At the time of writing (September 1974) it was not clear whether it would make no response at all, try and perhaps punish the helicopter crew for espionage, or—more probably—try to work out some intermediate course of action that would be intended to prevent the wrath of either the Chinese radicals or the Soviet military from assuming dangerous proportions.

Apart from particular incidents such as this one, the Soviet game appeared basically to create and maintain a military presence (including about 50 ground divisions) near the Sino-Soviet border that would deter Peking, "militarist" and "expansionist" though Soviet propaganda alleged it to be, from taking military action either against Soviet Asia or elsewhere in Asia (by way of exploiting the American disengagement). These forces would also be in a position to put pressure on the border, or even advance deeper into China, if Moscow decided that such action would serve a useful purpose, such as tipping the balance in favor of "healthy forces" (the Soviet term for pro-Soviet foreign Communists) involved in a succession struggle following Mao Tse-tung's death. In the meantime, even though the Soviet leadership is genuinely concerned over and angered by Peking's anti-Soviet stance and general behavior, the Chinese can be and are being manipulated as a convenient demon and adversary figure in Soviet domestic and foreign propaganda (in the contexts of the Warsaw Pact and the international Communist movement, for example). Moscow is happy to be able to demonstrate to Peking from time to time that in the last analysis the Soviet Union is more important to the United States than China is, and that therefore the American connection is of only limited utility to Peking for anti-Soviet purposes; examples of such demonstrations are the series of Soviet-American summits and the fact that the Middle Eastern crisis of late 1973 (in which Moscow was obviously involved to one degree or another) predictably compelled Secretary Kissinger to postpone a scheduled visit to Peking. In addition, as already indicated (in Chapter VIII) the Soviet Union is conducting intensive political activity in various parts of the world in opposition to or in competition with China.

The Chinese game is essentially to deter Soviet attack through conventional and nuclear military modernization combined with the creation of a network of international political relationships, with the United States in particular, that tend to set a high political price on any possible Soviet military action against China. In a more positive way, Peking is of course carrying on vigorous political and diplomatic activity in many parts of the world with the purpose of enhancing its own influence and reducing Moscow's, and where appropriate of demonstrating its own alleged ideological superiority. In addition to that, Peking vigorously exploits the charge of Soviet "revisionism" and of Soviet threats to China and other countries as well for purposes of domestic political mobilization and foreign propaganda.

Obviously wars, even major wars, have broken out over issues and policies far less serious than those that now exacerbate the relationship between China and the Soviet Union. There is unquestionably a possibility of a Sino-Soviet war. Since China's marked strategic inferiority makes it virtually "unthinkable" for Peking to launch such a war, the initiative would almost certainly be essentially with the Soviet side. Opinions in Moscow are apparently divided, among both the civilian and the military leaders, as to whether it would be advantageous on balance to attack China; to date the opponents and the negative arguments have obviously prevailed.

The basic argument in favor of such an attack goes to the effect that the Peking leadership is mortally hostile to the Soviet Union and is becoming an increasingly serious military threat to it, especially in the nuclear missile field, that this problem outweighs the consequences of taking military action to cope with it, and that it is desirable to act soon before the problem grows even more serious. Successful military action might not only blunt the Chinese threat but teach Peking a valuable lesson, influence its future leadership and policies in a pro-Soviet direction, and make China an example that would demonstrate to the rest of the world the folly and dangers of an anti-Soviet posture.

The negative argument goes roughly along these lines. China has a formidable defensive capability and at least some ability to retaliate against the Soviet Union with both nuclear and conventional forces; Moscow could not be certain of knocking out enough of Peking's nuclear weapons with a first strike to avoid an "unacceptable" Chinese second strike. In the course of such an exchange, the Soviet Union's military posture with respect to the United States would be significantly, perhaps seriously, impaired, an important consideration regardless of whether the United States supported China to the extent of attacking the Soviet Union. The political consequences of a Soviet attack might be equally serious over the long run. Far from being coerced or persuaded, even by Soviet military pressures short of an actual attack, into adopting a pro-Soviet line, the Chinese leadership and people would probably become more bitterly anti-Soviet than ever. A Soviet attack would have a negative effect, in all likelihood a strongly negative one, on Moscow's political standing virtually everywhere in the world, including the international Communist movement and the United States (even if the American stress on détente with the Soviet Union prevented any strong action by the United States against the Soviet Union on behalf of China). There could be no certainty in Moscow that military action, however drastic, could achieve anything resembling a "final solution" of the Chinese problem. China could probably recover and resume the contest, as some other defeated nations have done in the past (although to be sure not after a large-scale nuclear attack, such as might accompany a major Soviet military operation against China). The prospect of a protracted adversary relationship with China, and one exacerbated by Soviet military action, can hardly appear very attractive in Moscow. From this perspective, therefore, it would be wiser to manage the Chinese problem by various combinations of political and military measures short of actual war and hope for better days after the passing of Mao Tse-tung.

To most outsiders at any rate, the arguments against the wisdom of a Soviet attack on China appear far more persuasive than the arguments in favor. It is of course normal for some one to see no sufficient reason for two third parties to fight each other, and yet fights constantly occur at various levels of violence. Therefore, to repeat, a major Sino-Soviet war must be considered a realistic possibility. This is particularly so since the Soviet leadership appears to feel increasingly apprehensive about Peking's growing nuclear capability and to have recovered from whatever deterrent effect was produced initially by China's improved relationship with the United States. A reasonable estimate and forecast would be that a major Soviet attack on China will not occur, especially if the United States takes measures along the lines suggested in the previous section, but the possibility of such an attack cannot be ruled out.

Assuming that there is no Soviet attack on China, the outlook is for a continuation of the existing tense adversary situation for a while longer, at least as long as Mao Tse-tung is alive. One reason for thinking so is his fixation on his ideological campaign against Soviet "revisionism." Another is the fact that for historical reasons the leadership of the Chinese party and armed forces is about to pass predominantly into the hands of North Chinese, to whom on account of obvious geopolitical considerations the Soviet Union (rather than the United States or Japan) tends to appear as the major foreign threat, although probably not one against which it would be advisable to take the initiative. On the Soviet side, it is likely that some leading figures, including Brezhnev, have become so hostile to the Chinese as to be unlikely to make any major accommodation with them, at least during Mao Tse-tung's lifetime. The outlook therefore is for continued confrontation and rivalry for the time being.

On the other hand, although there are advantages to both sides in this state of confrontation there are also important risks and disadvantages, including the common need to conciliate the United States. Conversely, there would be advantages to reaching an accommodation. Barring a sharp worsening of Sino-Soviet relations, as a result of a Soviet attack on China for example, there is therefore an obvious possibility that confrontation will be replaced sooner or later by accommodation. Just as the Brezhnev leadership tried to reach an accommodation with Peking shortly after the overthrow of the obsessively anti-Chinese Khrushchev, it might try the same thing again after the death of the obsessively anti-Soviet Mao. If not, there is still the possibility that the passage of time, if it does not bring further exacerbation, will not only remove antagonistic leaders on both sides but soften attitudes to the point where an accommodation becomes feasible. This would require that each side outgrow a great deal of its current view of the other, as well as its felt need to exploit the other as a demon figure for domestic and external consumption. All this appears a reasonable possibility for the 1980s.

If a Sino-Soviet accommodation should occur, it might very well include (not necessarily simultaneously) some sort of agreement on the disputed border, a mutual pull-back or thinning out of troops, other forms of arms control, a cessation of ideological and political polemics, cooperation or at least mutual toleration rather than active rivalry in third areas, and a resumption of Soviet aid (economic, technical, and perhaps even military) to China. Of these the idea of cooperation in third areas seems the least likely. If an accommodation should take place along some such lines as these, it would presumably emerge in the context of a trend toward moderation and flexibility in the domestic politics and foreign policies of both parties. It would probably not involve a restoration of the Sino-Soviet alliance, which now exists on paper only and will expire in 1980 unless renewed or extended, to anything like the reasonably full vigor that it enjoyed in the early 1950s. For these reasons, a Sino-Soviet accommodation would not necessarily be a bad thing for the United States or Japan, unless it went to the point of an entente aimed at one or both of them.

Three and a Half Powers

The previous sections of this chapter, which revolve around China, point to the conclusion that China will be a significant power in Asia, whether in the rest of the world or not, and that Peking will be in a reasonably good position to play an active role in the international politics of the region. Actually, the argument is a circular one; China was made the focus of the preceding sections because of a belief that it has such a potential and that a demonstration of this fact—or probability—was desirable. A more difficult question is whether China's role will be constructive—that is, conducive to international stability—as well as active. On the whole, the best answer appears to be a cautious affirmative. There is a reasonable likelihood of a trend toward moderation in Chinese politics and foreign policy, as already suggested, and there are important military and political disincentives to a bellicose or expansionist Chinese role in Asia. This applies mainly to overt, formal, military activity outside China's borders, but informal or covert activity (such as support for "people's wars") also appears to be on a long-term downward curve. China, in short, appears likely to be a great power (not a "superpower") in Asia and to recognize the responsibilities that go with that status, at least to a reasonable degree. Indeed, as already suggested it may be essential to international stability and the effective operation of a multipolar balance in Asia, in the long run, that China play such a role.

Japan is now, and is likely to remain, essentially what may be

called a semi-power, or upper-level middle power. It obviously has
great economic strength and influence, although the oil crisis of
late 1973 demonstrated dramatically how vulnerable it is in this
respect. But it has virtually no foreign policy as yet, very little political influence, and no military capability beyond a modest defensive one. This situation could of course change as a result of a
Japanese decision to rearm on a large scale, and in particular to
acquire nuclear weapons (which would probably have to be based
entirely at sea). Under present conditions, such a decision would
be a political impossibility for any Japanese government. Some
drastic change in Japan's internal or external environment would
be required for it to become a possibility; one scenario that suggests
itself in this connection is a major Sino-Soviet war. As long as it
does not rearm, or acquire significant international political influence in some other way, Japan is likely to maintain something resembling its present relationship with the United States, which is
basically friendly in spite of the "shocks" that it has experienced
and which of course includes a military alliance. It is possible that
a left-wing Japanese government might repudiate the alliance and
try to adopt a posture of "equidistance" from the three major
powers.

The United States will presumably remain a "superpower,"
and as President Nixon indicated a Pacific power in the sense that it
will maintain significant air and naval forces on islands to the east
of the Philippines. Its political and economic interests in the Far
East, including continental Asia, will probably also continue to be
significant, although not necessarily at a level as high as in the past.
The American military presence on the continent of Asia and the
offshore islands, including Japan and Okinawa, will probably continue to decline and eventually approach zero. American ground
forces are not likely to fight in Asia again in the "foreseeable" future, and even air and naval action in support of friendly governments is likely to be conducted, if at all, much more reluctantly
and circumspectly than has sometimes been the case in the past,
notably in Indochina.

The Soviet Union will presumably remain a "superpower" and
a true Far Eastern power (the latter to a greater extent than the
United States, because of geography). Whether it will become a
true Pacific power, in direct rivalry with the United States, remains
to be seen. The outcome will obviously depend to a large extent on

the future of Soviet foreign policy and military growth in general, and of the Soviet Union's relations with the three other powers. On the whole, the outlook appears to be for a cautious but significant expansion of Soviet activity and influence in the Far East and the Pacific, barring the special situation of a major Sino-Soviet war.

It is practically certain that significant roles in Far Eastern international politics will be played, at various lower levels of power and influence, by other powers beside these four. Obvious candidates for such roles are Australia, India, Thailand, the Democratic Republic of Vietnam (especially if it succeeds in gaining permanent control over substantial additional areas of Indochina), and Indonesia. The combined effect of the policies and actions of these states, and the other regional states, on the international politics of East Asia is likely to be significant, and on balance constructive. It should be possible for them, singly or in combination, to avoid "domination" by the three major powers or Japan even if domination is attempted.

The combined effect of the policies and actions of the four principal powers (including Japan) and the less powerful states ought to be conducive, over time, to the operation of multipolarity and international stability. The rules of this game may be complex and will probably take considerable time to work out. But the outlook appears reasonably encouraging, always barring a Sino-Soviet war and making allowance for the special case of Indochina. Apart from these two problems, the main ones that might be seriously disruptive of international stability in Asia would be Japanese or Indian rearmament on a large scale, with nuclear as well as conventional weapons. It is entirely possible that disruptive international forces such as these, if they materialize at all, may turn out to be a less formidable problem for the countries of the region than their own domestic difficulties, which may become acute in some cases.

Whatever the exact shape of the future may turn out to be, Asia will unquestionably remain one of the most important, complex, and interesting regions of the world. Its international politics, as well as the other principal aspects of its life, will continue to deserve thoughtful attention, from Americans as well as others.

Suggestions for Further Reading

Since the subject of this book is vast and complex, the length of a reading list dealing with it could be extended almost indefinitely. This would be undesirable, however, both because of the obvious advantages of brevity and because of the fact that much of the available material is either of rather poor quality or too specialized to be listed here. The comments that follow will accordingly be brief and selective. It should not be assumed that I consider any relevant title not listed here to be substandard in some way; for one thing, there are undoubtedly some such titles with which I am not familiar.

Much of the best writing on current Asian international politics, as already indicated in the preface, is contained in articles appearing in the better newspapers; obviously these cannot be itemized here, except to say that the articles by Selig Harrison on Japan in Asia (referred to in Chapter XI) appeared in *The Washington Post* for February 25, 26, 27, 28, March 1, 2, 4, 1973. Similarly, much valuable writing appears in the form of periodical articles, but these cannot be detailed here; any writer who feels offended by this omission can take comfort from the fact I am leaving out some articles of my own as well. A key to this field is of course a good periodical guide, such as the *Bulletin of the Public Affairs Information Service* or the annual *Bibliography of Asian Studies* published by the Association for Asian Studies (which includes books as well as articles in Western languages). Likely places in which to look for articles on Asian international politics include some of the general periodicals on world affairs, notably *Foreign Affairs* (New York), *Orbis* (Philadelphia), *International Affairs* (London), and *The World Today* (London). Useful periodicals on Asian affairs include *Asian Survey* (University of California, Berkeley), *Pacific Affairs* (University of British Columbia), *The China Quarterly* (London), *Pacific Community* (Tokyo), and *Far Eastern Economic Review* (Hong Kong; also publishes a yearbook). *Problems of Communism* (Washington) publishes occasional articles relevant to the subject of this book. Any student of military affairs and their impact on international politics (as well as vice versa) cannot

afford to overlook the valuable publications of the International Institute for Strategic Studies (London): *Survival, The Military Balance,
Strategic Survey,* and the *Adelphi Papers.*

Some books that provide useful general background for the study
of contemporary Asian international politics are: Paul H. Clyde and
Burton F. Beers, *The Far East: A History of the Western Impact and
the Eastern Response (1830–1970),* Fifth Edition, Englewood Cliffs,
N.J.: Prentice-Hall, 1971; and Akira Iriye, *The Cold War in Asia: A
Historical Introduction,* Englewood Cliffs, N.J.: Prentice-Hall, 1974.
A helpful general book dealing mainly with the foreign policies of the
Asian states is Wayne Wilcox, Leo E. Rose, and Gavin Boyd, eds.,
Asia and the International System, Cambridge, Mass.: Winthrop Pub-
lishers, 1972.

On the Cold War and Soviet-American relations, a good brief
survey is David Rees, *The Age of Containment: The Cold War, 1945–
1965,* New York: St. Martin's Press, 1967. Invaluable and fascinating
material can be found in the first volume of George Kennan's memoirs
(George F. Kennan, *Memoirs, 1925–1950,* Boston: Little, Brown, 1967).
Although rather impressionistic, Adam B. Ulam, *The Rivals: America
and Russia since World War II,* New York: Viking, 1971, can also be
recommended.

There is no general book on Soviet politics or foreign policy that
can be unreservedly recommended. Two informative recent studies of
the Soviet Union's general role in Asia are Geoffrey Jukes, *The Soviet
Union in Asia,* University of California Press, 1973; and Charles B.
McLane, *Soviet-Asian Relations,* Columbia University Press, 1973.
Among the most useful works on Sino-Soviet relations are Donald S.
Zagoria, *The Sino-Soviet Conflict, 1956–1961,* Princeton University
Press, 1962; William E. Griffith, *The Sino-Soviet Rift,* The M. I. T.
Press, 1964; William E. Griffith, *Sino-Soviet Relations, 1964–1965,* The
M. I. T. Press, 1967; and Harold C. Hinton, *The Bear at the Gate:
Chinese Policymaking under Soviet Pressure,* Washington: American
Enterprise Institute and Stanford, California: Hoover Institution, 1971.

The foreign policy of the Nixon administration, including of
course its Asian policy, is dealt with in two recent books by distin-
guished journalists, on the basis of "inside" information: Henry
Brandon, *The Retreat of American Power,* New York: Doubleday,
1973; and Tad Szulc, *Innocents at Home,* New York: Viking, 1974.
Mr. Szulc's analysis of the American side of the Vietnam negotiations
is seriously in error on one important point. He says that Kissinger
made an important concession—that North Vietnamese troops need
not leave South Vietnam—for the first time during his visit to Moscow
in April 1972, whereas in reality the American demand for their

withdrawal had been dropped by October 1970. Some valuable recent books on various aspects of American Asian policy are Bernard K. Gordon, *Toward Disengagement in Asia: A Strategy for American Foreign Policy*, Englewood Cliffs, N.J.: Prentice-Hall, 1969; Robert Scalapino, *American-Japanese Relations in a Changing Era*, New York: Library Press, 1972; Roderick MacFarquhar, ed., *Sino-American Relations, 1949–71*, New York: Praeger, 1972; and Gene T. Hsiao, ed., *Sino-American Détente and Its Policy Implications*, New York: Praeger, 1974.

The best recent general book on Japan is Zbigniew Brzezinski, *The Fragile Blossom: Crisis and Change in Japan*, New York: Harper and Row, 1972. The "superstate" thesis is advanced in Herman Kahn, *The Emerging Japanese Superstate: Challenge and Response*, Englewood Cliffs, N.J.: Prentice-Hall, 1970. Also useful are John K. Emmerson, *Arms, Yen and Power: The Japanese Dilemma*, New York: Dunellen, 1971; Donald C. Hellman, *Japan and East Asia: The New International Order*, New York: Praeger, 1972; and F. C. Langdon, *Japan's Foreign Policy*, University of British Columbia Press, 1973.

There has been some excellent writing on the politics and foreign policy of the two Koreas; Gregory Henderson, *Korea: The Politics of the Vortex*, Harvard University Press, 1968; David C. Cole and Princeton N. Lyman, *Korean Development: The Interplay of Politics and Economics*, Harvard University Press, 1971; Young C. Kim, ed., *Major Powers and Korea*, Silver Spring, Md.: Research Institute on Korean Affairs, 1973; and Robert A. Scalapino and Chong-Sik Lee, *Communism in Korea*, 2 vols., University of California Press, 1972. The best general book on the Korean War is David Rees, *Korea: The Limited War*, New York: St. Martin's Press, 1964.

Among the useful general books on Chinese politics are Jürgen Domes, *The Internal Politics of China, 1949–1972*, New York: Praeger, 1973; Harold C. Hinton, *An Introduction to Chinese Politics*, New York: Praeger, 1973; and A. Doak Barnett, *Uncertain Passage: China's Transition to the Post-Mao Era*, Washington: Brookings Institution, 1974. On Chinese foreign policy and various aspects of it, Michael Lindsay, *China and the Cold War: A Study in International Politics*, Melbourne University Press, 1955; Harold C. Hinton, *China's Turbulent Quest: An Analysis of China's Foreign Relations since 1949*, rev. ed., Indiana University Press, 1972; Neville Maxwell, *India's China War*, New York: Anchor Books, 1972; and Melvin Gurtov, *China and Southeast Asia—The Politics of Survival: A Study of Foreign Policy Interaction*, Lexington, Mass.: D. C. Heath, 1971, can be recommended.

Two especially valuable recent books on South Asia are Norman D. Palmer, *The Indian Political System*, 2nd ed., Boston: Houghton

Mifflin, 1971; and William F. Barnds, *India, Pakistan, and the Great Powers,* New York: Praeger, 1972.

On Southeast Asia in general, Lucian W. Pye, *Southeast Asia's Political Systems,* rev. ed., Englewood Cliffs, N.J.: Prentice-Hall, 1974; Bernard K. Gordon, *The Dimensions of Conflict in Southeast Asia,* Englewood Cliffs, N.J.: Prentice-Hall, 1966; Peter Lyon, *War and Peace in South-East Asia,* Oxford University Press, 1969; and Mark W. Zacher and R. Stephen Milne, eds., *Conflict and Stability in Southeast Asia,* New York: Anchor Books, 1974, are useful.

There is of course a vast literature on the Indochina crisis, much of it polemical and almost worthless. Among the best books on this subject are Dennis J. Duncanson, *Government and Revolution in Vietnam,* Oxford University Press, 1968; Joseph J. Zasloff and Alan E. Goodman, eds., *Indochina in Conflict: A Political Assessment,* Lexington, Mass.: D. C. Heath, 1972; Gene T. Hsiao, ed., *The Role of External Powers in the Indochina Crisis,* Edwardsville, Ill.: Southern Illinois University Press, 1973; and Sheldon W. Simon, *War and Politics in Cambodia: A Communications Analysis,* Duke University Press, 1974. On the American role, a good survey is Peter A. Poole, *The United States and Indochina from FDR to Nixon,* Hinsdale, Ill.: Dryden Press, 1973. The most convenient version of the famous Pentagon Papers (United States government documents on the American involvement in Vietnam from the mid-1950s to the mid-1960s) is *The Pentagon Papers,* New York: Bantam Books, 1971. The Johnson administration's decision to begin disengaging from Vietnam is ably described in Townsend Hoopes, *The Limits of Intervention,* rev. ed., New York: McKay, 1974.

Index

ABM, 186, 208
Acheson, Dean, 35, 47, 81
Afghanistan, 246
AFPFL, 18
Afro-Asian Conference, 24–25
Aidit, D. N., 22
Aksai Chin, 15, 65, 66, 73
Albania, 73, 122
Algiers Conference, 24–25
Alliance Party, Malay, 260–61
Anderson, Jack, 180
Antiballistic missiles, 186, 208
Anti-Fascist People's Freedom League, 18
Arab states, 123–24, 201–3, 215
arms control. *See* SALT
ASEAN, 117, 252, 253, 261, 268–69
Asia: de-colonization of, 11–25; U.S. containment policy for, 51–58; collective security of, 116–21; Nixon's policy for, 128–30; shifting U.S. priorities in, 174–83; Japan's role in, 227–29; Southeast, 247–72; future multipolar balance for, 273–95
Asian and Pacific Council, 128, 268
Asian-African Conference at Bandung, 23–25, 65, 68
ASPAC, 128, 268
Association of Southeast Asian Nations, 117, 252–53, 261, 268–69
Australia, 270
Ayub Khan, Mohammed, 16–17, 75, 233–36

balance of power in Asia, 273–95
ballistic missiles, 39, 189–92, 207
Bandung Conference, 23–25, 65, 68
Bangkok. *See* Thailand
Bangla Desh, 118, 179–81, 235–39, 243–45
BCP, 248–51
Bengal, 232
Beria, Lavrenti, 35–36
Berlin, 38–39, 205

Bhumibol Aduldet, King, 252–54
Bhutto, Zulfikar Ali, 181, 234–37, 240–44
Bonn. *See* West Germany
Borneo, 260
Brandt, Willy, 187, 205
Brezhnev, Leonid: and Vietnam War, 40; and Third World, 41; and Sino-Soviet relations, 108–9, 112–17, 120; and détente, 187, 194, 196, 199, 202, 208; and India, 242; "collective security" system of, 270; hostility to Chinese, 292
Brezhnev Doctrine, 104, 111
British: de-colonization by, 17–20; in Southeast Asia, 269
Bruce, David, 110, 141, 283, 287–88
BSPP, 248–50
Burma, 18, 21, 247–52, 278

Cambodia, 78, 82, 107–8, 141–42, 150, 157–63, 167–73
Canada, 162
Castro, Fidel, 208
Chiang Ching, 108
Chiang Kai-shek, 28–29, 34, 43–45, 50–52, 175
China, People's Republic of: and India, 14–15; supervision of revolutions in Southern Asia, 23; Soviet vs. American interests in, 33–34; alliance with Soviets, 43–50; U.S. containment policy for, 51–58; foreign policy toward Asia, 59–77; border disputes, 60–61, 191; disputes with Soviets, 70–77; and Indochina War, 80; confrontation with Soviets, 97–124; "tilt" toward U.S., 111–16; détente with U.S., 125–48, 194; and European security, 203–5; and Japan, 217, 221–26; and Pakistan, 239–40; and Burma, 250–51; and Malaysia, 261–62; role in Southeast Asia, 270–71; political trends since Cultural Revolution, 274–78; future outlook for, 278–93; future of relations with

The dramatic confrontations and shifting alliances of the two great superpowers, and their sometimes disastrous consequences for lesser nations, are set forth in this searching analysis of political developments in the Far East since the Second World War. Professor Hinton skillfully presents the grand design of events in Asia: the period of American ascendancy giving way to an era of Soviet-American strategic parity, which has in turn been succeeded by a multilateral balance of "three and a half powers"—the Soviet Union, the People's Republic of China, the United States—and Japan.

Part I (1945-1969) describes Japan's re-emergence after the Second World War, decolonization and nation-building in south Asia, Mao Tse-tung's decision to "lean to one side"—the Soviet Union's—in the Cold War, and the American policy of trying to contain and isolate the People's Republic of China. The roots of the Sino-Soviet dispute and American involvement in Vietnam are discussed. Part II (1969-1974) examines in more detail the potentially dangerous Sino-Soviet confrontation, American military withdrawal from Vietnam, the United States' policy of détente with China and the Soviet Union, and recent developments in Japan, India, Pakistan, and Southeast Asia.

Professor Hinton believes that many factors will work toward making China a very great influence on the rest of Asia in the future, but that economic and technological limitations will probably prevent it from acquiring an influence equal to that of the United States and the Soviet Union. He